The Drama of W. B. Yeats: Irish Myth and the Japanese Nō

THE DRAMA OF W. B. YEATS

IRISH MYTH AND THE JAPANESE NŌ

Richard Taylor

YALE UNIVERSITY PRESS

NEW HAVEN AND LONDON 1976

Library of Congress catalog card number: 75-43336

International standard book number: 0-300-01904-1

Set in IBM Adjutant.

Printed in Great Britain by Biddles of Guildford.

Published in Great Britain, Europe, Africa, the Middle East,
India, Pakistan and South East Asia by Yale University Press
Ltd, London.
Distributed in Latin America by Kaiman & Polon, Inc., New
York City; in Australasia by Book & Film Services, Artarmon
N.S.W., Australia; in Japan by John Weatherhill, Inc., Tokyo

aina anadyomene

Contents

Preface

The daring experiments of W. B. Yeats in both dramatic content and form are easily the most interesting, and perhaps the most important, developments in the English-speaking theatre between 1890 and 1940. Only now do we begin to see the full significance of his work in the flowering of the anti-illusionistic drama known as the Theatre of the Absurd. Existing attempts to analyse and criticise Yeats's career as a dramatist, however, have suffered from a number of difficulties, most notably from an incomplete understanding of his borrowing from the Japanese Nō. In the notebooks and manuscripts of Ernest Fenollosa edited by Ezra Pound between 1913 and 1916, and in Fenollosa's early publications, Yeats encountered exciting new ideas which he seized upon for the long sought-after regeneration of the English theatre. Unfortunately, no-one has attempted to ascertain exactly which ideas were in fact borrowed, and which rejected, nor to compare those ideas with Yeats's dramatic practice in the early plays.

The developing naturalism of European stage practice had brought with it a strong reaction against the representation of exterior or surface reality, and lyric drama, both symbolist and expressionist, developed as a manifestation of subjective reality or consciousness in which imagination and poetry were returned to the theatre. The growth of *avant garde* drama was undoubtedly as much influenced by the contemporary revolution in staging technique and production method as it was by the various philosophies and aesthetic theories of the day, or by the construction and technique of the Japanese Nō. In order to document the precise pattern of Yeats's development as a dramatist, it is important to ascertain exactly what ideas were borrowed from Nō tradition, how accurately those ideas had been transmitted, and what effect they had on the already established course of Yeats's theatrical innovations.

It is particularly important to come to understand the Nō itself, the scope of its theatrical possibilities, and its relevance to the development of modern European forms. As one moves further away in time from the preoccupations of playwrights at the beginning of the present century, one tends to lose sight of their framework of reference, and so misjudge or misinterpret earlier conditions.

> The Western discovery of the classical Japanese theatre was, by necessity, as late and as sudden as the Japanese discovery of Western industrialism, and has tended to produce the same over-enthusiastic response. Re-reading the earlier critical accounts in English, one wonders that incomprehension could turn so quickly to idolatry, and if, perhaps, the two are not aspects of the same position. It should be possible to respect the serenity of *noh* while admitting its lack of theatrical vitality and the technical expertise of *kabuki* while deploring its lack of content.[1]

Not only is historical perspective lost in such a judgment, but it is also likely that Nō, for example, is being narrowly judged by the standards of western drama. A definition of 'theatrical vitality' is plainly the operative factor here, and for the purpose of a truly comparative study it would be far better to examine the particular vitality that Nō does possess, as well as the qualities and conditions which brought it into prominence at a particular point in the history of Western theatre. A critical analysis of Nō drama is both a valid undertaking in its own right as well as in providing critical perspective and vocabulary for approaching Yeats's dance plays, particularly in focusing attention on lyrico-musical composition and techniques of performance rather than on the thematic concerns of the texts alone. The intention is not merely to document instances of direct influence, but rather to understand the qualities of Nō which invited assimilation.

All too often Yeats criticism tends to be excessively impressionistic rather than judicial; that is, expressive of an almost visceral reaction to the work, or worse yet,

a pretext for the spiritual autobiography of the critic.
The plays themselves greatly benefit from a more rigorously
objective approach, and one which attempts to balance consideration of romantic subject matter and theme with that of
symbolic structure and anti-illusionistic production method.
The greatest stumbling block has been the inadequacy of
critical vocabulary when dealing with the question of abstract art and its ability to get beyond or apart from the
experience that inspired it and even from the consciousness
that created it. Terms such as non-representational are
somewhat misleading in that all human expression is representative of something, whether of the physical world or of
some emotional-psychological experience. Some confusion is
inevitable between the vocabulary of romantic artists and
objective critics. More difficult still is the need to
distinguish among levels of reality - temporal, imaginative,
and absolute or spiritual - as they are variously perceived
by author and audience. Since there is no solution to the
problem I have tried to avoid ambiguity by clarifying the
context in each case or reminding the reader of alternative
judgments and interpretations. Because the thrust of the
present undertaking is to assess the evolution of Yeats as
a dramatist, I have examined each play in order of its composition, not so much as a self-sufficient object or integer,
but in its relation to a developing mode of expression.
The plays are grouped together into three major phases:
Early Plays (1892-1910), Plays for Dancers (1914-20), and
Late Plays (1920-39). Before taking up the dance plays,
however, there is a discussion of Yeats's introduction to
the Nō through the offices of Ernest Fenollosa and Ezra
Pound, and a contrastive analysis of Nō drama in its own
right. The overriding contention is that Yeats was primarily influenced by the general plot organization of actual
Nō plays and their concentration on a single image or symbolic design and that it was his own adaptation of that basic
form in recreating his perennial themes that enabled him to
break through the impasse of traditional dramatic conceptions.
Each of the four plays for dancers is examined in relation
to its Japanese original, and the late plays are seen as
extensions and elaborations of these achievements.

     The editorial conventions used throughout hardly need
a word of special notice, except perhaps for the consistent
retention of the traditional Japanese form for personal
names, surname first. Similarly, I have used the modern

convention for indicating vowel length in Japanese words
rather than retaining the occasional use of the circumflex
as it sometimes occurred in earlier published work.

Nothing of the present study would have been possible
without experience gathered as a spectator at something
over a hundred individual Nō performances and from private
conversation with professional and amateur actors alike.
Above all, my thanks and appreciation are extended to
Mesdames Itō Shō and Itō Yonekō who together have worked
unselfishly for many years to introduce foreigners to Nō
drama through the International Nō Club of Japan. They
were particularly kind and generous during my year in Tokyo,
answering questions and arranging meetings with others who
were of incalculable help in my research. Mr. Ōtsuka Fumio,
a dedicated amateur performer, is another who during that
year was unfailingly kind and helpful in my aesthetic ini-
tiation; his translation of a modern Nō appears below. Miss
Oda Yori, for many years a close friend, has always shared
with me her enthusiasm for the art of Nō, and without her
constant assistance, the present work would never have come
into being. I should also like to express my gratitude to
Lady Blackett and the late Lord Blackett who generously put
at my disposal a writing desk of great character and a house
in London to go with it. Dame Ninette de Valois was most
generous in taking time from an extraordinarily busy sched-
ule to answer my numerous questions, and Mr. Norman Marshall
was very helpful in providing a clearer and more balanced
perspective on recent theatre history than texts alone could
furnish. Professor Jay Ruben read an early draft of the
chapter on Nō drama, kindly pointing out a number of errors,
and Dr. Robert Welch was very helpful in guiding me through
the intricacies of Irish heroic literature and its early
translators. Mrs. Margaret Folarin and Dr. William Allen
both read through the entire manuscript and offered a number
of perceptive and sensible suggestions for its revision. In
every case I am grateful to the scholars who have gone before
and freely acknowledge my many debts to them. Neither they
nor those mentioned above should be held responsible for the
errors and miscalculations into which my own judgment and
wilfulness may have led me. I am grateful to the Trustees
of the Ezra Pound Literary Property Trust and heirs to the
Ernest Fenollosa estate for permission to work with unpublished material in the Alderman Library of the University
of Virginia, the Beineke Rare Book and Manuscript Library

of Yale University and the Houghton Library of Harvard University. The editors of *Ariel* and *Paideuma* as well as Macmillan of Canada have given their permission to include material in the present volume which was originally published by them, and in the same way I must thank Dartmouth College for a Faculty Fellowship which allowed me six months' liberty from teaching to embark upon the project.

I am grateful to the Macmillan Company of London and Basingstoke for permission to quote passages from *'Noh' or Accomplishment* by Ernest Fenollosa and Ezra Pound. I am grateful to M. B. Yeats, Miss Anne Yeats and the Macmillan Company of London and Basingstoke for permission to quote passages from the works of W. B. Yeats.

I am grateful to the Macmillan Publishing Co., Inc. for permission to quote from the following. *Autobiography* (Copyright 1916, 1935 by Macmillan Publishing Co., Inc., renewed 1944, 1963 by Bertha Georgie Yeats); *Essays and Introductions* (© Mrs W. B. Yeats, 1961); *The Letters of W. B. Yeats*, edited by Allan Wade (Copyright 1953, 1954 by Anne Butler Yeats); *Variorum Edition of the Plays of W. B. Yeats*, edited by Russell K. Alspach (Copyright © Russell K. Alspach and Bertha Georgie Yeats, 1966); *Variorum Edition of the Poems of W. B. Yeats*, edited by Peter Allt and Russell K. Alspach (Copyright © 1957 by Macmillan Publishing Co., Inc.); *A Vision* (Copyright 1937 by W. B. Yeats, renewed 1965 by Bertha Georgie Yeats and Anne Butler Yeats).

1.

W. B. Yeats: Early Plays

> I shall not trouble to make the meaning
> clear - a clear vivid story of a strange
> sort is enough.[1]

Before his acquaintance with the form and technique
of Nō drama, Yeats had written eleven separate plays and
had seen each of them performed on the stage. Several had
been produced in more than one version, and it is only
reasonable to examine the range and direction of his early
experiments in both content and form before embarking on
the larger question of influence and assimilation from the
Nō. Yeats's early stage practice is of particular importance in assessing influences on his work, and the historical context of his ideas must be kept in mind. Separated
from the illuminating background of contemporary theatre
practice, his plays appear almost irrelevant and pose a
baffling, if not impenetrable, problem to criticism.
Like many other dramatists of the period Yeats worked
with both antique and exotic forms, and was particularly
concerned with the ideal synthesis of the arts that Richard
Wagner had originally advocated. Attempts at the revival
of lyric drama were not restricted to the writing of new
plays in verse, but were extended to the creation of a new
dramatic form in which symbolic significance of action,
schematic relationships of character, sculptural quality
of the playing area, rhythm of bodily movement, harmony of
music and song, patterns of colour in costume and setting,
and unifying texture of language would join together in the
expression of some hidden truth or reality of the imagination.

If the spectacle of that expression were both beautiful and sublime, understanding and acceptance of the larger reality beyond it would surely follow. Up to 1910 Yeats made concerted attacks on the problem of dramatic form and technique. Each play was a new experiment and was revised again and again until its texture and execution was wrought into as perfect a balance with the potential of its conception as was artistically possible. None of the plays, however, was wholly successful in achieving the ideal dramatic form that he sought. The failure was essentially conceptual, and however much his basic characters and situations were refined and elaborated upon, Yeats could only approach or suggest a condition of being which was separated from the illusion of reality found in conventional Renaissance drama.

Instead of working with a traditional drama of conflict and character analysis, Yeats began by projecting simple images of moral or spiritual insight and value. His early plays do not rely on the unravelling of a loosely thrown dramatic knot, but rather on the intervention of a supernatural agency in an otherwise realistic situation, and his break with the dramatic conventions of Shakespeare and Ibsen in pursuit of abstract passion, mood and atmosphere, led him to a conception of theatre as ritual, a demonstration or celebration of cosmic forces which condition the reality of daily life. Ritual drama is above all a group art in which historical or mythological events are both recreated and their significance for the community is emphasized through the focus of aesthetic structuring. Although tragic implications may figure in ritual drama as in the case of *The Bacchae* or *Samson Agonistes*, the importance of the form is in the revelation of 'what is' or 'what should be' in terms of the public good, a demonstration of the touchstone and ordering principle on which the stability of the community rests. Such group art requires an audience of initiates or participants, and Yeats was at great pains throughout his lifetime to induce a larger community to share his private visions of universal order. Influenced by the Pre-Raphaelite and Aesthetic movements which had urged both a return to functionalism and the establishment of a closer bond between life and art, Yeats began exploiting folk material and heroic legend, but the fact remained that both worlds were somewhat alien to his audiences of honest townsmen. Even more so in our own time and condition, understanding of his work is acquired rather than instinctive, and his

drama must always remain somewhat foreign. During the
early years his plays were either projections of a degraded
present, whose limiting circumstantial realism is exposed
by sudden juxtapositioning with the Ideal, or direct evo-
cations of ancient heroes. More often than not, his antique
and exotic subject matter was realized within established
historical forms; particularly the medieval and classical
Greek. As his proficiency and confidence developed, however,
Yeats began to experiment more widely in search of an ideal
concept of theatre and valid counter-reality. Among his
many public pronouncements on the subject was the lecture
on 'The Reform of the Theatre' that he gave in March 1903,
outlining the goals of the Irish National Theatre Society:

1. To present plays that generate intellectual excitement.

2. To make speech even more important than gesture.

3. To simplify acting technique.

4. To simplify both the form and colour of scenery
   and costume.[2]

As an alternative to naturalism in the theatre and
illusionistic method, Yeats encouraged both peasant plays
which cut below the drawing-room drama of the period, and
his own idealizations of heroic action which were heavy with
symbolic significance. In both he sought a dramatic art
that sprang from the life of a people whose inherent sense
of drama was highly sophisticated and who delighted in musical speech and extravagant language. There was still a
peasant culture in Ireland at the turn of the present century with a living speech of marked inflectional patterns
and also possessed of simple, human responses, as well as
a sense of wonder and kinship for an environment that was
held to be antecedently spiritual. Within this culture the
natural and supernatural worlds were equally accessible, the
figures of myth and legend as real as tramps and tinkers,
and there was an imaginative life that had not yet succumbed
to modern experience. The Celtic element in literature
advocated by Yeats represented irrationality and a revolt
against the materialism of the nineteenth century. In his
essay on the subject, Yeats emphasized the passionate imagination of Richard Wagner as a driving force in the Symbolist movement which had found its expression in England
in the work of William Morris and the Pre-Raphaelites, in

France with Villiers de l'Isle-Adam and Mallarmé, in Belgium
with Maeterlinck, and also had had some influence on Ibsen
and D'Annunzio.

The life of the spirit or soul was to be the proper
subject of serious literature and the recognition of truth
and beauty accomplished through the suspension of every-day
reality. Lyric poetry alone was not sufficient to establish
concrete images and represent the new vision, but together
with symbolic action, stylized stage design, and dramatic
gesture, a symbol could be created that would linger in the
mind and generate intellectual excitement. Yeats held that
drama was a means of expression, not a special subject matter, and as literature, it should reflect essential and unchanging aspects of experience.

> A farce and a tragedy are alike in this that they are a
> moment of intense life. An action is taken out of all
> other actions; it is reduced to its simple form, or at
> any rate to as simple a form as it can be brought to
> without our losing the sense of its place in the world.
> The characters that are involved in it are freed from
> everything that is not a part of that action; and whether
> it is, as in the less important kinds of drama, a mere
> bodily activity, a hair-breadth escape or the like, or
> as it is in the more important kinds, an activity of the
> souls of the characters, it is an energy, an eddy of life
> purified from everything but itself. The dramatist must
> picture life in action, with an unpreoccupied mind, as
> the musician pictures her in sound and the sculptor in
> form.[3]

Theoretically, at any rate, Yeats was on very firm ground,
but the characteristic subject matter with which he worked,
the contrast between immortal beauty and the ignominy and
mortality of human life, was rendered anything but concrete
by the vague rhapsodic tone and elegiac verse of his early
plays. Rather than the struggle of a dream with the world,
the first plays merely projected the static dream alone,
the romantic longing and spiritual hunger of Pre-Raphaelite
art. 'As Yeats saw it, the aesthetic function of the literary
symbol was not rational, but ritual: an "arrangement of
colours and sounds and forms" (*Essays*, p.191), which evokes
an infinite emotion.'[4] As Yeats gained experience of the
theatre, however, he turned from the evocation of generalized

ecstasy to the more dramatic delineation of a specified
spiritual order. Rhythm and pattern still predominated,
but action and abstract representation of opposing forces
came into relief. Problems of production method increased
as the symbolic nature of the characters and circumstances
became prominent, yet the action and circumstances had to
be both recognizable and convincing to an uninitiated audience.

> Tragedy itself has become problematic. There are, that
> is, no longer any absolute, overriding, external, easily
> discerned criteria by which one judges whether a given
> man and a given destiny are tragic. The tragic becomes
> strictly a matter of viewpoint, and - important as a
> problem of expression - strictly an inward, spiritual
> problem. Something becomes tragic only by the suggestive
> force of expression, and only spiritual intensities can
> lend the pathos of tragedy to it ... This is why the
> heroism of the new drama has grown more stylized, more
> rhetorical, than in the old: the heroism of the hero
> must be asserted consciously.[5]

The problem of expression in Yeats's view centred upon
the primacy of the actor, the quality of language in the
literary text, and the effectiveness of the visible scene.
His first thought was to simplify acting techniques, especially in poetic drama, but also in prose plays which
stress a remoteness from every-day life. It was William Fay
(1872-1947) who really instituted the acting style that
characterized the Irish National Theatre and his avowed
intention had been 'to enforce the most rigid economy of
gesture and movement, to make the speaking quite abstract,
and at the same time to keep a music in it by having all
the voices harmonized.'[6] William Poel had long been experi-
menting with rhythmic speech and choric harmony in his productions of Shakespeare, and Fay had been much impressed by
performances of the Comédie Francaise, especially so by the
effectiveness of formalized movement and rhetorical delivery.
Yeats came to understand the strength of the method on seeing
Sara Bernhardt and De Max play *Phèdre* in 1902. He wrote of
the astonishing pauses during which the performers merely
posed statuesquely, and of the amazing rhythmic progression
of gesture that created its own emotional climaxes. Beyond
the main characters 'stood a crowd of white-robed men who

never moved at all, and the whole scene had the nobility of
Greek sculpture, and an extraordinary reality and intensity.'
Yeats was captivated by techniques that refined heroic action
into ritual, suggested states of mind rather than describing
circumstances, and invited the imagination to share in the
emotion they delineated. The methods were carried over into
the style of the Irish players and by 1903 they were known
for the simplicity and self-consciousness of their acting.
A combination of awkward amateurishness and formal art gave
their work a refreshing spontaneity, almost impulsiveness,
in comparison with the fussy stage-business and perpetual
motion of the commercial theatre. The speaker was the only
person on stage to gesture or move, for example, while the
others stood still and listened; on their first appearance
in London the reviewer for *The Times* (8 May 1903) compared
their conventions to those of the Italian marionette theatre
and Sada Yacco's Japanese company.[8] Not only was there an
arresting strangeness in their deliberate and measured movement, but there was also an alluring stillness in which
magnificent words and rhythmic speech reasserted their proper
values.

Yeats insisted that simplicity of melodic line and
cadence was the secret of both clarity of enunciation and
expressiveness. The tonal scale for musical declamation
was to be restricted in range and a distinction between immortal and human speeches established by moving from whole
note to whole note in elevated recitation as opposed to the
more naturalistic and elaborate use of semi-tones in ordinary
speech. For some years, Yeats had been interested in techniques of verse speaking, and particularly in attempts to
rediscover the principles of chanted recitation. 'Mr. Dol-
metsch and Miss Florence Farr', he wrote, 'have been working
for some time to find out some way of setting serious poetry,
which will enable us to hear it, and the singer to sing
sweetly and yet never give a word, a cadence, or an accent,
that would not be given it in ordinary passionate speech.'[9]

Yeats's preoccupation with music and rhythmic speech
is a product of his belief that feeling or emotion is as
much present in lyric patterns of sound as it is in the
meaning of words and that the musical quality of poetic
language must be emphasized in order to realize the full
truth of lyric images. Rather than conceiving of the musical patterns inherent in rhythmic speech as independent
sense images or symbols, Yeats emphasized their incantatory

effects:

> The purpose of rhythm, it has always seemed to me, is to
> prolong the moment of contemplation, the moment when we
> are both asleep and awake, which is the one moment of
> creation, by hushing us with an alluring monotony, while
> it holds us waking by variety, to keep us in that state
> of perhaps real trance, in which the mind liberated from
> the pressure of the will is unfolded in symbols.[10]

Like the suspension of movement and gesture in acting which
creates pauses that the dialogue of the characters or imagination of the audience might fill, the incantation of
verse excites the imagination by creating a rhapsodic or
elegiac tone and frees it from commonplace concerns. 'If
the real world is not altogether rejected, it is but touched
here and there, and into the place we have left empty we
summon rhythm, balance, pattern, images that remind us of
vast passions, the vagueness of past times.'[11] In Yeats's
early plays at least, verse is the unifying, ecstatic element that evokes abstract passion, the 'living duration'
that Adolphe Appia found in music, and itself creates the
moment of exalted reverie in which ultimate recognition is
meant to take place.

As early as 1889 Walter Pater had suggested the ideal
of lyric unity as the basis of dramatic construction, and
in agreement with the Wagnerian tradition advocated the
balancing of plot and logic of event with rhythm and pattern.

> A play attains artistic perfection just in proportion as
> it approaches that unity of lyrical effect, as if a song
> or ballad were still lying at the root of it, all the
> various expression of the conflict of character and cir-
> cumstance falling at last into the compass of a single
> melody, or musical theme. As, historically, the earliest
> classic drama arose out of the chorus, from which this
> or that person, this or that episode, detached itself,
> so, into the unity of a choric song the perfect drama
> ever tends to return, its intellectual scope deepened,
> complicated, enlarged, but still with an unmistakable
> singleness, or identity, in its impression on the mind.
> Just there, in that vivid single impression left on the
> mind when all is over, not in any mechanical limitation
> of time and place, is the secret of the 'unities' - the

true imaginative unity - of the drama.12

Plays need not be written in verse to achieve unity of lyric
effect, however, and cadenced prose, as in the case of plays
by J. M. Synge, for example, is equally adaptable to such
musical construction. In fact, the same effect can be super-
imposed on a play whose text is not itself rhythmical, through
a careful selection and ordering of production technique as
in the work of Appia and Craig, Reinhardt and Meyerhold, or
any of the other producer/directors of modern theatre.
Within the wider context of lyric tradition, on the other
hand, Yeats's drama was basically poetic and versification
was used as a fundamental means of expression.

It is obvious that the Irish theatre was much more
oriented towards author and actor than producer/director,
and that both scene and acting technique were to be subordinated first to the spoken word and ultimately to the
intellectual content of the play. Yeats went on to discuss
the suitability of scenery; costumes were to be relegated
to the simplest decorative designs and limited to two or
three colours:

> As a rule the background should be of a single colour,
> so that the persons in the play wherever they stand, may
> harmonize with it, and preoccupy our attention. In
> other words it should be thought out not as one thinks
> out a landscape, but as if it were the background of a
> portrait, and this is especially necessary on a small
> stage where the moment the stage is filled the painted
> forms of the background are broken up and lost. Even
> when one has to represent trees or hills they should be
> treated in most cases decoratively, they should be little
> more than an unobtrusive pattern. There must be nothing
> unnecessary, nothing that will distract the attention
> from speech and movement.13

Yeats preferred the platform stage of speech and gesture to
the proscenium stage of pictures and realistic effects; his
ideal of stage design was to suggest an imaginative reality
through architectural form and decoration while avoiding
a meretricious and vulgar illusionism, and the degree of
distortion from naturalistic effect should depend on the
particular play to be produced. The participation of the
spectator in the imagined reality of scene and action was

a very important factor, and Yeats sought an 'aristocratic'
audience; that is, a select and cultured group who would
enter into the spirit of the new aesthetic form and assist
at the recreation of universal truth about human experience.
The theatre audience itself had to be created, since there
was no central passion or belief in contemporary society
that might be invoked, and Yeats fully appreciated the advantage of a small, intimate auditorium, both in establishing
rapport between actor and audience and in eliminating the
grosser tendencies of popular drama.   The *débâcle* of William
Todhunter's poetic play, *The Comedy of Sighs*, which opened
in 1894 at the Avenue Theatre then under the management of
Florence Farr, had been a stern lesson, especially so as it
was underlined by the huge success of his earlier pastoral,
A Sicilian Idyll, at the clubhouse theatre in Bedford Park
(1891), an enclave of aesthetes on the outskirts of London.
A small auditorium was perfectly suited to the kind of un-
popular play Yeats was interested in presenting, and because
of the proximity of audience and actor it did not matter so
much whether there was central staging as in the Godwin
production of Todhunter's *Helena in Troas* at Hengler's
Grande Cirque (1886), a platform stage as in Poel's Shakespearean revivals, or even the baroque proscenium stage of
the contemporary realistic theatre.   In his review of the
first performance at the renovated Abbey Theatre, John
Masefield mentioned that 'it had been the wish of Mr. Yeats
to have a projecting stage, in the manner of the Elizabethan
theatre, but it was found that the projection in such a
small building would occupy too much space.'[14] On the
other hand it is interesting to note that intimacy of
stage action was not uniformly welcome in the initial years
at the Abbey and that a scrim was occasionally used to re-
establish the Wagnerian 'mystic gulf' between auditorium
and stage, and to stress the symbolic overtones of a remote,
fictional world. By 1904, Yeats's ideas on lighting were
also very well defined:

> If one remembers that the movement of the actor, and
> the graduation and the colour of the lighting, are the
> two elements that distinguish the stage picture from an
> easel painting, one will not find it difficult to create
> an art of the stage ranking as a true fine art.
> Mr. Gordon Craig has done wonderful things with the
> lighting, but he is not greatly interested in the actor,

and his streams of coloured direct light, beautiful as
they are, will always seem, apart from certain exceptional
moments, a new externality. One should rather desire,
for all but exceptional moments, an even shadowless light,
like that of noon, and it may be that a light reflected
out of mirrors will give us what we need.[15]

The pattern of Yeats's development as a dramatist was
obviously set at a very early date. It merely remained for
him to discover themes and subject matter, character relationships and symbolic designs, which stylized production
method would project as ritual. The earliest of the plays
merely rely upon the dramatic revelation of the mystery or
miracle plays and the constructional features of the medieval morality. In both *The Countess Cathleen* and *The Land
of Heart's Desire* the slight plots only serve to establish
the surface reality of a peasant culture, while the moral
virtue and emotional intensity that are ultimately advocated
are those of a heroic or ideal world whose miraculous intervention exposes the degradation of temporal limitations and
human aspirations. *The Countess Cathleen* is a very interesting case in that its construction, however rough or primitive, is rather powerful. During a famine the Devil con-
trives to remove all possibility of alleviating the people's
suffering. His followers, disguised as Merchants, offer to
buy souls, but the Countess sells her own to ransom theirs.
Throughout the many revisions, the major conflict remains
focused on the opposition of Good and Evil as represented
by the Countess and the Merchants, while the peasant world
of Shemus Rua has no other function than to provide variety
and establish a sense of reality which substantiates the
figure of the Countess and her concern for the people. In
the middle and later versions the rustic scenes are balanced
by those which show the poet's love for Cathleen, and again
focus attention on her representative function rather than
on individualized character. In the final analysis however,
the drama fails, not so much because the action and outcome
constitute a cliché, but because there is no temptation,
the heroine is not faced with viable alternatives. The
Countess *is* Good; she represents the ideal image of Goodness
in the material world. The play attempts to particularize
heroic self-sacrifice, but the ritual of its action and
outcome neither startles the imagination nor induces sympathetic identification.

At least in *The Land of Heart's Desire* Mary Bruin's
dissatisfaction with the dreary round of duties and dull-
ness in a thoroughly pedestrian existence is a more readily
shared situation or attitude of mind. Yeats avails himself
of the contemporary distinction between physical and supernatural worlds, and the peasant culture of an unspecified
past time makes the action quite plausible, however slight
it may be. More importantly, the triumph of the Sidhe over
the temporal world is imaginatively extended. The carefree
animation of the other world is mentioned several times in
the dialogue, and it erupts on the scene with the magical
song and dance of the faery child who carries Mary off.
There is a viable choice between valid alternatives, but
the choice is neither ennobling nor tragic, for Mary, in
herself, has little importance whatever, although she is
more developed as a character than Cathleen. As in *The
Countess Cathleen*, the conflict is between a spiritual and
material existence, and the triumph of the spiritual world
is unexceptionable.

The direction of Yeats's development as a dramatist is
already obvious. In *The Land of Heart's Desire* the more
diffuse construction of *The Countess Cathleen* is reduced to
a single, climactic action in which characterization achieves
a better balance between surface reality and archetypal representation. As Yeats himself commented in a later preface
to revised texts of the two plays (1912): They are,

> I think, easier to play effectively than my later plays,
> depending less upon the players and more upon the pro-
> ducer, both having been imagined more for variety of
> stage-picture than variety of mood in the player. It
> was, indeed, the first performance of 'The Countess
> Cathleen', when our stage-pictures were made out of
> poor conventional scenery and hired costumes, that set
> me writing plays where all would depend upon the player.[16]

From the very beginning Yeats paid close attention to the
more plastic means of theatre production and achieved
striking effects with character contrasts; the Countess and
the evil Merchants at the inn of Shemus Rua, the Priest and
Faery Child in the Bruin cottage. His settings were simple,
but stylized; the background painted flat to suggest something of the unreality of the scene. The emphasis on uncertainty or mystery as to the true nature of the Merchants

and the Faery Child serves to cut across the superficially
realistic situation and leads effectively towards an ultimate revelation, while the harmonies of ballad meter and
natural speech rhythms are thrown into relief by the inclusion of music and song. Both timpani and harp are called
for in the 1895 version of *The Countess Cathleen*, and must
have come into their own during the newly-created scene in
which the angelic host is revealed and the Countess apo-
theosized. The single lyric, 'Who will go live with Fergus
now', is to be chanted by the old nurse, Oona, in each of
the revisions from 1895 to 1908, while singing and dancing
play an even more important role in *The Land of Heart's
Desire* where the lyric, 'The wind blows out of the gates of
day', is sung three times to mark the progress of the action,
and the dance of the Faery Child is the distinguishing image
of its power and nature. Again, the artifice of imaginative
and anti-naturalistic modes is relied upon to suggest a
transcending of surface reality.

　　The Shadowy Waters, on the other hand, constitutes an
entirely new departure for Yeats and a direct assault on
the problem of expressing a counter-reality. For the first
time since the narrative verse of *The Wanderings of Oisin*
Yeats chose to deal directly with the imagined reality of
the heroic world and to encompass it in an extended verse
drama. In its earliest form the dramatic poem concentrates
on Forgael's single-minded quest for the absolute life of
the spirit, and the dramatic action is at best artificial,
for there is little real conflict or opposition. As Forgael
wanders through a mysterious and supernatural seascape
guided by the souls of the dead incarnated as birds, his
men board another vessel and take it as a prize. Her consort slain, the Queen, Dectora, tries to incite Forgael's
men to mutiny with a promise of earthly reward in her kingdom upon their return. They are already discontented and
anxious because of their captain's mystical preoccupations,
but Forgael subdues their will by means of magic and casts
a spell on Dectora in which she conceives an archetypal
love for him that is compared to the mythological relationship between Aengus and Edaine. After mechanical interruption by the now drunken sailors, Forgael forsakes the temptation of Dectora's embraces in order to continue his pursuit
of the supernatural, and Dectora sacrifices all earthly
pleasure by accompanying him on his quest, proclaiming him

her King. What dramatic conflict there is in the play finds
its expression in the opposition of temporal and spiritual
existence, but the attraction of the supernatural remains
merely a matter of assertion. The actual situation is only
controlled by magic, and the self-sacrifice of both Forgael
and Dectora is ultimately a matter of faith. The alchemical processes symbolized by the action are emphasized by
the unreal setting and the alienation techniques Yeats
specified for production. On whatever level one wishes to
read the allegory however, it constitutes one of Yeats's
central visions as to the relationship which the hero/arti-
fex bears to both the physical and metaphysical worlds.
Union with an incarnation of the ideal feminine principle
is not an end in itself, but rather a stage in spiritual
development for both.

   Later revisions of the play demonstrate Yeats's tendency to accommodate his vision to traditionally realistic
norms and to elaborate on the intellectual import of the
action. In the acting version the scene is no longer man-
ifestly supernatural, and Forgael waits to be guided by the
souls of the dead. The spirit world, however, eludes him.
The attempted mutiny of his men is both realistic and spontaneous while Aibric's unquestioned loyalty acts as a
measure of Forgael's serious intent. The two men discuss
the inherent futility in the search for ideal woman, and as
soon as Dectora appears she is disclaimed as the object of
that search. Yet their union is fated, and Forgael's heroism is founded in his acceptance of this substitution.
The two characters are said to be caught in a net of fate
woven by the gods, an image that appears again to some
effect in *Deirdre*, and as Dectora rails, Forgael plays the
magic harp. The new thematic orientation is emphasized in
the keening for Iollan, Dectora's vanquished consort: 'The
King's dead, long live the King', and Forgael asks: 'Do
you not know me, lady? I am he / That you are weeping for.'[17]
In kindling Dectora's love Forgael replaces Iollan; a
woman's natural love elevates and maintains him. Rather
than a denial of temporal existence as in the original dramatic poem, the final version celebrates physical life.

   It would also appear that Yeats had wider symbolic
correspondences in mind when choosing Forgael and Dectora
as archetypal figures for his ritual drama. Forgael (or
Forgall) is the generally accepted name of Emer's father
and Dectora (also Dechtere and Dichtire) was Cuchulain's

mother. According to Lady Gregory's account of 'The Birth
of Cuchulain',[18] Dectora, sister to Conchubar and wife of
Sualtim, was stolen away supernaturally on her wedding day
by the god Lugh of the Long Hand and returned under mysterious circumstances one year later with a son who came to
be known as Cuchulain. The child was acknowledged by the
mother's husband, but its mysterious origins were also insisted upon through claims of a supernatural sire. There
is no overt attempt to associate the action of *The Shadowy
Waters* with Cuchulain, however, for the man of physical
action and artistic imagination is well represented in Forgael, and the symbolic action of the play centres on sexual
attraction between man and woman as a reflection of that
between the natural and supernatural worlds. In both versions of *The Shadowy Waters* it is obvious that the hero
assumes supernatural power and thus fulfils his nature.

Without recognizable dramatic conflict and action, *The
Shadowy Waters* relies wholly on the quality of its literary
text and method of production for its validity on the stage.
The original version was a concerted attempt to achieve imaginative unity and to transcend Walter Pater's concept of
art as a universal flux of impressions by creating a 'fire-
born mood' which exists beyond temporal limitations. Its
verbal music and sensuous ornamentation help to animate an
otherwise monotonous rhapsody or reverie and derive from
Pater's pronouncements on the unity of lyric effect. The
use of archetypal figures and heavily weighted symbols from
occult lore also adds an element of intellectual depth and
owes much to Villiers de l'Isle-Adams's symbolic drama,
Axel, while the slow posturing prescribed for the actors
and the mysterious, unnatural speeches imply undiscovered
significance much in the manner of Maurice Maeterlinck's
static theatre. In all, the severe restriction of place
and action, the limited colour scheme of blues and greens
with accents of copper, and the ground-swell of verse are
carefully calculated to achieve the unity of a choric song.
One of the most imaginative devices of all was the use of
the magical harp as a symbol for supernatural power which
could not otherwise be projected on the stage. Just as the
nature or quality of life among the Sidhe was projected
through the singing and dancing of the Faery Child in *The
Land of Heart's Desire*, so the supernatural power of the
artifex is presented through the music played upon the
magical harp given him by the Fool of the Wood. The device

was openly attacked as artificial, and Yeats replied (1906):

There is no reason for objecting to a mechanical effect
when it represents some material thing, becomes a symbol,
a player, as it were. One permits it an obedience to
the same impulse that has made religious men decorate
with jewels and embroidery the robes of priests and
heirophants, even until the robe, stiffened and weighted,
seems more important than the man who carries it. He
has become a symbol, and his robe has become a symbol
of something incapable of direct expression, something
that is superhuman. If the harp cannot suggest some
power that no actor could represent by sheer acting, for
the more acting, the more human life, the enchanting of
so many people by it will seem impossible. Perhaps very
wonderful music might do that if the audience were musicians, but lacking the music and that audience it is
better to appeal to the eye. The play will I hope, be
acted as on its first production, with a quiet gravity,
and a kind of rhythmic movement, and a very scrupulous
cherishing of the music of the verse.[19]

The early version of *The Shadowy Waters* was produced
privately for a convention of the Theosophical Society
(London 1900) where it was well enough received, but the
public performance of the later acting version (1906) was
something of a disaster. The audience was neither prepared
to participate in the ritual, nor to perceive its occult
wisdom. In a letter to Stephen McKenna, John Synge puts the
case rather well:

I do not believe in the possibility of 'a purely fantastic, unmodern, ideal, breezy, spring-dayish, Cuchulainoid
National Theatre'. We had *The Shadowy Waters* on the stage
last week, and it was the most *depressing* failure the
mind can imagine - a half-empty room, with growling men
and tittering females. Of course, it is possible to
write drama that fills your description and yet it is
fitter for the stage than *The Shadowy Waters*, but no
drama can grow out of anything other than the fundamental
realities of life which are never fantastic, are neither
modern nor unmodern and, as I see them, rarely spring-
dayish, or breezy or Cuchulainoid.[20]

Yeats could hardly be expected to agree with Synge's implied
definition of the fundamental realities of life, but in
every revision of the play, he did seek a more convincing
dramatic conflict and concreteness of detail which inevitably
compromised his original conception. He ruthlessly pruned
away much of the occult imagery and otherwise impaired the
play's lyric unity by sacrificing the incantatory verse to
a more naturalistic speech rhythm. Instead of sinning with
greater strength against theatrical convention and creating
a new dramatic form, he continued to accommodate his subject
matter to a basically realistic and logical progression of
dramatic events. Instead of radically refocusing his perceptions of psychological or spiritual experience, Yeats
attempted to arrive at their expression by imitating naturalistic action. The presence of the irrational may well
be inferred from a reversal in the logic of naturalistic
events, but its quality and nature can only be exhibited
by direct presentation. Unfortunately, Yeats missed the
point in his revision of *The Shadowy Waters*, and it was not
until some years later that he recognized the impasse toward
which he was working.

Between the publication of *The Shadowy Waters* (1900)
and its first public performance (1904), Yeats worked on
four other plays. Like *The Land of Heart's Desire*, the
first of these, *Cathleen ni Houlihan*, is little more than
the presentation of a simple, naturalistic scene in which
the advent of a supernatural apparition provides a concrete
image of an abstract idea or emotion. The brief intensity
of the play is a great advance on the diffuseness of *The
Countess Cathleen*, and a similar telescoping of *The Shadowy
Waters* might well have proved a more successful means of
revision than his uneasy compromise with circumstantial
realism. The characters and situations of *Cathleen ni
Houlihan* are hardly sketched in when the Poor Old Woman
enters, bringing with her an air of foreboding and mystery.
Her unnatural answers to civil questions emphasize the
presence of dramatic irony and her songs 'I will go cry with
the woman' and 'Do not make a keening', substantiate a
growing mood of melancholy, even of enchantment or madness,
which finally overcomes Michael Gillane who chooses pat-
riotism and death over marriage and material ease. Unlike
either *The Countess Cathleen* or *The Land of Heart's Desire*,
the choice forced upon Michael was immediately real to an
Irish audience and involved an option fundamental to their

lives. The theatrical success of the play was not altogether
due to the relevance of its subject matter or to the personification of Mother Ireland, however, but rather to the
accomplishment of progressive patterning and lyric unity
which gives way to transcendent revelation at the end.

To a lesser degree, *The Pot of Broth* relies on the same
combination of relevant content and lyric treatment, even
though it is the only one of Yeats's many plays which has
neither supernatural revelation nor fantastic setting, and
deals wholly with the natural world of traditional comedy.
Instead of the projection of absolute values, comic inversion is employed to satirize those of a bourgeois-oriented
society; the outcast Tramp gulls Sibby Coneely through an
appeal to her avarice and vanity. With the help of Lady
Gregory, Sibby's peasant mentality is accurately observed
and credibly rendered, while the glamour of the Tramp's
ready speech and of his songs, 'There's broth in the pot
for you, old man' and 'My Paistin Finn is my sole desire',
builds to its inevitable climax as the cumulative effect
of progressive intensification.

In construction *The Hour-Glass* returns to the pattern
of medieval morality and creates a world of imaginative
reality, such as that of *The Countess Cathleen* and *The
Shadowy Waters*, rather than the naturalistic setting of a
localized, peasant culture as in *The Land of Heart's Desire*,
Cathleen ni Houlihan and *The Pot of Broth*. The strong sense
of an antique past in all his plays, whether explicitly
medieval, heroic, or merely indefinite, effectively removes
the action from naturalistic considerations. The central
incident of the play is taken from Irish legend and the
action represents the opposition of reason and intuition in
apprehending the nature of the circumambient universe. The
major revisions of the play differ from the original in the
change from prose to verse, and from the Wise Man humbling
himself to the Fool and being saved, to his courageous acceptance of God's Will regardless of consequences and subsequent salvation. The pattern is exactly that of *The
Countess Cathleen* - revelation, sacrifice/submission and
salvation - and the elaborate situations and dialogue of
both plays are equally necessary in order to suggest the
inner struggle of the main character. In *The Hour-Glass*
the basic tension is between the Wise Man and the Fool,
whose very names help to render them archetypal and representative rather than realistic and individual. The

struggle of reason with intuition for ascendence over the
mind of man is shown in the interviews between the Wise
Man and his pupils, his wife and the Fool. After the revelation of God's Angel which demonstrates the vanity of his
earlier views, the Wise Man is made to confront the success
of his teaching in each refusal to admit belief in the supernatural. With each episode the tension mounts, and the
allegorical nature of the play becomes even more evident.
In order to insist more emphatically on the character of
the Fool as a principle of the mind rather than a human
being, he is given a mask 'in the old Italian way',[21] and
the Angel who appears to the Wise Man is also masked in
the version of 1912.[22] Although not particularly original,
the image of the symbolic butterfly is a particularly happy
concrete detail which reaffirms the play's general mood of
innocence and accommodates itself very well to the prevailing
anti-illusionist mode of production.

   Not only were visual effects utilized in distancing
both Fool and Angel from the human condition and directing
audience attention toward the allegorical action - the redemption of reason through emotion or intuition - but vocal
effects were also invoked. In the later poetic version
irregular line lengths were introduced into the dialogue
which characterize the mounting human emotion, and Yeats
advocated delivering the Angel's speeches on pure musical
notes set down beforehand and rehearsed: 'On the one occasion, when I heard the Angel's part spoken in this way with
entire success, the contrast between the crystalline quality
of the pure notes and the more confused and passionate
speaking of the Wise Man was a new dramatic effect of great
value.'[23] As in earlier plays, lyrical unity was founded
in archetypal characterizations, allegorical structures,
patterned language and poetic imagery while the cumulative
effect was further heightened by the artificiality of the
Pupil's song, 'Who stole your wits away'. The production
method, especially in the later version, follows that of
The Shadowy Waters in its reliance on a symbolic and harmonious colour scheme of olive-green, purple and red-brown
against the ivory screens designed by Edward Gordon Craig.
One begins to recognize a characteristic tension in Yeats's
early drama between a basically realistic and logical progression of dramatic events which imitates naturalistic
action and the allegorizing effects of highly stylized stage

conventions. The peculiar weakness of *The Hour-Glass* is
its lack of relevance to the modern predicament. Outside
of *Cathleen ni Houlihan* perhaps, none of Yeats's early plays
convince unless one already accepts his premises about the
fundamental realities of human existence. Each play is
carefully worked out to overcome its conceptual disadvantage,
but the impact of the psychic truth to be projected and of
anti-illusionist technique is greatly diminished by the
need to make the action plausible.

    The King's Threshold is a further exploitation of the
relationship between intuition, now embodied in the poet
Seanchan, and reason or political wisdom, incarnated in the
King. At the same time, the play is a further experiment in
the wrong direction. Again, the action takes place in an
imagined past whose authority lies in legend, and the dis-
integration of the heroic order is represented by the poet's
expulsion from the King's council. Since the hero represents virtue itself, there is no alternative but to inten-
sify his opposition to vice, and the dramatic action remains
on the surface, leaving little room for any imaginative
participation of the audience. Nor is heroic transcendence
really possible as we have seen in *The Countess Cathleen*,
when the protagonist is an allegorical abstraction rather
than a particularized Everyman. In such a conception it is
the outcome of the action which carries the burden of meaning and not the quality or nature of the experience. In
The King's Threshold there are only two alternatives: either
the King capitulates as in the original version and poetry
is acknowledged as legislator in the practical affairs of
men, or Seanchan dies, as in the final revision of the play
which is certainly more faithful to reality as we know it,
since poets are rarely prime ministers. The play's most
serious flaw lies in the limitation of its outcome to such
an either/or proposition and particularly in the circumstances of the later version where attention is drawn away
from the main theme of poetry's rightful place in the world
of affairs to the personal courage and tragedy of Seanchan,
the hero. *The King's Threshold* is certainly one of the
most naturalistic presentations among the early plays and
its strength lies in the rich sense of multiplicity of
action, observation, and satire with which Yeats was able
to elaborate the basic plot. Instead of either supernatural
revelation or personal apotheosis, Seanchan's inner struggle

is presented as a tension between delirium and vision as
the poet approached the Dionysian ecstasy that precedes his
death. The movement of the action is further projected by
the choric effect of his pupils and their implied commentary as they move from a stage of innocence to understanding
and also by the successive levels of temptation to end his
hunger strike in the encounters with Mayor (and Cripples),
Chamberlain (and Courtiers), Princesses, Fedelmn, and finally
the King himself. One wonders, in fact, if the play is not
perhaps inspired by *Samson Agonistes*. In any case much good
use is made of the opportunity to caricature a cross-section
of social pretensions and false values in the play, and Yeats
was able to present on stage his own quarrel with an unpoetic
and uncomprehending Dublin audience. More than any of the
earlier plays which had used episodic construction, *The
King's Threshold* is obviously modelled on the form of classical Greek drama, and it is not surprising that Yeats should
have taken up the translation of *King Oedipus* after the first
version was published.

The formal construction and dramatic conception of *The
King's Threshold* does contribute to whatever lyric unity the
play possesses, but so naturalistic a representation depends
far more on the laws of cause and effect, the logical progression of events, and the presentation of acceptable human
motivation than on stylization of language, acting technique,
or staging. There is, as always, in Yeats's plays a close
control of language, imagery, and rhythmic patterning, and
the action is punctuated strategically with songs: 'There's
nobody'll call out for him' and 'The four rivers that run
there', but the lyrics are somewhat gratuitous and devoid of
significance in their actual context. Apart from the songs
in *The Land of Heart's Desire* and *Cathleen ni Houlihan*, which
themselves intimate supernatural or mysterious experience,
Yeats had never succeeded in using songs as an integral part
of the action and meaning of his plays. In every way *The
King's Threshold* is a more traditional dramatic conception
and treatment than any of the earlier work, and it was more
successful on the stage than many of the more radical experiments, but its success was purchased at the expense of
its universality and import. The truth it manifests is of
little interest to anyone and has no relevance to modern life
at all. At best it is a theme treated indirectly and sub-
jectively while Yeats was yet to find his characteristic expression and new dramatic form in direct and objective
treatment of abstract ideas and states of mind.

At the same time that Yeats was writing *The King's Threshold* he was still working with *On Baile's Strand*, a play that was to prove itself far more successful and satisfying as a compromise between conventional Renaissance form and experimental technique in expressing the conflict between the natural and supernatural worlds, both directly and objectively. The original version of Yeats's play also concentrates on the perennial opposition of male and female in the enmity of Aoife towards Cuchulain, which results in her son's challenge of mortal combat to the bemused hero. The Celtic legend as recorded by Lady Gregory under the title 'The Only Son of Aoife', ends with a classical recognition and reconciliation, while in the major versions of Yeats's play the frenzied hero fights and kills his own son before their relationship is revealed to him. Cuchulain's youthful, sweet victory over Aoife is emphasized in the first published version and eventually results in bitter self-destruction; the heroic assertion is shown to be inherently self-defeating. The outline of action appears to be an inversion of Forgael's victory over Dectora through magical song, and of her subsequent acquiescence to the spiritual quest and mystical union with the artifex/hero. Cuchulain's end is tragic; he is seen to be the victim of inexorable fate which he confronts heroically and futilely in his fight against the waves. The weakness of this version is in its lack of credible motivation and the vagueness of its underlying theme. The revision of 1906 further emphasizes the role of Conchubar and his claim to Cuchulain's fealty. The oath of allegiance exacted by Conchubar is an abandonment of Cuchulain's spontaneous and heroic nature and marks the capitulation of the heroic world to the exigencies of time and reason. 'It is significant that it is the cries of "witchcraft" which tip the scales. We can see the change as an extreme formulation of the life of instinct and the denial of reason - in essence, a magical conception of life.'[24] There can be no role for the true hero in the debased world of Conchubar's new dispensation, and fittingly, Cuchulain's last act is his heroic assault on the symbol of human experience which has overcome him. The double vision of archetypal self-destruction is enormously powerful, while the emphasis on actual conflict and a tragic fall from undivided being rather than ritualised mythic action, judiciously avoids dramatic situations antithetical to the values and experience of the audience. The role that Conchubar plays

in the revised version of *On Baile's Strand* is very similar
to that of the Wise Man in *The Hour-Glass*, abstract reason
unredeemed by inspired intuition, but in the later play
reason is the antagonist, and the spontaneity of the hero
more forcefully celebrated at its expense. Unlike *The
King's Threshold* where the decision to exclude the poet from
the King's council marks the dissolution of the heroic world
and unity of being, Cuchulain denies his own nature and puts
an end to the fulfilling union of opposites for all time.
On Baile's Strand parallels the Judeo-Christian myth of
original sin and the fall from grace, while its multiplicity
of implications and compactness of design is a great advance
on the more artificially drawn out and unsatisfactory morality plays. For the first time Yeats has conceived characters and situations which work together perfectly, both
on the level of circumstantial reality and also as symbolic
representations of universal significance. A very real
dramatic intensity is achieved through the integration of
complex thematic material, an intensity which was noticeably
lacking earlier in the separate treatment of individual
themes. The play is certainly Yeats's most significant and
successful experiment since *The Shadowy Waters*.

One of the most interesting technical achievements of
On Baile's Strand, and yet another link with his experiments
in *The Hour-Glass* and *The King's Threshold*, is the use of
Fool and Blind Man as both sub-plot and chorus. The conception may well derive from Yeats's enthusiasm for *King Lear*,
but his Fool is more a figure of folklore, as are the Cripples in *The King's Threshold*, and they serve a more symbolic
purpose within the play than either the use of Fool or sub-
plot in Shakespeare, even though they accomplish a similar
function in providing a vivid sense of variety and multiplicity in events. Fool and Blind Man not only reflect and
comment on the relationship between Cuchulain and Conchubar
as representing instinctive action and reason, but they also
demonstrate the direct correspondence between heroic and
folk traditions. In their role as chorus they provide both
a perfect induction and frame for the dramatic action, as
well as comic detachment, and in their representative nature
they focus attention on the symbolism of character and situation. In terms of Yeats's development as a dramatist it
is important to note that the original characterization of
Fintain, a blind man, and Barach, a fool, is more completely
expressed in the final version, especially in the fool's

speeches, and that the archetypal significance of the characters is emphasized by suppressing personal names and
giving each a mask. In order that the point not be missed,
Yeats added a note to *Plays for an Irish Theatre* (1911):
'The same Fool and mask (from *The Hour-Glass*), the Fat Fool
of folklore who is "as wide and wild as a hill" and not the
Thin Fool of modern romance, may go with a masked Blind Man
into *On Baile's Strand*.'[25] The schematic construction of
the play has been criticised as mechanical, but through the
superimposition of such formal patterning, circumstantial
reality was successfully transcended, and a poetic image
of the human condition came into being. Without the Fool
and Blind Man we would become involved in a purely personal
tragedy, rather than the ritual presentation of man's plight
as he is seduced by time and nature to contradict the transcendent aspect of his own character. More than in any of
the early plays, the personages of *On Baile's Strand* are
symbolic and draw their meaning directly from their actions
and interrelationships.

     Just as the Fool and Blind Man naturalize the action
of the play with their earthy comedy, The Chorus of Women
insists on a supernatural element and the awesomeness of
religious ritual. Their role is much more conventionally
choric in the Greek tradition, and their intervention at
critical moments of the action provides an excellent aesthetic balance to the encapsulating scenes of Fool and Blind
Man which mediate between the real world of the audience and
the higher plane of heroic reality. Yeats was obviously
moving away from his early dependence on direct supernatural
intervention, conventional naturalism and lyric unity in his
freer experimentation with direct expression of experience
and states of mind. The surface reality of *On Baile's
Strand* is both sharp and vital, yet the consistency and control of language still attests to the presence of lyrical
unity which is emphasized by the songs of both Fool and
Chorus: 'Cuchulain has killed Kings', 'May this fire have
driven out', and 'When you were an acorn on the treetop'.
The dramatic validity of the dialogues, however, is under-
cut by the insistent unreality of the production method, and
the anti-illusionism of the play's conception is further documented in a later preface to *Plays in Prose and Verse* (1922):

     'On Baile's Strand', though produced for the first time
     at the opening of the Abbey Theatre in December 1904, was

planned when I had no hope of that, or any, theatre, and
the characters walk on to an empty stage at the beginning
and leave that stage empty at the end, because I thought
of its performance upon a large platform with a door at
the back and an exit through the audience at the side,
and no proscenium, or curtain; and being intended for a
platform and a popular audience.[26]

On Baile's Strand was perhaps the most popular of all Yeats'
plays, and it is still highly regarded in many quarters with
good reason; the possibility of a balance between surface
realism and symbolic import had been realized.

Although popular on the Abbey stage in its day, *Deirdre*
is a much more limited success because of the severe res-
trictions imposed by its dramatic conception and treatment.
The action opens in the middle of things, and an outline of
the legend is rehearsed by the chorus who recount the background and present circumstances of Deirdre's life as well
as intimating its inevitable outcome. In acknowledging her
fate, attention is immediately focused on the manner in whic
it is met, and Deirdre dominates the action of the play whic
presents the drama of her inner being and, incidentally, an
image of ideal heroic action. However fixed her fate may be
her character remains uncertain to the end, and her plight
is quite recognizably personal. Yeats's insistence on natural emotion and human psychology makes *Deirdre* one of the
most readily accessible of his plays, and, I think, accounts
for its popularity at the Abbey.

The essential conflict is the opposition of honour and
passion in the heroic world, a typically antithetical vision
of public versus private morality, inner versus outer.
Deirdre and Naisi return to Ireland in good faith, and the
honourable intentions of Conchubar are reiterated again and
again through Fergus. The chorus of women who set the scene
are much more certain of the High King's actual intentions,
however, and the fact that Fergus himself had been tricked
by Conchubar into abdicating the throne is not to be overlooked. Fergus represents an older and more perfect order
in opposition to Conchubar whose quarrel with Naisi is represented as the conflict of age with youth. Like the longing of fallen man for spiritual perfection, age is goaded
by the image of youth, and Conchubar destroys Naisi in order
to obtain what he can never possess. The spectacle of
Conchubar's frustration is a characteristic evocation of the

human condition, and it is beautifully balanced by Deirdre's
transcendence of temporal limitations in her acceptance of
heroic decorum. Both Naisi and Deirdre keep faith with
heroic tradition, whereas Conchubar breaks the oath in which
they had believed. Controlling her passion and refusing
to give in to expediency, Deirdre achieves a transcendent
and heroic stature. Ironically, she wins her end by app-
ealing to Conchubar's sense of decorum and the honour due
to her position, when, in fact, he has little faith in her
apparent change of heart. Nor is she false to herself in
those speeches which gain her an honourable death. The
abrupt shift after Naisi's end from pleading, passionate
woman to cold detachment and mastery of the situation is so
much an apotheosis as to seem a supernatural intervention.
At this moment Deirdre is an exact parallel to the image
of Aoife as Cuchulain speaks of her in *On Baile's Strand*,
and approaches the condition of their archetype, the goddess
Fand.

Within so static a drama of ideas and ideals, however,
and where the narrative element of realistic plot progression
is avoided, there is a great tendency to monotony. In a
note published in *The Collected Works* (1908), Yeats himself
confessed:

> The principal difficulty with the form of dramatic struc-
> ture I have adopted is that, unlike the loose Elizabethan
> form, it continually forces one by its rigour of logic
> away from one's capacities, experiences, and desires,
> until, if one have not patience to wait for the mood, or
> to rewrite again and again till it comes, there is rhet-
> oric and logic and dry circumstance where there should be
> life.[27]

The verse of *Deirdre* is highly textured in keeping with his
earlier views on lyrical composition, and songs mark the
progress of the action as well as decorating and heightening
the poetic text: '"Why is it", Queen Edain said', 'Love is
an immoderate thing', and 'They are gone, they are gone'.
But language alone is hardly sufficient to galvanize dramatic structure into life and Yeats solved the problem by
interposing a chorus between action and audience and raising
simple stage properties to the level of images which serve
as paradigms of the dramatic action itself.

Without the use of the chorus, *Deirdre* might well have failed both as an experiment in the search for a new theatrical form and as a viable stage play. The property images serve as a necessary catalyst in the crystallization and reassertion of dramatic tensions, while The Chorus of Women mediates between the surface action and its archetypal significance, much in the manner of the Fool and Blind Man of *On Baile's Strand*. A symbolic sub-plot is no longer necessary because the relationship of characters, motives, and situation in *Deirdre* itself constitutes an archetypal pattern, but The Chorus of Women provides an absolute moral standard by which to judge the action. They not only set the scene and rehearse background information in a traditional way, but they also interpret the action and imply the fate of the participants. In the dramatic sense they are removed from the action itself, but in their intimations of omniscience they actively manipulate the reaction of the audience. At one and the same time they are identifiable as limited human beings and also suggest the uncanny presence of supernatural knowledge. They are both women and priestesses who direct our attention to the reality of the surface action at one point and to the archetypal nature of the ideal action at another. Without them we might overlook the formalization of conflict and resolution into a metaphorical pattern.

The brazier of fire, which is also the symbol of The Chorus of Women, becomes an active presence in the play and together with the chessboard, dominates the scene. The action is carefully divided between antithetical images - the subjectivity of the hearth and the objectivity of worldly encounter - while their visible presence is a continual reminder of the opposition between passion and honour. Yeats also employs literary symbols within the text; rubies and dragons vie for our attention with forest birds and hunting nets, not only within the text of the play, but also in the stage business, for Deirdre arms herself with her jewels and Naisi is entrapped on stage. On the other hand, the symbolism of brazier and chessboard operates on several levels at the same time. The fire, for example, is as much associated with domestic religious ritual and with the moral touchstone provided by the chorus as it is with personal passion, both public and private. The chessboard is a projection of human experience in society and through the allusion to Lugaedh Redstripe and his seamew wife it also becomes an emblem of heroic decorum and acceptance of the inevitable. The chess-board functions as an image of foreboding, and a very necessary element of variety and tension is added to an otherwise near-static situation, while the fire represents stability and protection. The use of the mysterious and exotic dark-faced soldiery represents a further effort at theatrical symbolism and heightening of tension. Both the inescapability of Deirdre's fate and its insidious origins are visually asserted and emphasized.

To a very great extent *Deirdre* is a measure of Yeats's development as a practical man of the theatre, for the play depends as much upon staging and production for its effectiveness as upon its literary text. Its greatest achievement, however, is the imaginative combination of expressive elements that attempt to direct the attention of the audience from the individual tragedy of a particular character to the ritual significance of the archetypal pattern on which the drama is based. Presentation of the passionate moment is substituted for narration, and the central character, again like Milton's Samson, triumphs in defeat through the demonstration of moral integrity. What happens is no longer as important as the quality of the happening, and the audience is immediately thrown back on the texture of language as a considered means for expressing the forces that come into play. The stylization of acting technique and of the visible scene is equally important in heightening the effectiveness of Yeats's double vision: the power of youth versus the degradation of age, and the transcendence of heroic action versus the debasement of selfish motivation.

Whatever the theoretical success of the play, *Deirdre* falls short of Yeats's achievement in *On Baile's Strand*. The drama remains a very personal tragedy in spite of the creative efforts to balance realism with symbolism, and the interplay of ideas is largely obscured by rhetorical language. Admiration for Yeats's experimentation should not blind us to the fact that the play is rather heavy going in the study as well as on stage. Such idealization of the heroic world would be more acceptable to an audience of Dryden's time than in our own, and however imaginative the expressive devices, the simple dramatic tension is over-extended. Ultimately, our interest flags. On the other hand, *Deirdre* is Yeats's first success in conceiving a new and experimental form of drama, but such a judgment is only possible in retrospect. In the light of later developments

we now recognize *Deirdre* as the first important attempt at
a new form of drama since *The Shadowy Waters*, and a prototype of the plays for dancers. The play did not appear to
have satisfied Yeats however, and instead of pursuing the
experiment farther at that time, he turned to other possible
forms and conceptions of drama. Together with *On Baile's
Strand*, *Deirdre* marks a definite stage in Yeats's development as a dramatist since it is also the last of his plays
in a serious mode before his introduction to Nō drama in
1913.

While *Deirdre* was being revised, a radically new version of *Where There is Nothing* was also in preparation.
The Unicorn From the Stars is certainly a more accomplished
play than the earlier effort, yet neither are wholly success
ful in projecting the desired Nietzschean vision of astrin-
gent joy or in asserting the negation of pure spirituality.
Where There is Nothing was originally written and published
under great pressure in order to save the plot from being
pirated, but its revision as *The Unicorn From the Stars* is
a concerted attempt to find an alternative to the heroic
world of high seriousness as a medium for Yeats's themes.
The realistic world of folk comedy was a natural choice,
expecially since the form had proved so popular on the
Abbey stage. The text of *Where There is Nothing* had little
to recommend it for the experiment, except perhaps in its
basic naturalistic approach to the perennial opposition
between the dictates of spiritual vision and the conditions
of temporal life. The quality of the hero's vision is only
implied by the extent of the heresy he commits and the degree of fanatical zeal that is aroused, while the play is
loosely constructed of episodes linked by a strong central
character, and progresses linearly through the climax of
Paul Routtledge's sermon to its inevitable resolution and
ironical tragedy. *The Unicorn From the Stars* is much more
carefully worked out, and the basic shift from a priest/hero
to a country craftsman is underlined by the addition of an
effective sub-plot which both parallels the main action and
provides a further inversion of the conventional world of
affairs in the values of tinkers and tramps. Johnny Bocach
reinterprets Martin Hearne's mystical vision in terms of
political conflict between England and Ireland, and the
opposition of golden lion and unicorn from the stars replace
the vaguely episodic construction of the earlier version.
The physical reality of the coach which the hero is building

and its political implications, are played against the romantic possibility of Martin's visions, while Martin himself
mediates between the practical reality of both Thomas Hearne
and Johnny Bocach on the one hand and the psychic preoccupations of Andrew Hearne and Father John on the other.
Martin's second vision, however, reserves the cosmic battle
to the mind alone and insists on revelation, rather than
reformation or revolution. His accidental death is rendered
both artificial and anticlimactic since martyrdom is at best
ineffectual when the conflict is not of this world. Altogether, the spiritual reality of mystical vision is incon-
clusively established and co-exists uncomfortably with the
circumstantial reality of the play's basic conception.

Exact correspondences between temporal and spiritual
activity can be set up within naturalistic drama, but the
metaphorical design of *The Unicorn From the Stars* is all too
obvious. The symbolism of artisan and golden coach is mechanical and lifeless, Martin Hearne is too little developed
as a character, and the images alone are incapable of communicating a felt or shared experience to the audience. As
in so many of the early plays, the desired state of being is
outlined and described rather than actually expressed or recreated in imagination. In order to make its point, the
plot of *The Unicorn From the Stars* is elaborately contrived,
whereas realistic drama requires a degree of inevitability
in its action. Very few experimental techniques are employed
in the play, but stylistic unity is achieved through the naturalism of dialect speech rhythms. Not surprisingly, there
are two songs, ' O come all ye airy bachelors' and 'O, the
lion shall lose his strength', but both arise naturally from
the action and contribute directly to the contrast of serious
dialogue and boisterous comic activity which save the drama
from total failure. Certainly it is the spontaneity of the
play's ironic observation of rural life rather than its realization of conflict between spiritual and temporal being that
gives the work whatever vitality it possesses. The one important contribution of *The Unicorn From the Stars* to Yeats's
development as a dramatist is the exploration of symbolic
possibility in the figure of the Irish tinker and his inversion of bourgeois values. Yeats developed the idea farther in several later plays and led the way to the establishment of tramp or beggarman as anti-hero and major
literary type of our time.

In *The Green Helmet* Yeats turned sharply from folk

comedy and experimented with the world of myth patterns and cycles. Rather than using Celtic legend as a basis for either heroic tragedy or ritual drama, Yeats combined several tales in such a way as to celebrate Cuchulain's heroic stature and at the same time to satirize human weakness or folly in the lesser characters. The action of the play is derived from three separate tales: 'Bricriu's Feast', 'The War of Words of the Women of Ulster', and 'The Championship of Ulster'. Each of the legends is recorded in Lady Gregory's *Cuchulain of Muirthemne.* The quarrel among the three warriors as to which should wear the green helmet, symbol of primacy, is settled in the play by Cuchulain's ingenious idea of filling the helmet with ale and sharing it equally among themselves. The renewal of that quarrel among their wives is settled by giving each a separate entrance to the hall in order that no one of them might take precedence over another. The third episode shows Cuchulain's real transcendence as hero for he alone is willing to accept the consequences of his actions, to play the game fairly and to laugh unconcernedly in the face of death. The mysterious Red Man who challenges him to a beheading tournament is obviously meant to be considered responsible for the earlier quarrels and to be associated with the figure of Bricriu, god of discord. The suppression of his actual identity in Irish myth also emphasizes the character of the play as a ritual of regeneration. The Red Man, symbol of disharmony and destruction is set in direct opposition to Cuchulain, who is associated with the Green Man of nature through the image of the green helmet. Not only is 'The Championship of Ulster' assimilated into the action, but the influence and overtones of *Sir Gawain and the Green Knight* is also present in the revised version of *The Golden Helmet.* The separate episodes which demonstrate Cuchulain's heroic magnanimity and spontaneity as a universal model of human conduct are brought together in a myth pattern of daring, death and regeneration. The supernatural revelation of the Red Man is as striking as that in any of the earlier plays, and the drama is particularly successful in reaching the required climax through the cumulative effect of ebullient comedy. It is particularly interesting to note that *The Green Helmet* was conceived as a curtain-raiser for *On Baile's Strand*, which constitutes its antithesis in both mood and theme.

The method of construction is as much a new departure

for Yeats as the matching of a comic mode with heroic action, and we see in *The Green Helmet* not only the comic counterpart of *Deirdre* but also a perfect distancing effect in myth patterning. Heroic characters can be rendered representative, and even archetypal, by ordering their actions into a pattern or design that parallels some recognizable cycle of human activity or experience. In *Deirdre* Yeats had attempted a structure which stood as a metaphor for the personal conflict and inner tensions of the central character, while in *The Green Helmet* he discovered the effectiveness of symbolic design in intimating the abstract force behind accidental circumstances.

    The Green Helmet is equally as interesting in its textural details and production method as it is in dramatic conception and construction. The songs that are included are far more closely related to the basic movement of the play than earlier examples. Instead of merely marking off the major divisions, the songs in *The Green Helmet* provide dramatic climaxes in themselves. Laegaire establishes the theme in the first episode with the swaggering lyric, 'Laegaire is best', and in the second the quarrel among the three wives was originally borne out in their self-conscious songs. A later revision of the play suppressed this elaboration, however, and intensified Emer's claims to Cuchulain's primacy among the heroes by giving her the magnificently rewritten lyric, 'Nothing that he has done', which crytallizes the conflict and leads inevitably to the climactic scene of riot and discord. The chaos and anarchy of the situation are broken, however, by the mysterious, supernatural figures who invade the scene and the action is effectively shifted to another level of reality, now that the hidden forces which had instigated the early conflicts are made manifest on stage. The cat-headed men who are associated with the moon and dressed in dark purple are an extension of the dark-faced and exotic soldiery of *Deirdre*, and their dramatic function is much the same. Another of the devices through which Yeats makes his point is the carefully controlled colour symbolism of the whole production. The characters, except for the supernatural figures, are dressed in various shades of green and associated with the luminous, green sea, which is visible through open windows. At the end of the play, even the eyes of the cat-men are meant to reflect the colour green, while the house in which the confrontation between the two worlds takes place is red-orange. Unlike the earlier use of effective colour schemes for mood and atmosphere, the colours of *The Green Helmet* add valid symbolic significance and independent presence, just as the symbols of brazier and chessboard had done in *Deirdre*. As the alexandrines inspired by Wilfred Scawen Blunt's *Fand* give lyrical unity and pattern to the play, so the colour scheme complements the action and dramatic conception. In 1908 Yeats documented his concern for stage design and debt to Gordon Craig's ideas, as well as his reliance on plastic means of production to reshape experience and meaning within a dramatic counter-reality:

> We staged the play with a very pronounced colour-scheme, and I have noticed that the more obviously decorative is the scene and costuming of any play, the more it is lifted out of time and place, and the nearer to faeryland do we carry it. One gets also much more effect out of concerted movements - above all, if there are many players - when all the clothes are the same colour. No breadth of treatment gives monotony when there is movement and change of lighting. It concentrates attention on every new effect and makes every change of outline or of light and shadow surprising and delightful. Because of this one can use contrasts of colour, between clothes and background or in the background itself, the complementary colours for instance, which would be too obvious to keep the attention in a painting. One wishes to make the movement of the action as important as possible, and the simplicity which gives depth of colour does this, just as, for precisely similar reasons, the lack of colour in a statue fixes the attention upon the form.[28]

The use of stylized stage setting and costume in Yeats's early plays should not be overlooked as an indication of his development as a playwright, especially since they served as so important a means of distinguishing the reality of the stage action from that of everyday life. In the earlier plays the sets presented very real interiors which gave on to the counter-reality of stylized nature; real incidents were set against an unreal image of the natural world. Through open windows and doors, for example, the great spaces of flat painted forest were perceived, but the uneasy juxtaposition did not keep the stage scene from dissolving into a vague and unspecified area of imagination. Yeats's later reliance on folk legend and heroic myth did ground the action in local reality, and it also allowed a freer use of anti-illusionist technique which differentiated image from object, the ideal from the actual. The stage action itself became more and more representative of truth or experience which existed only in imagination as Yeats was groping toward an expressive and highly symbolic form of theatre. Unfortunately, the techniques with which he had experimented refused to arrange themselves into a coherent and balanced pattern that suited his developing thought.

After the publication and first performance of *The Green Helmet* in 1910, several years passed before Yeats attempted another play. On his introduction to the classical Nō drama of Japan during the winter of 1913-14, he was again inspired to write for the stage, and his first efforts in a new theatrical convention were closely modelled on specific plays from the Fenollosa manuscripts which Ezra Pound was then editing. Nō drama offered him acknowledged prototypes of dramatic form and construction which successfully balanced theatrical effectiveness and esoteric significance, while it also evoked the authority of an antique and aristocratic tradition. The extent and accuracy of transmission through Pound and Fenollosa must be taken into account, however, before assessing Yeats's assimilation from the Nō.

2.

Fenollosa and Pound: Agents of Transmission

WHAT SPLENDOUR, IT ALL COHERES.[1]

Any number of difficulties stand in the way of assessing Yeats's assimilation of the Japanese Nō, and the problem of transmission through the hands of both Ernest Fenollosa and Ezra Pound is not the least of them. The achievement of Fenollosa as translator and commentator, and that of Pound as editor and enthusiast, can best be ascertained from the published volume, *'Noh' or Accomplishment* (1916), but the wider implications of Fenollosa's experience and thought need also to be examined, especially as they bear on the immediate attraction and relevance that his work had for men such as Pound and Yeats.

Ernest Fenollosa (1853-1908) was a man much attuned to the intellectual and aesthetic developments of his time, and he became a central figure in the transmission of knowledge of Oriental art and thought to the west. He died suddenly of a heart attack at the age of fifty-five, and his unpublished manuscripts concerning the Japanese Nō and Chinese poetry were eventually entrusted to Ezra Pound who acted as literary executor. In turn, Pound transmitted both the material and his enthusiasm to W. B. Yeats during the winter of 1913-14.

Ernest Fenollosa was an ideal student of Nō; his background as Professor of Philosophy at Tokyo University and his particular interests in aesthetic speculation, as well as an extraordinary sympathy for Japanese culture and expert knowledge of Oriental painting and sculpture, provided

intellectual authority for his approach to the classical
theatre as both spectator and performer. Unfortunately,
his work was completed during the early years of the modern
revival of interest in Nō and some time before classical
Japanese drama was to become a legitimate object of scholarly enquiry and discussion. Even without the help of accurate philological scholarship, however, he was in an
excellent position to contribute significantly to the study
of Nō. Not only had he perceived a basic and all-pervading
aesthetic principle in the synthesizing and harmonious design or structuring of individual sense images which constitutes an archetypal image or symbol of reality, but he
also had personal training as a Nō performer, and might,
therefore, offer an analysis of the relationship between
music and choreography in performance and the poetic quality of the text. Because of his untimely death such promise
went unfulfilled, however, but enough of his ideas carried
over into his one published essay on Nō, and even in the
later work edited by Ezra Pound, to be accounted a considerable contribution to the transmission of Nō and of its
understanding in the west.

One only has to read the descriptive article Fenollosa
published in 1901 to recognize the authority and completeness of his presentation in comparison with those of earlier
commentators. In the opening paragraph he suggests the
areas of enquiry which need to be considered for complete
coverage of the subject: Nō drama 'has never yet been
studied as a whole, even as literature, and never in its
wealth of aesthetic features, music, costume, spiritual
meaning, action, nor in its origin, its history, and its
present condition'.[2] The essay touches on all facets mentioned with the exception of the literary character which
is too complex for easy generalization, and emphasizes an
outline of origins, historical development and present
conditions. Long before other western commentators, Fenollosa demonstrated his understanding of the crystallization
that Nō drama had undergone during the Edo period as compared with its earlier vitality and creativity, and he also
voiced his disagreement with contemporary Japanese scholars
who maintained that actors had not created the plays unaided,
but that they merely added music and choreography to texts
prepared by Buddhist priests.

The Fenollosa essay which Pound incorporated in its
entirety in *'Noh' or Accomplishment* under the title

'Fenollosa on the Noh' (1903), gives some indication of
the character of Nō as an art form while focusing attention
on its historical development using Greek drama, medieval
mystery plays and Kabuki as points of comparison and contrast. Fenollosa recognized the complete grasp of spiritual being in the plays, and the last stage in perfecting
the form was presented as the addition of epic incident
and the celebration of cultural values which further affected the development of literary structure. He did understand, however, that the origin of Nō is to be found in
earlier dance performances which gathered to themselves
music and song (poetry) as both accompaniment and expressive elements. He concluded: 'The beauty and power of
Noh lie in the concentration. All elements - costume, motion, verse, and music - unite to produce a single clari-
fied impression. Each drama embodies some primary human
relation or emotion; and the poetic sweetness or poignancy
of this is carried to its highest degree by carefully ex-
cluding all such obtrusive elements as a mimetic realism
or vulgar sensation might demand. The emotion is always
fixed upon idea, not upon personality'.[3] Considering that
the essay is historically oriented, it does offer some excellent generalization on the nature of Nō, but not sufficient detail for any accuracy or depth of understanding.

Fenollosa's notes were fragmentary and incomplete,
never having been unified coherently as was the case with
the rough draft of *Epochs of Chinese and Japanese Art* which
he prepared before his untimely death. Without a thorough
knowledge of the subject, Ezra Pound was very naturally at
a disadvantage in attempting the articulation, analysis,
and elaboration that Fenollosa might have supplied had he
lived to undertake the complete study he envisioned. As
Pound noted in Appendix II: 'Many facts might be extremely
interesting if one had enough knowledge of Noh, and could
tell where to fit them in.'[4] In fact, the use of various
appendices did not solve the problem. The plot summaries,
for example, are inaccurate, even incoherent, and seem to
have been chosen at random for their interest as remarkable
examples of dramatic conception or stage technique. The
other information is largely miscellaneous and completely
unassimilated, while the western notation of music for
Hagoromo is a wholly inadequate redaction.

Part I of *'Noh' or Accomplishment* constitutes Pound's
efforts at making sense of Fenollosa's notes and first

appeared independently in *The Drama* (May 1915).[5] The
greater part of the text, which was illustrated by the
fragmentary translations of three plays, is directly quoted from Fenollosa's diary notes, and a translation of
passages from *Utai tō Nō* by Ōwada Tateki. Passages att-
esting to the historical and social conditions of classical
drama are freely mixed with recorded conversations and miscellaneous information on Nō tradition and staging. The
organization of the material is highly questionable, and
however accurate the individual facts are, they have little
cumulative effect or importance. The personal observations
of the editor are far more interesting in that they reveal
an intuitive grasp of several important aspects of Nō, even
though there is no explicit understanding of detail. Pound
was willing to suspend his disbelief in spiritism and ghost
psychology, for example, in order to enter into the world
of Nō, and he was also struck by the larger encyclopedic
intention of the conventional cycle of five plays:

> The Noh holds up a mirror to nature in a manner very
> different from the Western convention of plot. I mean
> the Noh performance of the five or six plays in order
> presents a complete service of life. We do not find,
> as we find in Hamlet, a certain situation or problem
> set out and analysed. The Noh service presents, or
> symbolizes, a complete diagram of life and recurrence.[6]

He was certainly prepared to accept the anti-realistic
method of Nō production and recognized the sculptured se-
verity of musical composition, but this led him to believe
that the less substantial Fenollosa drafts, even the grossly
incomplete ones, were sufficiently fleshed out in performance through movement and gesture. On introducing the
translations he admonished:

> The reader must remember that the words are only one
> part of this art. The words are fused with the music
> and with the ceremonial dancing. One must read or
> 'examine' these texts 'as if one were listening to
> music'. One must build out of their indefiniteness a
> definite image. The plays are at their best, I think,
> as image; that is to say, their unity lies in the image -
> they are built up about it as the Greek plays are built
> up about a single moral conviction.[7]

Pound also admired the poetic sensibility of the plays, the
expression of emotion within each text as well as the use
of allusion and subtle suggestion: 'Our own art is so much
an art of emphasis, and even of over-emphasis, that it is
difficult to consider the possibilities of an absolutely
unemphasized art, an art where the author trusts so impli-
citly that his auditor will know what things are profound
and important.'[8] Whether through Fenollosa's description
or his own analysis, he understood that the unity of emotion
which Nō projects depends upon the intensification of basic
images through poetry, music and dance: 'the red maple
leaves and the snow flurry in Nishikigi, the pines in Taka-
sago, the blue-grey waves and wave pattern in Suma Genji,
the mantle of feathers in the play of that name, Hagoromo.'[9]

     What Pound understood of inherent literary structure
within individual plays is another, and very important,
matter. Without some sense of the constructional patterns
which constitute Nō form, it would be impossible to judge
the completeness of Fenollosa's drafts or render the proper
balance and interplay of prose and verse within passages of
description, dialogue and reverie. Pound's only reference
to form is the comment: 'A play very often represents
someone going a journey. The character walks along the
bridge or about the stage, announces where he is and where
he is going, and often explains the meaning of his symbolic
gestures, or tells what the dance means, or why he is dancing.'[10] No description could be more grotesque or more
misleading, even one of mere physical action on the stage.
It is true, however, that Fenollosa had given scant attention to the intricacies of literary construction in his
published writings, but it is unlikely that he would have
felt the need to record his first-hand knowledge of lyrical
composition in his notebooks. So subtle and complex a construction as the poetic text of Nō is easily warped beyond
recognition in recasting it into another language unless
due attention is paid to its original forms, and Pound often
misconceived the lyrical movement and composition of the
plays while editing the prose drafts. His division of
speeches into prose and verse is altogether arbitrary, almost haphazard, whereas each Fenollosa draft was either
entirely in prose or a line for line translation of the
Japanese verse form. For example, the truncated text of
Shōjō lumbers along in heavy prose while the delicacy and
spontaneity of the verse in Japanese provides much of the

joyful and exquisite effect for which the play is famous.
The ending of *Hagoromo* in the Fenollosa-Pound version is
another distinct disappointment; it lapses back into dull
prose just at the point where poetry and dance should join
together to raise the lyric intensity of the ritual performance to its apotheosis.

Pound considered his work with the translations as
'recreations' and the following letter to Harriet Monroe
from London, dated 31 January 1914, shows his arbitrary
criterion for recasting the language of Fenollosa's drafts
as prose or poetry:

Here is the Japanese play for April. It will give us
some reason for existing. I send it in place of my own
stuff, as my name is in such opprobrium we will not mention who did the extracting. Anyhow Fenollosa's name
is enough.

These plays are in Japanese, part in verse, part in
prose. Also I have written the stuff as prose where the
feet are rather uniform. It will save space and keep
the thing from filling too much of the number.

There's a long article with another play to appear in
The Quarterly. This *Nishikigi* is too beautiful to be
encumbered with notes and long explanations. Besides I
think it is now quite lucid - my landlady and grocer
both say the story is clear *anyway*. Fenollosa, as you
probably know, is dead. I happen to be acting as literary executor, but no one need know that yet awhile.

I think you will agree with me that this Japanese find
is about the best bit of luck we've had since the star-
ting of the magazine. I don't put the work under the
general category of translation either. It could scar-
cely have come before now. The earlier attempts to do
Japanese in English are dull and ludicrous. That you
needn't mention either as the poor scholars have done
their bungling best. One can not commend the results.
The best plan is to say nothing about it. This present
stuff ranks as recreation. You'll find W.B.Y. also very
keen on it.[11]

Years later, when considering a revised edition of *'Noh'
or Accomplishment*, 'copper-bottomed and guaranteed correct
in every detail', he wrote to Glenn Hughes from Rapallo on
9 November 1927:

> Don't know whether you know the work (pub. by Macmillan,
> now out of print). I think Fenollosa did a lot that
> ought not to be lost. I had not the philological com-
> petence necessary for an ultimate version, but at the
> same time Mrs. F's conviction was that Fen. wanted it
> transd *as* literature not as philology.

*   *

> One wants a Jap on the job, and one wants a Jap who
> knows Noh. I shd. like to protect Fenollosa from sonzov-
> bitches like ----- and in general from the philologs who
> were impotent till Fen. showed the way (via y.v.t.) and
> who then swarmed in with inferior understandings.

*   *

> At present it is the scattered fragments left by a dead
> man, edited by a man ignorant of Japanese. Naturally
> any sonvbitch who knows a little Nipponese can jump on
> it or say his flatfooted renderings are a safer guide to
> the style of that country.[12]

There can be no doubt that Fenollosa was more interested in presenting Nō as a living art form than as a philological study. In fact, until recently there was little
certainty that he even had enough Japanese to work out the
translations for himself. Although he lived in Japan for
nearly seventeen years altogether, he was known to have
used an interpreter up to the very end of his time there,
especially when attending Nō performances and taking lessons
in chanting and dance. While making a special study of Nō
under Umewaka Minoru (1827-1909) and his sons during his
second sojourn in Tokyo (1897-1901), Hirata Tokuboku (1873-
1943), a student of English literature and young colleague
at the secondary school where Fenollosa was teaching English,
undertook this duty. Furukawa Hisashi, a noted scholar of
modern Nō history, quotes Hirata in *Ō Bei Jin no Nōgaku ken
Kyū* (European and American Studies of Nō): 'We prepared an

outline based on my account of the play, and I discussed it
with him, but in the case of *Hagoromo* at least, he worked
out the lyrics, and one can see that the translation is
complete.'[13] However highly qualified Fenollosa was in
other respects, he could have had but little pretention to
scholarly philology. On the other hand he was intimately
familiar with Nō stagecraft, and his training in performance as principal actor may possibly account for the in-
accuracies of the published translations which are not
attributable to the internal corruption of the Japanese
text from which he worked. Amateurs were often given only
the famous passages or 'arias' to learn, that they might
be performed outside the theatre as a kind of cultural
accomplishment, and unless preparing for a full-scale amateur production, students were also taught from heavily-cut
scripts which merely sketched in the introduction and development sections of a play and concentrated on the noted
scenes and dramatic climaxes. *Han-Nō*, half performances
or conventionally truncated versions, were also common on
the professional stage, as they are today, and it is entirely possible that Fenollosa had translations of these
fragments among his papers. Roy Teele has recorded the
recollection of Umewaka Takuyo, one of Minoru's sons, that
Fenollosa commonly studied such selections rather than
whole plays.[14]

Other failings of the Fenollosa-Pound edition can be
traced directly to the unsettled state of Nō drama during
the time that Fenollosa was seriously interested in it,
from 1898 to 1901. The fall of the Tokugawa Shogunate (1868)
and the undisciplined desire for westernization that followed in its wake, seemed to indicate that traditional Nō
was doomed. The troupes of actors attached to the courts
of feudal lords were disbanded and individuals were driven
to other work in order to make a living. Priceless collec-
tions of ancient texts, costumes, masks and properties were
dispersed and sold for what little they would bring. For
seven years there were no performances given anywhere in
the land, but in 1873 Umewaka Minoru began to perform again
on a stage reconstructed at his home in Tokyo, and so laun-
ched the revival of classical drama. Umewaka had been a
performer of secondary *(tsure)* roles in the Kanze guild or
school at the Shōgun's court, and he was determined to continue the tradition of his own family and of his art. His
success in finding private patronage among the survivors of

the feudal aristocracy drew other actors out of their en-
forced retirement. As nationalist feeling reasserted itself, public theatres were built by subscription and
supported by paying audiences, while private lessons were
offered to amateurs interested in Nō as both an art and a
cultural accomplishment. Traditionally, a performer's
training was by strict and precise imitation of a master
in both chanting and dance. Both the art form and attitudes
towards it had long since been rigidly formalized and prescribed. Objective enquiry into the history and development of Nō, as well as critical analysis, was unthinkable
up to that time, and the scientific/scholarly methods so
widely applied to the study of literature and theatre in
Europe were only just becoming available to Japanese scholars.

During the Edo Period (1603-1868) the Nō had crystal-
lized to a large extent while being preserved as an element
of established order. The myth had grown up that Nō had
remained unchanged and unchangeable in every detail since
its almost spontaneous creation some three hundred years
earlier. In fact Nō drama had developed steadily from the
time of its emergence as a separate and popular form in the
fourteenth century to its final condition as an aesthetic
ritual in the seventeenth century. Only after becoming a
moral and spiritual exercise which affirmed both cultural
values and the social order that patronized it was Nō cut
off from interaction with a dynamic and public audience.
It is not true, however, that Nō did not continue to change
throughout the whole period of its existence. After reaching its characteristic modern form Nō drama underwent a
continual process of refinement which affected, among other
things, the shape of the playing area, systems of notation
and the tonal scale in which lyrics are chanted. The earlier
periods of Nō history were fertile and creative, whereas the
taste and judgement of the Tokugawa era selected and preserved only the most effective and expressive examples of Muromachi imagination. For example, only the most abstracted and
powerful masks were copied and used during this period, while
the solemnity and import of Nō was greatly stressed by slow-
ing down the pace or basic rhythm of performance. Records
show that modern productions take nearly two or three times
as long to perform as those of Muromachi times (1336-1603).
A repertory of canonical plays was established according to
contemporary views, and the texts themselves, especially

those of the older works, underwent major revisions, even
the reassignment of entire roles from one personage to another, which reflected the prevailing literary tendencies
and mores of the times.[15] Not only were texts corrupt, but
the training of performers also depended on a secret tradition within schools or guilds of actors in which lyrics
and knowledge of acting techniques were transmitted orally
from master to pupil, sometimes only from father to eldest
son or heir. Manuscript texts as well as printed editions
of doubtful origins passed freely among amateurs and pro-
fessionals, while definitive editions had never been attempted and authoritative readings of individual plays diff-
ered from school to school and from generation to generation.
The soundness of any given script was highly doubtful in
Fenollosa's day; it might be an outright abbreviation on
the one hand or reflect any degree of corruption and revision
on the other. Considering that he was not fluent in either
contemporary or classical Japanese and that he completed
his study of Nō before the methods of modern scholarship
were brought to bear on the subject, we should recognize
that the fragmentary nature of his notes was not wholly
responsible for the failings of the 1916 volume.

Among the pioneer publications in the serious study of
Nō, Fenollosa was probably only aware of the general collection of plays, *Yōkyoku Tsūkai* (The Complete and Annotated
Edition of Nō Plays) which was edited by Ōwada Tateki (1857-
1910), an instructor in Japanese Classics at Tokyo University. The eight-volume edition appeared in 1892 and contained some 230 plays. Every title that Fenollosa is known
to have worked with is, in fact, represented in that collection. Ōwada's texts can hardly be considered definitive,
but they were a beginning and could have provided substantial
authority for a translator or editor interested in transmit-
ting knowledge of Nō to a Western readership. In 1903 Ōwada
published a further six-volume collection, *Nō no Shiori* which
contained written stage directions *(kakatsuke)* for ninety-
one plays. It is doubtful that Fenollosa knew of this work
or of the enlarged nine-volume edition of texts containing
270 plays with commentaries, *Yōkyoku Hyōshaku*, which Ōwada
brought out in 1907-8. In any case, it is fairly obvious
from the varying states of incompleteness of his published
translations that he used a number of different and less
scholarly sources.

The textual authority and reliability of translations included in *'Noh' or Accomplishment* is mixed. The texts of *Sotoba Komachi* and *Kayoi Komachi*, for example, are so fragmentary as to be almost unintelligible. They contain less than a third of the lines proper to each. Had Pound only known the work of Noël Peri and his excellent translation of *Sotoba Komachi*, which was published in 1913,[16] he might have been more circumspect. From the prior scholarship in English which was available to Pound, however, he had every reason to rely completely on the Fenollosa material at hand. It is unfortunate that he did not know, for example, that the translations of *Suma Genji*, *Shōjō*, *Chō ryō* and *Genjo*, which he did choose to include in the 1916 volume, are accurate in so far as they go, but in each case nearly a third of the lines proper to the play are omitted. Of the other translations included, only the following might be considered complete texts: *Kumasaka*, *Nishikigi*, *Kinuta* and *Aoi no ue*; while *Tamura*, *Tsunemasa*, *Hagoromo*, *Kagekiyo* and *Kakitsubata* suffer in varying degrees from the omission of speeches, and even whole sub-divisions of the literary form. *Tamura* is perhaps the most fragmentary of these plays, and even Pound must have been aware of the deficiency as he could compare his text with that of Marie Stopes and Sakurai Jōji, which is not only more complete and accurate, but frankly acknowledged by them as a *résumé* rather than a translation. The opening speeches are incomplete in Fenollosa's text, but the conspicuous omission in both versions involves set speeches describing the battles of Tamura Maru which accompany the mimetic dance of the principal actor. In *Hagoromo*, too, a sequence of five speeches which constitute an important literary/musical section and incorporate a climactic dance, is omitted altogether. *Kagekiyo* suffers less conspicuously, but miscellaneous speeches have been cut out, and some important poetic details are missing, as is also the case in *Tsunemasa* and *Kakitsubata*. Fenollosa's translation of *Kagekiyo* compares well with that of Stopes and Sakurai, and both are much less complete than either the Waley version or later work which is based on more scholarly, modern editions. In any case, completeness is only one aspect of the accuracy of translation, and one finds that the poetic strength and immediacy of the Fenollosa-Pound *Suma Genji*, for example, renders it a fine translation, however fragmentary the text.

Certainly the state of the texts prohibited the recognition of generalized structure and defied critical analysis in any effort to come to terms with the details of Nō form. It is amazing that Pound's few generalizations on the nature of Nō drama are so correct, and undoubtedly his major contribution to the process of transmission was the force of his poetic imagination, which not only recreated the originals, but also popularized them. He was bound to err on the question of scholarly accuracy, but his intuitive understanding and technical accomplishment infused the language of the rough drafts with something of its original life. Comparison of the published versions with Fenollosa's drafts show them to be reasonably faithful to the originals in every respect; the extensive changes of wording are almost invariably directed towards poetic and dramatic effects.

One of the interesting discoveries in the unedited translations is the presence of extensive production notes and marginalia taken down at actual performances, which indicate something of the staging and acting techniques involved.[17] From the notes and comments on the plays which Pound included in the 1916 volume, it is obvious that he made some use of the marginalia, but it remains one of the great failings of the edition that this material was not included in its entirety. Pound omitted all discussion of the translations as plays, and although he admonished the reader to fill out the text with imagined elements of music and movement, one is given almost no help at all in doing so. The effect of Pound's editorial practice in this case is to reduce the plays to a literary text by suppressing their character as theatre art. As one can see from the following play, Fenollosa was at some pains to retain indications of the literary/musical forms and voice-styles of delivery, as well as descriptions of stage movement and musical orchestration. The word 'cat' is used to refer to the musicians and the curtain mentioned by Fenollosa is a curtained frame which represents the hut in which Atsumori's ghost appears, while *'Sura'* are the shades of warriors killed in battle who are condemned to eternal combat with ghostly foes in the other world.

IKUTA ATSUMORI

by Motoyasu

grandson of Ujinobu

Cats and part of chorus come in first. Small hut with straw roof, sage green curtain brought on stage, back, C, front of cats.

Old name of piece - Ikuta.

Shite. Taira no Atsumori (ghost).
Kogata. His child.

Then in silence comes Kogata. Stands forward right - then Waki who stands back left - ordinary costumes. (Saw this again May 19th 1901) (5 days after landing).

Waki. An attendant of Honen Shonin.

Scene in Yamatsure   1st
        Settsu   2nd

They wait some time. Waki begins to speak, without cats. Recitative chant. Waki in ash blue gray, with touches of deep tawny yellow. Kogata costume is green blue and brown.

There is no variation of intoning through-out this speech.

Waki. (Kotoba) I am one who serves Honen Shonin in Kurodani. And the one here is the child of Atsumori who was killed in Ichi no Tani. Once when Shonin was going down to Kamo, he found a baby about 2 years old in a box, under a pine tree. He had a great pity for the child, he took it home, and cared for it greatly. Now he has grown to be ten years old; and, as he is complaining that he has no parents, Shonin spoke about this to the audience who came to his preaching. Then a young lady came up to him and

said; 'This is my child'.
And, on asking, he found
that this is the child of
Atsumori. Hearing this,
the child wishes to see the
figure of his father, even
in a dream. And now he has
been going to Kanio no
Miojin for worship these
seven days. Today is the
time for fulfillment, so I
take him now to Kanio no
Miojin to pray. Now we
have arrived. Pray well!

Here the back rank of
chorus comes in.

Kneeling with beads
before him, high
voice praying.

Kogata. (Sashi) The red
fence of the divine temple
seems very holy. And the
stream round about is pure.
Now I rely on the deep
blessing of the god.

During the *long* chorus,
both are kneeling.
Music of cats now begins.
Chorus slow with inter-
vals. Chorus expands.
Something may have been
omitted from text here.
Cats here stop.

Chorus. (Uta) Even in a
dream, please let me see
the shadow of my father.
If I pray to the end thus,
I shall not be devoid of
blessing. O God of Tadasu!
let my wish be fulfilled!

The two face across
front of stage.

Kogata. (Kotoba) What!
Strange! While I was
sleeping a little, I had a
divine dream just now.

Waki. (Kotoba) How happy!
Please tell about the divine
dream.

Kogata's speech very
rich and powerful
(has improved).

Kogata. A new voice from
the inside of that jewelled
temple told me to go to the
forest of Ikuta in Tsu no

The two standing,
facing across front.

Accompaniment of full
cats. Cats begin the
music. Waki sings this
Michiyuki alone, slowly.

During this Waki walks
about a little.
(1901, curtain is
dropped at this
point).

Waki front centre,
acts, looking about.
(At end of speech 2
go off right).

Curtain is let down.
Very young man with
mask appears, looks
18 yrs old. Tall
black hat, rich cos-
tume. White and gold
hakama, blue and gold
overdress.

         love
(color, received, idea,
act, intellect).

Kuni, from now; if I wish
to see my father even in a
dream. This was the divine
dream.

Waki. What a strange thing
this is! we need not return
to Kurodane. I will accompany you to Ikuta no Mori.
Please prepare soon.

Michiyuki. (Uta) Going
out from the temple of Kamo
in the shadow of mountains,
we hasten to Yamazaki; and
crossing the misty Minase-
gawa, and the wind being
cold to our travelling
clothes, and the autumn
having come, we have now
arrived at Ikuta no Mori
in Tsu no Kuni; which it
was only yesterday that we
thought to visit.

Waki. (Kotoba) As we made
haste, this is already the
Ikuta no Mori in Tsu no
Kuni. These scenes of the
forest and the flowing of
the river are much better
than we had heard in the
capital. What an interes-
ting *meisho* this is! The
fields over there must be
Ono of Ikuta. We shall
draw near, and look at them.
As we look here and there,
now the sun has set. What!
A light is seen yonder!
Perhaps it may be a house.
We will go and take lodging
there.

He is sitting in hut.
(kuo manoru yukori)
guhaku = gu = poverty-
stricken.

Very weird singing.
During singing Waki
rises and faces Shite.

Kogata runs to him,
grasps sleeve.

Fine voice singing.

Kogata kneeling at
corner of hut, not
touching. (1901
clasping his arm).

Rich strong chorus.
Waki sits off front
right.
This chorus quite
long.
At end of chorus
Shite turns and
looks fixedly at
Kogata.
(1901 - during chorus,
looks at boy and weeps)
(the separate).
pink = nade hiko,
nade = patting.

Shite. (Sashi) Go Min!
Go Min! The five possess-
ions of man! are all empty.
How shall we love this our
body! The mystic spirit,
which dwells in agony, flies
under the moon. And the
poor bewildered wraith, that
has lost its body, is whist-
ling to the autumn wind.
What a solemn occasion!

Waki. (Uta) Strange! In
this cottage a very flowery
young Knight who wears
armor shows himself. What
does it mean?

Shite. (Kotoba) (half singing) How foolish is the
heart of man! Did you not
come here to see me? The
ghost of old Atsumori came
here, though I am ashamed
to tell it.

Kogata. (Uta) O! Atsumori?
Is he my father? So saying,
he ran up to him even uncon-
sciously   ,   and   .

Chorus. Clinging to the
sleeves, he wept so much
that he lost himself. O
this is too much, for a person of sorrows. But may
there be some means of
making this meeting in the
dream a real thing?

Shite. (Uta) How misera-
ble! Though you are a

Shite soon faces
audience, still sit-
ting. Sometimes looks
aside at child. Some-
times turns toward him.
(1901 Shite sings only
looking at child very
emotionally).
(Towards last, looks
away for a moment -
face fixed forward on
floor).
(1901 Shite's costume,
purple hakama with gold
fans and waves on it.
Green and gold outer
dress over; underneath
No dress of many rich
colors, mostly blue
and gold).

The two remain facing
each other, some time.
Then Kogata goes back
right front.

Atsumori comes forward
from hut *(kirocho Fugetsu)*
begins to dance very slowly
at first. Often pausing
as if to think - as if
listening to chorus.

When they speak of leaving
capital, walks slowly rear,
down to farther end of
bridge, then pauses.

After 'Suma' begins to come
back. Comes rapidly forward

flower-child of mine, like
a pet pink, left in the
world, how pitiful it is to
see you in these worn-out
black sleeves! (the child's)
As you are so faithful to
me, you carried your steps
to Kanio no Miojin, and
prayed to see your father
even in a dream. Miojin
had pity on you, and sent a
messenger to King Em. King
Em, by his order, gave me
some leisure, so the meeting
of father and child will be
only this time.

Chorus. Through the moon-
shiny night now will we
speak of those days.
(Kuse) But in the first
Heiki was at the top of its
glory. In the play of
flowers, birds, winds, and
moon (i.e. poetry) and in
this play of flutes and
strings, they passed their
springs and autumns. But
suddenly they were defeated
by an unexpected enemy.
Even the Emperor and the
whole family, leaving the
capital of flowers, went
to the shore of the Western
sea, and, on the way, which
was not so familiar to them,
crossing mountains and seas,
they became the inhabitants
of the country, for a while.
But again they returned to

to centre. Dances with
fan for sword.

Cats begin to become
boisterous.

Centre

Shite dances strongly.
Flute now begins for
first time and *very loud*.
Chorus becomes loud and
excited. Dancing of
ghost always restrained.
Goes into corner.

Centre. Dancing slowly.
'Strong voice', almost
crying.

Chorus and cats very
loud.

S. stamps right back.
Then comes rapidly for-
ward to right corner.
Much dance, with no
words and full cats.
Stamps. Gazes off
back right, then speaks.
Waves fan. Most power-
ful part of dance begins.
Cats and chorus. Whirl-
ing. Shakes head, draws
sword.
This means that the Sura
are themselves the enemy
of Atsumori as of any man
in torment.

Suma, and arrived at the
forest of Ikuta in Ichi no
Tani - and the whole family
were very glad that here it
is quite near to the capital.
At that time -

Shite. The forces of
Nariyori and Yoshitsune -

Chorus. Rushed like clouds;
and, though they fought for
a while, Heike was at the
fall of fortune. They were
scattered, and scattered,
and I had cast away my body
in Ikutagawa, where the sorrows are deep. O it is vain
to tell the story!

Shite. (Uta) How happy!
Though in this vain dream
meeting, the father and the
child touch their sleeves
together.

Chorus. O hearts hard to
separate!

Shite. (Kotoba) What is
that over there? What!
Are you the messenger from
Em O? It was a leisure but
for a short time. Why are
you so tardy? Em O is very
angry now! -

Chorus. So he said, and
then, strange! A black
cloud suddenly rose up, and
furious fires broke out, and
swords fell down, and many
were the enemies of Shura
(asura) fighting, and a
great noise resounded through
heaven and earth.

The last dance
(seen May 19th 1901) is
strong, platform in
front. Dance with a
spear. Jumping and fighting. Despondency -
Jumps on platform.
No. This was the End
of K?
Sword dance rapid
then long pause right
back with sword in
hand.

Looks at sword,
then drops it.

Comes toward Kogata
with fan. Dances to
him with fan gestures.
Stops. Gazes. Droops.
Raises sleeve. Weeps,
turns, goes slowly back
to corner.
Kogata follows.
Touches him. One
agonized turn only.
Gaze. Then S. goes
down bridge. K. remains
gazing after at back corner.
Then K. turns and gazes off
right. Flute gives final
shriek at end of chorus.

Shite. How noisy are you!

Chorus. You are the enemies
of Shura, which are very
familiar to me in the mor-
ning and in the evening.
Thus saying, he unsheathed
his sword, and ran here and
there, and fought, scatter-
ing the fire-flowers. Then
gradually the black cloud
vanished, and the enemies of
Shura disappeared, the moon
was clear, and it has become
the sky of bright dawn.

Shite. How shameful. Thoug
you are my child! -

Chorus. To let you see this
my agony! Return quickly,
and pray for me! Thus saying, they separated their
sleeves, weeping and weeping
And the figure, which was
going out, vanishes like the
dews on the grass of *Ono*.

Having considered the quality of Pound's *aperçus*, the limitation of the manuscript material and the extent of information on performance that was available to Yeats, it still remains to explain exactly what there was about Fenollosa's notes that fired Yeats's imagination. From his use of specific Japanese texts found among the translations as models for his dance plays, it is obvious that he discovered in Nō a correlative or organizing principle for the separate breakthroughs he had already made in subject matter, symbolic construction and stylized/expressive stage technique; above all, a correlative in terms of romantic world-view and more particularly, in the role of art as mediator between temporal and spiritual being. It is, however, difficult to believe that Yeats could have developed his interest in, and understanding of, the Nō from the translated texts alone. Fenollosa's papers also included numerous drafts and transcriptions of public lectures on such subjects as Oriental history, religious philosophy and aesthetic values, while his published writing constituted a further elaboration of the same major ideas. Yeats could not help but respond to Fenollosa's appraisal of the spiritual and intellectual congruity between East and West that had become apparent for so brief a time after the turn of the century. His own values and preoccupations, like those of Fenollosa, had been conditioned by the very features of contemporary sensibility that signalled the *rapprochement* of Orient and Occident.

Fenollosa was as well qualified to be an interpreter in the dialogue between the two cultures as he was to be a student and exponent of Nō. He had read philosophy at Harvard:

That was the moment when John Fiske was expounding the theory of Evolution, as Herbert Spencer presented it, in popular lectures, a new conception of the unity in which all its phenomena were parts of an unbroken chain of cause and effect. Man was involved in this cosmic drama in which sun, stars, animals and plants followed one law of development from a common source, all the various forms of nature evolving from previous forms through the vast sweep of time from the primeval vapour.[18]

A new conception of religion was evolving from the scientific discoveries which had destroyed the old. As objective

evidence of spontaneous variation in organic forms over
vast periods of time gave rise to theories of natural selection and the mutability of species, the personal god of
the Old Testament, who had created the universe at a blow,
gave way to ideas of a more abstract, universal force whose
furthest manifestations were physical forms. The possibilities for individual realization of inherent spirituality
within so harmoniously poised a universe were limitless and
found their best expression in religious and aesthetic speculation. The 'Class Poem' which Fenollosa wrote for his
Commencement shows the world to be 'a progressive organic
unity in which the individual, if he will but reverence all
nature, can grasp the Ideal and synthesize Subject and Object, Force and Being to become absorbed, finally, in God.'[1]
By the time he took up an appointment in 1878 as Professor
of Political Economy and Philosophy at the newly founded
University of Tokyo, Fenollosa had also studied theology
at the Harvard Divinity School and painting at the Massa-
chusetts Normal Art School. The University courses which
he offered at Tokyo amply reflect the direction of his professional preoccupations:

Freshman - Synthetic Logic

Sophomore - History of Modern Philosophy to Hegel

Junior - Hegel with Side Glances at Spencer

Senior - Ethics, Aesthetics, and the Philosophy of
             Religion[20]

As Fenollosa developed his taste for, and understanding
of, esoteric Buddhism and Oriental art, he became an ardent
champion of traditional Japanese culture against the wave
of westernization that followed the Meiji Restoration, and
in 1886 he gave up his university appointment to become
Commissioner of Fine Art in the Imperial Government. Throug
the application of scientific method in his study of traditional painting and sculpture, he reconstructed the historical turns of aesthetic development against a background
of political and social conditions. The premise of his ar-
gument in 'An Outline of Japanese Art' which appeared in
1898 is very similar to that of Walter Pater in such works
as *Greek Studies* (1895) and *The Renaissance* (1877). With
reference to the decay of Fujiwara civilization in eleventh

and twelfth century Japan, he wrote: 'The drift of things
was towards an oligarchic tyranny. In religion, form and
ritual tended to supplant insight. In art, line became
weak, proportion abnormal, composition spotty. The pro-
fessors of mystic illumination found themselves heirs of
a prescribed iconography. In literature little was produced. In politics the emperor had become the plaything
of his ambitious ministers.'[21] In the same article he
also wrote of the supreme crisis in the history of China
which centred on the effort to readapt its mental machinery
in the face of political and social needs, to end political
corruption and the repression of the soul's spontaneity
that was disintegrating character:

Neo-Confucianism

A fourth effort was a revolution within the ranks of
Confucianism itself, which produced the famous Sung
philosophy, the most metaphysical and original of all
China's systems of thought. It undertook to explain
progress itself as a series of interactions between
extremes, during which the universe passes from abstract reason to self-realization in the human spirit,
thus reminding us strongly of the Hegelian idea and
dialectic. This philosophy of evolution, although Confucian in phraseology, was permeated throughout by
Buddhist principle, with which latter the pure idealism
of Tao has already thrown in its allegiance. Thus, for
the first time, an approximation was being made to a
unification of the three systems in absolute idealism.

Zen Idealism

But the most powerful factor in the new movement was
the nature of Sung Buddhism itself. This was the sect
of Zen, or Contemplation, which conceived of spirit as
a creator immanent in a double garb, acting with equal
clearness under the parallel series of orderly changes
in the worlds of soul and nature. In this respect it
foreshadowed the philosophy of Schelling. Its business
was to enfold in nature the infinite analogies of human
process. Its thought was the very substance of subtle
poetry. It anticipated our modern Western love of scenery. It took the spontaneity of nature for a type of
character.

The Art of Sung

The outcome of all these forces was the deliberate
making of art to be the most typical and inclusive manifestation of the spiritual life. For is not art the
meeting-point of man and nature? In her perfections
are mirrored as identical the two spontaneities. The
world is only one vast metaphor. Even Confucius had
asserted that the harmony of human living is a kind of
music. So the painter, at one with poet and priest, is
no mere skilful specialist, but an interpreter of the
great book of analogies into form's more permanent language.[22]

The meeting point of East and West, of Fenollosa and
Yeats, is in the Doctrine of Correspondences which underlies the symbolist aesthetic. The idealism of esoteric
Buddhism had become almost commonplace in European thought
through the syncretism of the Mystical/Occult revival of
the 1880s; the techniques of symbolism as a literary movement were based on systems of exact correspondences between
spirit and matter which were tenets of such cults as Theosophy, Hermeticism and Mystical Christianity. As early as
1886, A. E. Waite had suggested the relevance of art to
spiritual experience:

The doctrine of universal analogy as the basis of progressive revelation is a noble and beautiful hypothesis
which eminently recommends itself to reason, and once
properly understood it would be an inexhaustible fountain of purest inspiration for the poetry of the age to
come; it transforms the whole visible universe into one
grand symbol, and the created intelligence of man becomes
a microcosmic god whose faculties are in exact though
infinitesimal proportion with the uncreated and eternal
mind.[23]

In 1896 Yeats himself wrote:

The more a poet rids his verses of heterogeneous knowledge and irrelevant analysis, and purifies his mind with
elaborate art, the more does the little ritual of his
verse resemble the great ritual of Nature, and become
mysterious and inscrutable. He becomes, as all the

great mystics have believed, a vessel of the creative
power of God; and whether he be a great poet or a small
poet, we can praise the poems, which but seem to be his,
with the extremity of praise that we give this great
ritual which is but copied from the same eternal model.[24]

It was their shared belief in the redemption of spirit from
matter that Yeats responded to in Fenollosa, a celebration
of the spiritual idea and creative imagination; the denial
of those false gods of the post-Darwinian era, materialism
and progress. Fenollosa's views on the efficacy of artistic processes in reconciling subject and object, force and
being appeared in 1898. Buddhism of the Lesser Vehicle,
he wrote,

was a gentle, exoteric doctrine, which, while it insisted on the impermanence of earthly forms and hopes, in-
culcated a positive faith in man's spiritual capacities
and deliverance from the illusions of sense. The world
was no hopeless dream, as with the Hindu, but a store-
house of forms to be idealized.[25]

*   *

The noblest of problems was thus afforded to sculpture,
the majestic expression of the religious ideal in human form. But, naturally, it could not, like Greek
sculpture, aim to make its ideal immanent in the bare
human personality. It aimed at a form suggested, indeed, by the human, but transfigured by the requirements
of spiritual proportion.[26]

*   *

The influence of the exoteric Nara faith had been mildly
restraining - in fact, negative. It refused to recognize value in the transitory and the personal. It detached itself from activity of career, and, lost in its
dreams of bliss and form, was incapable of corrupting
abuses. Not such the esoteric Buddhism of the second
period. It sought for positive, concrete powers. Its
comtemplation was not passive, but creative and master-
ful. It professed to penetrate to the spiritual law

which underlies the healthiness of change. Its precept
was, not to eschew the world as illusion, but from within
to purify the world of its illusion - to evolve the
kingdom of spirit out of the kingdom of matter.[27]

The scientific and philosophical idealism that informed the romantic world-view of the late Victorian period
seemed to echo the values and sensibility of classical
Japan in which Fenollosa recognized ' a flash of human
genius at highest tensions, which in our records only the
sensitively organized Greek, and that for only a few centuries, ever reached.'[28] It was Zen philosophy which gave
classical Japanese art its essential form and character,
and while discussing the artistic possibilities of that
creed, Fenollosa delineated a complex of ideas and ideals
which must have appealed to Yeats:

Certainly the most aesthetic of all Buddhist creeds is
this gentle Zen doctrine, which holds man and nature to
be parallel sets of characteristic forms between which
perfect sympathy prevails. In this respect it is not
unlike the Swedenborgian doctrine of 'correspondences'.
But it goes much further than any European has ever done
in carrying out the details of the correspondence, in
freeing them from a narrow ethical purism. It has something of the openness and humanism of the Renaissance,
without its somewhat empty Paganism.

An extreme example of Zen is that books are injurious,
especially in the education stage. Therefore it dis-
cards even scripture reading, and cuts itself away from
the literature of its order. This is enough to condemn
it with Chinese scholars, who regard the written word
as a sort of sacred talisman. Yet it was partly to
break up the deadness of this very conceit that turned
Zen teachers to the value of a more vital writing,
namely, the Book of Nature. The neophite was to see for
himself how animals and birds, and rivers and clouds,
and mountains and rocks are built up and discharge specific functions. It is an attempt to reconstruct the
categories of thought *de-nono*, and that on the basis of
nature's organization. This is why the writer Kokko . .
leaps out with the first words of his joyous preface,
'Why do men love landscape? Because it is the place

where *life* is perpetually springing!' Life, that is it;
not a Confucian cupboard-full of dead weights and meters,
and the bones of social orders, ranged rank upon rank,
and ticketed in analytical order. The trouble with
Confucius is that he had acted as if the skeleton were
indeed life. He was probably better than his practice,
and took narrow ground as the only policy to convert the
feudal spendthrifts of his day. Had he foreseen that he
was defining an Imperial China for all time, we may well
believe that he would have propagated freer doctrine.
But his overzealous disciples had for ages intensified
his defects; and now they were openly clamouring that
the very way to learn how to live was not by watching
the heart beat and lungs expand, but to count the number of ribs. Such antithesis was one ground of Zen
educational policy.

Another great point of the Zen scheme was that, in taking
for his book the characteristic form and features of
nature, the student should have no guidance but his own
unaided intelligence. The wise teacher set him down
before rocks and clouds, and asked him what he saw. The
priest was examiner, if not preceptor. It was his very
purpose to let the mind build up its own view of the
subtle affinities between things; to construct an organic
web of new categories. In short, education must develop
individuality! This is why the great portraits of the
Zen priests . . . are so powerful of head and keen of eye.
For individuality, though a means, is really not an ultimate end, since behind the way of approach will loom
something of a common great spiritual system underlying
both man and nature. In this sense it is a sort of independent discovery of Hegelian categories that lie behind the two worlds of object and subject. Possibly,
the telepathic power of the teacher, and the whole Zen
enlightenment, worked through the perceptions of the
neophite, to bring him to this general unity of plan.

That such a doctrine should become a powerful adjunct of
poetry, from Shareiun, of Liang, to So-Toba, of Sung, is
due to its keen perception of analogies. All real poetry
is just this underground perception of organic relation,
between which custom classifies as different. This

principle lies at the very root of the enlargement of
vocabulary in primitive languages. Nature was so plastic and transparent to the eye of early man, that what
we call metaphor flashed upon him as a spiritual identity to be embodied at once in language, in poetry and
in myth. Zen only tried to get back to that primitive
éclaircissement. A word, like a thing, means as much
as you can see into it, and therefore lights up with a
thousand chameleon-like shadings, which of later days,
only the poet knows how to use with a hint of the original color. So in Chinese poetry every character has
at least *two* shades of meaning, its natural and its
spiritual, or the image and its metaphorical range. In
Chinese poetry we find extreme condensation, for every
word is packed with thought. Hence, also, the parallelism goes on to couplets or stanzas, contrasted in their
apparent yet alike in their real meanings.[29]

The very writing of *Epochs of Chinese and Japanese
Art* was based on the premise that art is 'the power of the
imagination to transform materials - to transfigure them',[30]
and Fenollosa's discovery of a larger metaphor in the design
or structure of a whole work of art is significant in terms
of the development of modernism, especially in poetry.
Through his study of Oriental art Fenollosa understood that
the synthesizing force of a central poetic image or conception was fundamental to the success of dynamic composition
in all art, and he outlined his thought in a monograph,
Imagination in Art (1894), which focused on the creative
faculty of thinking and feeling in terms of clear and unbroken images. Fenollosa proposed that art should be perceived as a synthesis of such objective integers.

But if, as can never happen by accident, each line, each
area, and each proportion between areas is such that it
positively assists the value and meaning of all the other
so that all can be seen in their intended force only
through this particular juxtaposition, then a single
artistic image crystallizes, so to speak, out of the
mass of units. When the areas cut by the lines are filled in with dark and light masses as with colors, a new
factor is added to the image, which factor not only must
not contradict the line-structure, but must even enforce
and clarify it. No doubt the relative importance of

parts can, in this way, become somewhat modified, and
their harmony enriched; but of themselves, without the
fundamental unity of the lines, mass and color can produce no clear image.[31]

He continued:

Imagination is creative. The image is individual, and
can never digest an intractable formula. Every element
that enters into an imaginative group must be plastic
and sensitive, full, as it were, of chemical affinities,
through which the just and crystalline balance can be
rapidly found. This mystery of genius, this quick
power of the imagination, which seems in a moment to
explore a million possible combinations, and to seize
upon the right one, is significantly called by Kant the
faculty of Judgement. By this he does not mean the cold
weighing of the intellect, but an almost intuitive
seizing upon the capacity for organization in one's raw
material.[32]

In 'The Nature of Fine Art' (1896), published along with
several other articles in various issues of a journal
called *The Lotos*, Fenollosa elaborated further on the properties of literary images:

Synthetic thinking demands a pregnant language; rich,
juicy, significant, full words, charged with intense
meaning at the center, like a nucleus, and then radiating out toward infinity, like a great nebula. This is
poetry, the making a word stand for as much thought and
feeling as possible, and that through the mutual modi-
fications of the successive words. No literary production which does not have this synthesis as its meanings,
principle, and illustrations, fact and ideal, the organic
fibre of the world, all packed away together in its
lightest phrases, plays a part in the sphere of literature as a fine art.[33]

Fenollosa was not alone, however, in having anticipated
Yeats's symbolic design, Eliot's objective correlative, or
Clive Bell's significant form; a basis for the reception of
such ideas had already been established in the wave of

Japonisme which swept across Europe, especially England
and France, from 1865 to 1895. Earl Miner has traced the
influence and assimilation of techniques from Japanese
block prints, especially stylization and the expressive
forms produced by a conscious disarrangement of composition
and the flouting of naturalistic perspective. The European craze for *ukiyo-e* had a marked effect on Impressionist
painting, and because the interchange of theories, techniques and critical vocabularies among the various arts was
an essential characteristic of the Impressionist Movement,
there was also an indirect effect on the literature of the
period. The later novels of the influential brothers
Goncourt are said to have been much affected by the canons
of Japanese art which taught the appreciation of arranging
colours and masses, while poets such as Oscar Wilde experimented with colouristic images in the creation of poetic
'studies' and 'impressions', after the fashion of Debussy
and Whistler. The influence of *ukiyo-e* prompted later
groups to turn directly to Japanese literature, and the
early Imagists in London (Flint, Hulme, Tancred, Storer,
Campbell and Farr) embarked on a study of Japanese poetic
forms, particularly the *haiku*, which was as much an inspiration to them as the *vers libre* of French Symbolism[34] and
led them to adopt suprapositioning and the creation through
plastic design of a presentational icon or structure of
images.

What brought Fenollosa to a serious and disciplined
study of Nō in 1898 was the recognition of the universal
principles which underlie Oriental philosophy and art. Here
again, sensuous rhythms and patterns of natural images are
so arranged and ordered as to charge objective images with
pure and intense emotion and to disclose by direct correspondence the pattern of ideal order which existed beyond
them. Fenollosa understood Nō as ritual rather than drama;
not an imitation of life, but rather a transfiguration of
its forms through human imagination in which universal antitheses are synthesized and reconciled. 'It is thus a
highly complex form of operatic art, whose aim is never sen-
sational or realistic, but to lift the beholder through a
refined appeal to several of his faculties, into a single
state of intense and imaginative emotional impression.'[35]

He was particularly struck by the techniques of visual
and aural 'spacing' in performance and the 'radiating' significance and unifying effect of a central image. He saw,

for example, the sustained pauses of Nō chant, musical accompaniment and dance as direct analogues of negative spacing in painting and the meaningful intervals between juxtapositions of concrete images in poetry. Introduction to the critical analysis of Nō is not uncommonly made by analogy with the art of formal flower arrangement *(Ikebana)* in which the composition must always follow the pattern of nature, while the three basic lines (branches or flower stems) of the arrangement are so stylized or abstracted as to sculpt the surrounding space into dynamic shapes whose relationships are as rhythmic and harmonious as those of the positive elements themselves. In the simplest arrangements the three flower stems or branches are taken to represent heaven, man, and earth; every composition, no matter how sophisticated, is a creative and artistic concentration of their ideal relationship and harmony. Fenollosa was fascinated by the idea that the lyric poetry, music, and mimetic dancing of a Nō performance were not only suggestive in themselves, but that they were also elements of a larger expressive design of composition. In his early study of Japanese and Chinese painting, as in his study of Nō, Fenollosa had recognized the characteristic achievement of Oriental art in its subordination of representative and analytical statement to the expression of an idea through stylization and subtle suggestion.

Ezra Pound's commentary in *'Noh' or Accomplishment* emphasizes the very points on which Fenollosa's understanding rests and his own speculation on poetic theory, not to mention his later practice, is very reminiscent of Fenollosa's pronouncements. There is no actual evidence that Yeats read all of Fenollosa's published works, nor even all of the manuscript material, but the principles extracted by Pound can be shown to have exerted a great deal of influence on Yeats's dance plays:

1. That Nō is concerned with an intense emotion fixed upon idea and not personality; a service of life, not the analysis of a set problem.

2. That unity of image through repetition and variation brings focus and intensification to the emotion expressed.

3. That Nō is a complete art in which poetry is assisted by music, dance and mime in expressing intense emotion.

Through his intellectual commitment to these principles, Yeats was influenced by the Nō, in which he discovered the capacity of dramatic conception and traditional structure to organize the raw material of his own art. Because of the many limitations in transmission through Fenollosa and Pound, the discovery was largely intuitive, and the only proof of the assertion rests on a comparison of Yeats's early experimentation with the actual features of Nō drama as an independent art form.

3.

The Japanese Nō: Art and Accomplishment

Other theatres are often said to be
a mirror of life, but Nō is an image
in the mirror which life approximates.[1]

In its long development Nō has assimilated a great
many elements from such antecedents as Chinese opera and
Japanese folk dance, popular mime and court music, Shinto
ritual and Buddhist philosophy, and has integrated them all
through performance, an achievement of technical balance
and overall harmony of expressive or evocative forms in dynamic tension. The production dramatizes the text, projecting an interpretation through plastic performance, and
realizes the given emotional intensity of the piece as a
single artistic unity. Each play concerns itself with the
truth of a particular human emotion or experience, but attention is generally divided between the universality of
the emotion and the nobility of the character who under-
goes the experience. Subjects such as the miraculous apparition of a compassionate god, the tragic death of a
youthful warrior, the thwarted love of a beautiful lady,
the pathetic derangement of a mind unbalanced by human
suffering or the frenzied gaiety of supernatural figures,
make of the drama a demonstration of noble values and
right conduct while the characters portrayed are identified with universal types.

Everything about Nō drama is non-representational, and
almost no attempt is made to evoke the temporal world. In
the larger number of plays the action is, in fact, removed
from the vulgarity of immediate representation by showing
the central figure *(shite)* in the act of recreating emotions

originally engendered by a dramatic situation, as they have
been refined by obsessive reflection over many, many years.
Indeed, it may even be the ghost or spirit of the protagonist lingering at the scene of a legendary or historical
incident, who is encountered by the secondary personage or
interlocutor *(waki)*. Through the interest shown by the
latter in the now famous associations of the place, the
shite reveals himself miraculously reincarnated in his
prior condition and recreates the passion of the original
crisis.

Ezra Pound understood from Fenollosa's notes that the
cycle of five plays which make up a complete Nō programme,
constitutes a closed scheme of human experience and recur-
rence. The two hundred and fifty or so plays in the modern repertory can be classified in a number of ways (see
Appendix), but the selection of Nō for a complete programme
and the order of their performance is invariably based on
an established cycle of subject matter and emotional experience:

1.	God Play	:	Joy and Happiness
2.	Warrior (Man) Piece	:	Refinement and Elegance
3.	Wig (Woman) Piece	:	Love and Attachment
4.	Lunatic (Mad) Piece	:	Sadness and Lament
5.	Finale (Concluding) Play	:	The Sublime

The human world of warrior, woman and psychological imbalance is not only penetrated by the presence of the supernatural, but also embraced and bounded by gods and beatific
vision on the one hand, and by fierce demons and the sublime on the other hand. Within that frame of reference the
joy and pain of the human condition is justified, and reality is illuminated through the demonstration of intercourse
between the two worlds. The intensity of emotion at the
core of each play is further excited by the thrilling and
direct presentation of the supernatural, and human passion
is ennobled, purified and refined through examples of joy
and happiness, elegance and restraint, love and attachment,
grief and lamentation, and manifestations of the sublime.
The pattern of subject and mood which is recreated in every
full programme clearly suggests a conception of universal
order, a golden chain by which the human condition is

reconciled with spiritual values. Within the larger structure a unique, yet multiple sense of reality is created;
the aesthetic and ethical orders coincide, the spiritual
unity of beauty and moral action are revealed.

In so far as one can generalize about so variable and
permissive a conception, the Appendix gives a fair outline
of the characteristic subject-matter, treatment and emotional qualities from which the plays of a complete cycle are
chosen, but it is not always possible to generalize on the
dance sequences for each subdivision because a single form
may not be common to all, or even most of the plays, so
loosely grouped together. Subdivisions of the five major
types are by no means fixed, and many plays are considered
to fall under more than one category. Another way of indicating the expressive range and symbolic scheme of a
formal Nō cycle is to offer a descriptive summary of representative plays, outlining the thrust of action and emphasizing the focus of emotional interest.

The text of a modern *kami Nō*, *Fukkatsu no Kirisuto*, will
be presented later in the chapter, and a different kind of
god play might well be examined more closely here. *Sagi*
(The Heron) is a very interesting congratulatory piece in
which the spiritual and natural orders are reconciled
through the confrontation of Emperor and Heron. Rituals
of rejoicing in the beneficence of an Emperor's reign are
not uncommon, and *Sagi* provides a rather splendid illustration of the type. The play opens with praise of the monarch
and an association of order under his governance with the
order of nature. The Emperor is abroad in the palace grounds
on a summer evening viewing the landscape garden and replen-
ishing his soul from its beauty when he sees a strangely de-
mure heron at the edge of a pine-bordered pool. The Emperor
commands that the bird be brought to him, but the Ministers
wonder to themselves about the extent of his sway over a
creature of nature whose element is the air itself, and not
the earth. The heron obeys, overcome with fear, and allows
itself to be captured and borne off to the Monarch while the
Ministers rejoice that the Law of Buddha and of the Emperor
coincide. As presented on the stage, the scene is especially
moving; the *shite*, dressed in white dancing robes with a
long white wig and a crown surmounted by a miniature bird
in flight, mimes the trembling and fluttering of the submis-
sive bird so subtly with his hesitating progress across the
stage toward the Emperor as though carried by the attendant

who follows, that the spectator is in complete sympathy
with his situation. Charmed by the bird's submission, the
Emperor confers upon it a high court rank as a sign of his
love and protection, and the heron dances its delicate joy
and gratitude. The chorus comments on the bird's loyalty
to established order and voices the Monarch's admiration
for the heron's control over his own nature in submitting
to temporal power. The bird is released and flies off,
joyfully; the audience is equally moved by the Monarch's
magnanimity. As with most *kami Nō*, the text is very brief,
but the performance enormously effective.

As a representative example of the Warrior piece,
Tsunemasa might well follow in a full cycle of plays. The
action opens with a priest who tells of the death of Taira
no Tsunemasa and of his present intention to dedicate at a
shrine the lute given by the Emperor to his favourite, the
now fallen warrior. The ritual is intended for the repose
of Tsunemasa's soul, but in fact conjures his ghost which
the priest perceives but dimly. The first encounter concentrates on the insubstantiality of the apparition and on
the ghost's longing for a return to the natural world.
Tsunemasa reappears, recounting his close relationship with
the Emperor and singing of the music played at court and
of its spiritual affinities in nature. Music is played
and the ghost participates in a court dance of midnight
revel while the chorus chants verses which expound the relationship between music and nature, culminating in the
image of the phoenix and his mate dancing in rapture to
the strains of a lute. Anguish then engulfs the ghost as
his momentary identification with life in the temporal
world is broken and he reverts to a re-enactment of the
ceaseless combat which characterizes the *Asura* world to
which his soul is consigned, until his material image is
blotted out by the growing darkness and he is once again
hidden from the eyes of men.

Another play of the second group, *Tamura*, offers a
more conventional structure and a more direct affirmation
of spiritual values. The monks who have travelled to a
famous temple at the time of cherry blossom, encounter a
youth sweeping the fallen flowers with a besom. He asso-
ciates the glory of the blossom with Kwannon, the Bodhisattva of Mercy, and relates the miraculous history of the
temple's founding, but not of its donor Tamura-maru. There
follows a dialogue on the beauties of the capital and a

rapturous description of the scene with spring blossoms
illuminated by the moonlight and the flashing waters of
the pure stream for which the temple was named. The section ends with a questioning of the youth's real identity,
his inner nobility being so at variance with his humble
demeanour. The boy disappears to return, resplendent and
masked, as Tamura-maru, who recounts his exploits in sub-
duing the Eastern tribes and routing the demon hosts of
the Suzuka mountains through the power of Kwannon. The
dance he performs suggests his encounter with the demons
and the choral ode moves on to praise the victorious power
of the Bodhisattva which works through him. It is more
usual for *shura-mono* to present vanquished warriors and
their torment in the life after death, but *kachi-shura*
(victory *asura*) such as *Tamura*, *Yoshima* and *Ebira* were
also popular among *samurai* in feudal times.

For *kazura-mono*, (wig or woman piece) of the third
category, it is even more difficult to choose a representative example since there are several recognized types.
Hagoromo is a ritual of a supernatural being whose dance is
the dominant feature of the piece. The lyric structure of
the play constitutes a variation of the traditional norm
which reinforces the vivacious and graceful character of
the drama. Fishermen open the action by chanting the beauty
of the scene in Mio bay with its pine-covered hills and
golden strand. Finding an exotic feather mantle on a pine
branch, the leader decides to take it home, but a Maiden
appears who claims it as her own. He persists, and the
revelation of her nature as a supernatural figure confirms
his resolve to keep it. Without the robe she cannot soar
to her home in the heavens, and her grief at being exiled
on earth is so poignantly expressed that his heart is soft-
ened and he claims a vision of her dancing in exchange
for the robe. He hesitates to return it at once, however,
fearing that she may not dance for him once she has it,
but she cannot perform the dance she had promised without
it. Her authority and nature are assured by her reply:
'Doubt is for mortals, in heaven is no deceit'.[2] Her dance
is one of quiet restraint, elegance and lyric beauty which
progresses unilinearly, whereas two contrasting states of
mind are normally presented through separate dances, and
ends with a choral description of her ascension and gradual
disappearance amid the mists of heaven. The outline of the
play has much in common with *kami-Nō*, but the character of

the dance and its emotional content identify it as a female-wig piece.

There are also a number of *kazura-mono* whose plot incidents concern human relationships and their implications, such as *Izutsu* (The Well-Curb) which is based on the love of Ki no Aritsune's daughter for Narihira, a gallant, but not altogether faithful, prince and poet. At the beginning of the play a priest lingers at a temple built on the spot where the two had lived, and a maiden, drawing crystal-clear water from a well in the courtyard, reflects on its purifying presence, recalls memories of the past, and hopes for religious enlightenment in the future. She shows the priest the nearby tomb of Narihira who had endowed the temple and, speaking of the passage of time since his day, she offers flowers at the grave and weeps. Prompted by the priest, she talks of Narihira's married life with Ki no Aritsune's daughter and of an affair with another woman from which he returned to his wife through her steadfast and selfless love. The Maiden also tells the story of two children who often peered into the well to see their faces mirrored cheek to cheek and who grew up to fall in love, herself and Narihira. After revealing her identity she disappears, but returns, as in the priest's dream, wearing Narihira's robe, to dance out the story of the love which was so strong that it survived her death. Looking into the well, she sees the ecstatic vision of his face reflected there, and her ghost fades away as the priest's dream is shattered by the first light of dawn. Not all wig pieces of this type are so congratulatory, however, and thwarted love is often the subject, although the obstacle is likely to be a conflict of duty or sheer hard-heartedness. In a few plays the drama is rendered more immediate by the direct presentation of a heroine who does not appear as a ghost recollecting her earthly life, and still others involve a broken old woman who remembers her youth. In all the plays, however, there is a basic contrast of moods, as in *Hagoromo* where the early grief and lamentation over the loss of the feather mantle resolves into joy and release at its return, or in *Izutsu* where the poignant loneliness of the figure who tends her lover's tomb for centuries after his death and recalls his infidelity, turns to an ecstasy of fulfillment at the vision of his face.

The final type of *kazura-mono* is well represented by *Kakitsubata*, another play which offers a version of the

Narihira myth. A priest travels to a distant province to
see the water iris at their prime and encounters there a
woman who speaks of the flowers' fame. A poem about the
iris by Narihira is quoted, and the woman asserts that he
had loved this spot best of all. The chorus sings of a
man bound by love who returns many times in his thoughts
to his beloved, and the woman turns to change costume on
stage for that of a great lady, the beloved of Narihira.
She sings of the clothes she wears and of their former
owner in a time past, confessing herself to be the spirit
of the flowers, an incarnation of remembrance. Narihira
is then said to have been an incarnation of music, and his
art to have reached even the inanimate objects of nature
through its magic, conferring upon them a blessing. The
story of the poet's life is recounted against lamentation
for his passing and the passing of a golden age, while the
Flower Spirit, who suggests Narihira's presence, dances to
the delicate poetry that ends the play.

The various subdivisions of *kurui-mono* (lunatic or
mad pieces) are even more diverse than is the case with
kazura-mono, but again there are three major types. The
first involves frenzy or derangement at the loss of a
child or lover and is well represented by *Sumidagawa* (The
Sumida River). Madness in this kind of play is usually
temporary and expresses itself in abnormal sensitivity and
susceptibility to surroundings, as well as fits of poetic
exaltation and frenzied gestures. In *Sumidagawa*, however,
the heroine does not become reunited with her lost child
as is usually the case, but discovers his death, and the
play ends somewhat tragically. A ferryman opens the action with news of great numbers of people to be taken across
the river for a solemn memorial service; a traveller from
the capital enters who wishes to make the crossing in order to continue his journey, but they wait for the arrival
of a mad woman he has recently seen who is also travelling
to the East. The woman appears, telling of her grief and
recounting the kidnapping of her young son. The ferryman
rudely takes advantage of her overwrought state and makes
sport of her before the company; she admonishes him for his
incivility, but is distracted by the sight of gulls on the river, associations of a poem by Narihira, and thoughts of her
son. Once in the boat the traveller asks about the gathering of people on the other shore, and the ferryman tells
the story of a slave-trader who had travelled that way the

year before with a tender boy who had fallen ill and could
go no farther. The local people had tended the lad as
best they could, but he had died and, as he had asked, was
buried on the spot. In a very moving dialogue with the
ferryman, whose former rudeness to her adds immeasurably to
the charged emotion of the situation, the heroine reveals
herself to be the mother of the dead boy and is pitied even
by the ferryman. She sings of the cruelty of fate and begins to dig ineffectually with her bare hands at the burial
mound in order to see the face of her son once more, but
she dissolves into bitter tears and laments the transiency
of life. The ferryman enjoins her to pray for the repose
of the boy's soul, which she does, and her prayers are answered, first by the voice of her son from inside the stylized structure representing the tomb, and then by the
fleeting apparition of the boy's ghost. All the plays in
this category tend to be still more intense and emotional
than those which precede, and they provide a climax of
passion for the complete cycle of plays.

The second variety of mad piece, *onryo-mono* (possession piece), is generally based on a ghost story in which
the souls of the dead are bound to earth by some particularly intense human passion. *Nishikigi* (The Brocade Tree)
is just such a ritual, and opens with the pilgrimage of a
priest and his companions to a distant northern province.
A man and woman of the place enter, calling attention to the
accessories they carry, a decorated stick *(nishikigi)* and
a length of cloth, and chant a poem of delicate imagery which
expresses their anxiety over a pattern gone awry, their guilt
their longing and the weight of time past. The priests question them about the accessories, and the symbolism of unrequited love is explained. The cloth is of so narrow a weave
that it will not meet about a woman's body, and the *nishikigi*
are tokens of courtship which a man leaves before a maiden's
gate each day, until she countenances his suit. If after a
thousand days she still has not received him, he must admit
defeat. The grave of just such a rejected suitor is pointed
out nearby, and the party removes there as the chorus sup-
plies associations of loneliness, chill autumn evenings and
dark mountain storms. The man enters the stylized grave
mound and the woman retires into conventionalized invisibil-
ity nearby. After the interval the priests prepare to pray
through the night, and the woman comes forward as though in
a dream or vision; the man is discovered inside the tomb,

costumed resplendently and masked. The figures now re-enact
their story, seeking repentance and release from their attachment to life, which in fact is granted them. They pledge
their love, and the mime finishes with a lively dance of joy
before the poetic vision dissolves.

Another kind of possession piece is represented by
Aoi no ue (The Lady Hollyhock), in which the revengeful
ghost is the personification of intense emotion which has
become an independent agent. The play opens with the announcement by a courtier that exorcism and physic have both
proved ineffectual in restoring the Lady Aoi to health, and
that a diviner is at hand to determine whether the possession spirit is that of a dead or a living person. In response
to the incantation, the jealousy of the Lady Rokujō enters
incarnated as a pathetic and beautiful, love-lorn noble woman.
The *shite* sings of her uncontrollable passion, the wheel of
retribution and the deceiving illusion of reality in life.
Her speech abounds in references to wheels and carriages
which constitute veiled allusions to the familiar story of
a humiliation visited upon Rokujō by the servants of Aoi
over standing-room for her coach at a festival. The *shite*
declares herself an invisible phantom, but the *mikko* perceives her dimly, and the figure answers by identifying herself. She sings of her love for Prince Genji and her
bitterness that his attentions have returned to his wife,
the Lady Aoi. Her jealousy mounts and she attacks the sick-
bed which is represented by a folded *kimono* on the floor,
then rushes out in a frenzy of passion. In the second
scene a priest is summoned to dispel the possessing spirit,
and his prayers summon forth the phantom, now manifest in
its true form with demoniac, horned mask and hammer-headed
staff. The dancing of the fierce spirit as it is controlled
and finally calmed by the invocations of the holy man, is
frankly spectacular and greatly overshadows the poetry of
the finale.

Still another variety of play generally classified
among *kurui-mono* of the fourth group is the *genzai-mono*
(earthly piece) which presents real action rather than an
action relived through recollection. Plays of this type
often concern warriors and battle, but differ widely in
mood and atmosphere from those plays of the second group.
A particularly effective example is *Kagekiyo* which opens
with Hitomaru, the daughter of Kagekiyo, travelling in

search of her aged father, a former Heike warrior, surnamed 'the hot-tempered', who now lives in exile in a far province. She speaks of her longing to see him and of her arduous journey. Kagekiyo then appears in his beggar's hut; he is now blind and destitute, an object of charity. He sings of his sad condition, and when Hitomaru approaches to ask news of her father, he recognizes her voice, but hides his identity out of genuine feeling for her. Encountering the village headman, Hitomaru and her attendant inquire after Kagekiyo and, discovering that the man who sent them on was in fact her father, Hitomaru breaks down and weeps. The headman assumes the office of intermediary, and Kagekiyo abuses him for interrupting his thoughts, but goes on to reflect on his fallen condition and burned-out passion. Softening, Kagekiyo agrees to entertain the headman with tales of former glory in battle, but the headman re-introduces Hitomaru, and a touching reunion follows. The old man explains that his deceit was to spare the girl her anguish at finding him so reduced by misfortune, and the chorus suggests his former glory as a famous warrior of the Heike. Kagekiyo is then asked to tell of his exploits at the battle of Yoshima, and he agrees, on condition that she then consent to return to her home without him. The ritual recreation begins, and the *shite* mimes from a seated position. The enfeebled movements, blind mask, and beggar's garb are all in sharp contrast to the matter recounted. He rises at the end of the recital and Hitomaru leaves, but not before Kagekiyo has placed a hand upon her shoulder as she passes; he is left alone on stage, weeping silently. The play is particularly powerful, but not all the pieces in this subdivision are quite so melancholy. There are a number, such as *Ataka*, which present more lively and decidedly dramatic action, and have more affinity in mood and tempo with plays of the fifth and last group.

Kiri Nō (finale or concluding pieces) are usually plays in which spectacular and lively dancing takes precedence over the text itself. Their place in the scheme of a complete programme constitutes a heightened recapitulation of mood and atmosphere, rather than meaningful action. By this point in a cycle of plays, the logical faculty of the audience is suspended, and the imagination is carried along more by patterns of music and moment than by the significance of events. *Kumasaka*, however, is a play with a

semblance of normal structure and text, and I give it here
as an illustration in order to contrast it with an example
of a more common type later on. The play springs from the
boyhood exploits of Yoshitsune, whose childhood name was
Ushiwaka, but the main character is the ghost of Kumasaka,
a famous bandit. A pilgrim priest sets the scene and encounters a colleague near Kumasaka's tomb who is really
the disguised ghost of the robber. Together they pray for
the dead, and the *waki* is then invited to spend the night
in a nearby cottage which he discovers has no holy images
upon the walls, but instead, weapons of war. The *shite* explains that before taking his vows he had been a bandit,
and the chorus continues the train of thought by extolling
the weapons of the Bodhisattvas and finally the superior
virtues of their holiness. The scene dissolves and, after
the interval, the *waki* encounters the vision of Kumasaka
who begins by lamenting his attachment to the world and
then recounts the details of a daring robbery at that very
spot. Ushiwaka, a boy of sixteen, however, happened to be
in the merchant's caravan and fought off the attack as one
possessed, his virtue being superior to the weapons of the
robbers. Kumasaka himself engaged the youth in combat, but
could not overcome him, and finally the agile boy drew
blood. Enraged, Kumasaka threw down his weapons to wrestle
with the boy, but could not come to grips with him and was
wounded many times. His strength of spirit drained, he
died. The choral narrative which the *shite* mimes is so
constructed as to raise the battle to a quite miraculous
level and suggests the sublime transcendence of human limitations through the strength of spiritual values.

    Shōjō represents another type of *kiri Nō* which provided
little more than a poetic base for spectacular dancing. The
plot incident is an obvious excuse, and the drama of the
performance is only evident in the relationship between poetic imagery and the dance itself. One version of this play
opens with the *waki*'s recital of a dream which had led him
to become a successful wine merchant. He speaks of a strange
customer who is never affected by the quantity he drinks, and
how, when asked his name, answers *Shōjō* (orang-utan). In
the second scene the *waki* awaits the arrival of the *shite*
by the mouth of a river, clipping chrysanthemum petals into
the wine. The *shite* appears, praising the wine of autumn
and the scent of white chrysanthemums, the moon and the
stars, and dances across the waves in delicate celebration

of ecstasy. The play ends in the benedictions of the Wine
Spirit, the real identity of the *waki*'s customer, and in
the bestowal of a miraculously replenished wine jar, a
magical fountain of perennial nature which is associated
with the unchanging character of the seasons, however varied
their cycle may be. With the *kiri Nō*, the cycle of themes
and moods which constitute a full programme, has also completed itself and returned at a more climactic level to the
original quality of the congratulatory piece or god play.
The emotions of the spectator have undergone both a cathar-
sis and refinement in the carefully articulated progress of
the performance. Strictly speaking, Nō is not a drama of
conflict but rather a purely theatrical experience in which
a unified vision of universal order is suggested through a
parallel cycle of emotional responses arising directly from
the presentation.

Indeed, it is not difficult to recognise the basic
similarity of Yeats's intention in his early plays, both in
presenting universalized human passions at moments of crisis
and in suggesting an ideal mode of existence. His plays,
however, are very different from Nō in their celebration of
spiritual ideal and the significance of human experience.
As Ezra Pound readily perceived, Nō is concerned with intense
emotion which is centred on an idea and not on character or
personality: human experience is raised to the level of
a spiritual or heroic ideal through strict aesthetic ordering, and rather than analysing psychological or social problems, a cycle of Nō plays outlines a complete service of
life or experience which reflects a traditional world-view.
Although Yeats was certainly interested in the more superficial aspects of the ghost psychology represented, I do
not think that the Japanese vision of human experience, with
its emphasis on the isolation of the individual and profound
melancholy in the face of mutability, had much effect on
Yeats's imagination. On the other hand, the subjective
apprehension of the ideal or archetype through images of
intense emotion must have been a revelation. His early
plays had attempted to present images of moral or spiritual
ideality, and the themes of the plays were often at variance
with the circumstances of the action. The attempt to be
representational often made the characters and situations
uninteresting in themselves, and the insistence on realistic action embarrassed the imaginative or ideal values that
were to be expressed. In general, the tragic implications

for human characters go undeveloped, and the action seems
weighted and artificial; that is, subordinated to a prede-
termined outcome or effect. It is only in *On Baile's
Strand* and *Deirdre* that conceptions of spontaneous human
passion in conflict with ideal or heroic norms are adequately
projected, and *On Baile's Strand* is further rescued through
stylization in the use of Blind Man and Fool, while *Deirdre*
falters because of an imbalance of tragic and ritual modes.
Yeats was not so much influenced by the idea of a complete
cycle of plays reconciling the individual to a particular
vision of order in the universe as he was by the effectiveness of universalizing and distancing techniques; especially
the localization of action, the use of historical or legendary characters and the recreation of action through the
imagination by the protagonist from a vantage point in time.
The form of Nō plays rather than their peculiar subject-
matter presented new possibilities for expressing his own
world-view. Perhaps the most significant characteristic of
the complete Nō programme for Yeats was the discovery that
its vision of human experience is not limited only to high
seriousness; Nō is rarely performed without its comic counterpart, Kyōgen (playful words).
     Even the self-contained and independent interludes
which are performed between separate Nō plays complement
the intention of the complete cycle. Kyōgen are not merely
farces used for comic relief, however, but present the lives
of common folk and the comedy of human imperfection as a
contrast to the exalted subjects of the more sombre and
ritualistic Nō. It is a comedy of situation which demonstrates the discrepancy between appearance and reality, and
usually ends with a Punch and Judy drubbing or wild flight
from the stage as the comic inversion is recognized and
reversed. Kyōgen sets out to expose human frailty, but
within a frame of reference determined by self-knowledge,
joy and reconciliation. It is a celebration of warmth and
human nature, and the buffoonery is often delicious, however
slight. The world of Kyōgen is vivid and down-to-earth,
peopled by cowardly gods, unctuous priests, dull-witted
masters, scheming servants, tyrannical wives, rebellious
children and cunning animal spirits, but the characteristic
moral inversions are well regulated and controlled by
aesthetic decorum and comic insight. While Nō makes one
aware of an ideal reality through its presentation of

ennobled human experience, Kyōgen underlines the comic in-
significance of everyday life. Toraaki Okura (1597-1662),
a master of Kyōgen and noted theoretician, comments: 'The
Nō transforms the unreal into the real; the Comic Interlude,
the real into the unreal.'[3] While Nō recreates the ideal,
Kyōgen encourages an amused detachment from the trivial and
ignoble, laughs gently at the nature of things as they are,
and directs serious attention away from the actual.

Yeats could not have known that *The Pot of Broth*
(1902) was in fact a very close approximation of Kyōgen,
and before he had been introduced to classical Japanese
drama he had already experimented with comedy as a means
of integrating the rich variety of actual human experience
with the ennobling values of ideal aspirations and actions.
Where There is Nothing (1907) and *The Green Helmet* (1910)
are far more complex and developed as plays than any Kyōgen,
and certainly much more sophisticated than *The Pot of Broth*
which need only end in Sibby Coneely's recognition of the
Tramp's imposture and a wild chase from the stage to become
indistinguishable from a Kyōgen plot. To be sure, Kyōgen
also requires a higher degree of stereotyping in characterization than can be found in the folk comedies of the
Abbey tradition, but from the single comparison with *The
Pot of Broth*, one can see that Kyōgen as a form had little
to offer Yeats in the way of startling dramatic conceptions
or techniques. Fenollosa had not been interested in Kyōgen
as a form, and there is very little information on the subject in his notebooks, but Yeats was aware that Kyōgen were
performed as interludes of contrasting mood and subject
matter between Nō plays, an integral part of a complete Nō
programme. In fact, he had already written *The Green Helmet* as a curtain-raiser for *On Baile's Strand*, and went on
to write several more comedies in his later career, one of
which was said to be inspired by Japanese Kyōgen, but even
there it is really the specific influence of Nō that we
discern; that is, outside the general confirmation of com-
patibility between serious and comic modes that was maintained in the complete cycle of five Nō plays and three
Kyōgen.

It is only by comparison with the internal structuring
of Nō that we can best assess the influences on, and originality of, Yeats's plays for dancers. It is very awkward
to generalize about a structure common to all Nō plays,
but it is possible to outline a general pattern of poetic

units which has been fixed to a large extent by tradition
(for precise details see Appendix). Within such a flexible framework, the dynamics of plot organization, musical
style and literary texture accommodate themselves to the
particular requirements of the subject, and one must bear
in mind that Nō is primarily a kind of music drama in
which mime, dance, music and chant are each at least equal
in importance to the poetic text. According to Motokiyō
Zeami (1363-1443), perhaps the greatest of Nō masters and
surely its finest theoretician: 'A Nō play should possess
three elements, *Shu*, *Shaku*, and *Sho*: *Shu* is to have adequate matter, *Shaku* to have harmony between the musical
composition and the plot, and *Sho* to have a suitable expression of words in harmony with the peculiar flavour of
the work.'[4]

In general, individual plays are constructed on a
tripartite principle of introduction-development-climax
or slow-lively-fast *(jo-ha-kyū)*, but one finds that the
development section can also be elaborated into a tripartite structure, making a division of five sections in all.
The same basic composition is used for the complete Nō
programme and for individual dance sequences within any
one play. Either three or five units are the norm in Japanese classical drama, and there is a very intimate relationship between the literary and musical structure of a
play. The opening section of a typical play is dominated
by a slow and regular rhythm, solemn and powerful, which
finds its most characteristic expression in the lyrical
description of locality by the *waki*, who is usually a
priest, pilgrim, or court official on some sort of journey.
Having arrived at a place associated with a famous legend
or historical incident, the development section begins
with the entrance of the *shite*, often disguised as a local
person, who introduces a different pitch and faster tempo.
His encounter with the *waki* brings about a recounting of
the famous legend or incident and mutual reflection on the
sorrow inherent in the human condition. Having accomplished
the induction of the audience into a scene of imagined
action, the *waki* retires to a seat at the front right corner of the stage, while the *shite* recreates the significant
mood of the original incident through mime and dance. If
the *shite* has been disguised up to this point, he exits and
changes costume for the brief finale of the piece which is
characterized by a fast and irregular rhythm. The second

entrance of the *shite* reveals his identity and former condition, while the dance performed recreates the crisis or
intense passion of the experience itself and provides a
vivid contrast in both nature and character with the earlier
posturing. Neither the use of transformations, nor the
'time machine' techniques, however, are absolutely essential to the success of Nō. It is rather the expressive
method of representation through dance and mime, music and
chant, which evokes an idealized reality. Musical composition reinforces the progressive intensification of feeling
through vocal styles of delivery and leads to a sustained
melodic section of complex rhythm, a scene of quiet grace
and beauty during which the first dance, or posturing, is
performed. The conclusion follows as a brief sequence dominated by an impelling, regular rhythm and an ecstatic dance
which acts as a contrasting restatement of images created
during the earlier performance. The central position of
that lyric passage is, in fact, a major historical development, and it was through the genius of Zeami's father
Kiyotsugu Kannami (1334-84), that an antecedent and independent form of lyric dance, Kusemai, was fused with Sarugaku,
a mimed verse narrative, thus forming the characteristic
features of Nō performance and creating a new theatrical
form, Sarugaku no Nō.[5] More important still in realizing
the universal is the objective distance obtained in the
subordination of all roles to that of the *shite*; an inno-
vation of Zeami which effected the future course of Nō as
an artistic accomplishment and created its ideal form.[6]
From the direct representation of a dramatic action, Nō
became the recreation of an intense emotion or psychological state, as a single actor interprets a dramatic poem and
creates a paradigmatic world of time, space and energy.
        Rather than the homogeneity or evenness of rich, golden
tone that was advocated by Walter Pater as lyric unity, a
Nō performance is a dynamic arrangement of poetic forms and
musical patterns that contrast sharply with one another,
shaping the reactions of the audience to the particular
action and universal theme. The introduction section is
musically complete in itself and opens with the *waki*'s
solemn announcement in formal, fixed rhythm, of subject,
situation, or circumstances *(shidai)* which is followed
by a flexible, prose-like statement of his name, social
condition, and present intention *(nanori)*. The relaxed

and lyrical travel-song *(michi-yuki)* that ends the section
normally describes the journey he is undertaking to a famous place and introduces seasonal imagery with its heavy
burden of emotional overtones in Japanese culture. The
formal entrance speech of the *shite (issei)* opens the development section which repeats the earlier pattern and leads
to a description of place or state of being *(uta)* depending
on the subject matter. A dialogue between *shite* and *waki*
(mondai) introduces the second subdivision and expresses
the feelings which motivate the speakers and leads through
a relevant narration to the *shite's* account of the significant action or experience *(uta)*. The third subdivision may
begin with a separate introduction leading to the *kuri* which
prepares the audience for the *kuse* or climax and emphasizes
a maxim or principle of religious doctrine relevant to the
central experience. In discoursing on its application to
the situation the *shite* dances out the intensity of the
emotion or experience which has been recreated in imagination. The *coda* takes the form of a monologue *(rongi)* which
expresses thought or feeling arising directly from the recreation of emotional experience. Again the musical development of the section is from formal declamation through
intermediate stages of musical form to an obvious lyricism
which is melodically free, yet balanced by a calmly insistent rhythm, a point of transition to the dominance of
rhythm in the finale section that follows. So impelling a
climax is achieved within the *kuse* where the first major
dance sequence occurs, that an additional lyric form is
needed to provide a musical resolution, retard the movement,
and allow it to come to rest. The concluding or fast section opens in a fixed rhythm with a temporizing re-intro-
duction by the *waki* and/or the formal speech of the transformed *shite (issei)* and maintains its rhythmic insistence
throughout. The further narration of the *waka* dwells on
the present condition of the *shite* and accompanies the climactic dance which is again accelerated by the special
fixed rhythm of the *kiri* (finale). 'Moreover, there is
a tendency to accelerate the tempo during a performance.
According to this principle, called *jo-ha-kyū* (slow-lively-
fast), a verse should begin slowly; the pace then gradually
increases, becomes fast, and finally retards and comes to
rest. Each successive verse begins at a faster tempo than
did its predecessor and continues its own cycle of speeds,

so that an *accelerando* gradually builds up through a whole
section or play. The gradual *accelerando* may even be applied to a whole programme of several plays.'[7] This basis
of lyrical composition, however, is found in recurring
patterns of contrasting forms which give way to one another
through the transition provided by passages of melodious,
but simple and flexible, recitative. The barest outline
of traditional structure demonstrates the essential simplicity of the scheme:

Jo.			*Shidai*			
			Nanori			
			Michi-yuki			
Ha.	i.	*Issei*	ii.	*Mondai*	iii.	*Kuri*
		Sashi		*Sashi*		*Sashi*
		Uta		*Uta*		*Kuse*
						Rongi
Kyū.			*Machi-utai*			
			Waka			
			Kiri			

The chanting of individual speeches *(utai)*, which
make up a Nō text involves the heightening and interpretation of the natural rhythms of verse through vocal dynamics
and melody as well as through rhythm pattern. There are a
number of distinct musical patterns which range from pure
speech, a slightly figured or heightened recitation of the p
etic line to those which vary as to characteristic pitch lev
and degree of melodic ornamentation, but more importantly
as to whether the basic rhythm pattern is fixed or not
(see Appendix for specific details). The range of vocal
styles extends from the slightly formalized intonation of
verse forms through highly inflected melodies to special
fixed rhythms in which each syllable is fitted to a single
beat, giving an effect of formal measure and majesty, or
to a single half-beat with a resulting sense of excitement
and tension, a pounding speed and regularity. The object
is to express the movement of thought in the mind of the

character through exact sense images and emotional suggestion. Nō is primarily concerned with the inner nature of
the individual's response to human experience, and characterization is implied by rhythmic and tonal control. The
performer's voice must convince that it reflects the mind
of the character without attempting to imitate the overtones of another person. An actor's voice is never changed
or disguised, and frankly sonorous male tones in obvious
middle age may represent the inner consciousness of a young
and delicate court beauty, or that of a deranged youth; even
inadequacies of voice are forgiven if a role is successfully
projected. It is not human emotions which are caught and
conveyed in the voice, but states of being which are suggested through patterns of rhythmic variation and melodic line.
In fact, it is the musical modification of the lyric forms
which becomes a primary vehicle of expression in Nō, a filter
that refines crude emotion and communicates it intelligibly
as sense imagery. The spectator experiences the integration
of the actual words into a musical flow which is itself the
movement of the play's basic emotion or mood. *Utai* never
reaches the fullness and fluid movement of pure song, nor
does it confine itself to a monotonously regular rhythmic
pattern, but follows the natural intonations of the verse
form.
     Japanese is a quantitative language, and has a very
regular syllabary, much like that of Italian. There is no
stress pattern inherent in either individual words or
phrases, and normal speech rhythms tend towards isochronous
syllables, although variation is freely attempted in emphasizing significant words and phrases. The standard verse
form of classical poetry is derived directly from the rhythm
and phrasing of refined speech and consists of distiches of
five and seven syllables separated by a caesura, which form
lines of twelve and fourteen syllables each. In general the
delivery of *utai* is related to an eight-beat musical
measure; in actual practice, sixteen half-beats, but the
music of Nō is remarkable for its free variation, and the
performer is not held to the authority of the musical bar.
The duration of syllable is often expanded or reduced both
to emphasize meaning and to reconcile the line length to
the measure. The intervals of the musical bar are not rigidly metronomic, but are subtly modified to avoid monotony
and gain emotional effect. The interesting and flexible

treatment of rhythm enlivens a performance with a very real sense of vitality and subtle invention.

All forms of *utai* may be sung in either of two tone systems which differ from one another in range and vocal technique (see Appendix). The distinction between the strong *(tsuyo)* and weak *(yowa)* modes is often compared to the difference between *recitativo* and *cantabile* forms in western opera. The strong mode is a highly intoned recitation which accomplishes upward movement to higher notes by straining the vocal chords, and because of the *sforzando*-like dynamics and intense *vibrato* employed, pitch intervals are inexact and unstable. Only two main tones are distinguishable: high and low. The strong mode renders a style of stately power which is particularly appropriate for the more formal god play or congratulatory piece. The weak *(yowa)* mode emphasizes melody and is particularly effective in projecting the heightened emotional subject matter of the more lyrical and elegant plays.[8] It is based on a full octave scale which has four main tones: high, middle, low and very low, as well as intermediate and transitional notes The designation of tone system for delivering a given speech is determined by context and desired effect, but as a general rule the descriptive and powerful subsections are recited in the strong tone system, while the lyrical and emotional passages are sung in the weak mode.

Still another dramatic technique of musical performance, and one which bears a direct relationship to Yeats's later practice, is the characteristic substitution of the chorus, chanting in unison, for the voice of the protagonist as he dances. In Nō the chorus may also act independently of the *shite* and function as accompaniment, impersonal commentator, or even as interlocutor, but in every case the massed effect of six, eight, or ten voices is a striking contrast to solo performance. Similarly, there is also a pattern of dynamic contrast in the intervention of musical accompaniment at strategic moments in the progress of the play. The orchestra *(hayashi)* consists of two hand-drums, a stick-drum and a flute; they accent the atmosphere and character of each drama through prelude music and accompaniment of the *shite*'s entrances as well as of the dancing at both the climax and conclusion of the performance. The use of percussion is also accompanied by rather alarming hooting cries or shouts *(kakegoe)* from the hand-drummers, which outline or mark the rhythm by an indication of the unsounded

strong beat, and stress the emotional tension of an action
through vocal colouring. A profusion of cries and drum
strokes during a moment of crisis produces a startling contrast with the silence and solemnity of other scenes, and
becomes a spur to the imagination of performer and spectator alike. The drums control the nerves of the audience
and a sudden burst or dense texture of sound creates an
almost unbearable excitement and expectation. Inner tensions, on the other hand, are created and extended during
the less exciting patterns of suppressed rhythm in the
musical score, where sequences of negative space are produced, created by sounds punctuating silence as when rain
slowly drips from the eaves on a summer night. The intervals which result are not unlike the moments of motionless-
ness during the performance of dances; the very stillness
is charged with tension and quiet expectation. Throughout
a performance, musical movement concentrates on the manipulation of interval and duration into patterns of satisfying psychological rhythms which inform the spectator's
responses and suspend his consciousness of conventional
time. An independent and ideal sense of relativity and
timelessness is created through suggestive rhythm.

From such an outline of poetic and musical composition
it should be obvious that in the strictest sense of the
word, the ritual of Nō is not really dramatic. There is
little conflict of any sort, and whatever logical progression does exist is determined by associations of feelings
and emotional states, not the inevitability of cause and
effect. In fact, the progress of the action presented on
stage represents a decided movement away from realism. A
Nō play always opens in objective exposition; the *waki*, a
dramatic foil, announces himself as a real person, in a
given time and place with a particular intention that brings
him to a famous spot. The audience accepts the projected
reality of the *shite* on his first appearance, although in
a majority of plays this figure is somewhat mysterious and
incompletely explained. At this point the narrative focuses
attention on a spiritual quality or emotion connected with
the famous incident that had occurred locally, and the shape-
changing potential of the *shite* becomes evident in his dis-
course with the *waki*. The strangeness of the *shite*'s re-
plies and the unexplained presence lead the *waki* to voice
the doubts of the audience as to the figure's true identity,

and the very nature of the Japanese language lends a further element of flexibility. Without personal pronouns there is no distinction between a third person narrative and one delivered in the first person. In talking about the emotion associated with the legendary incident, the narrator merges his identity with that of the original participant and attention is directed from the character experiencing the emotion to the quality of the emotion itself. As the *waki* retreats from the action altogether and seats himself in a reverie at one corner of the stage, the audience is left unconcerned by the fact that the dramatic reality of the action has receded into a shadowy region of dream or vision. As the *shite* focuses more intently on the central emotion and its ultimate significance, the rhythm of the performance builds towards a climax and stylized bodily movement extends itself into dance which projects abstraction as a concrete image. The poetry of the text, as well as the extended patterns of images and allusions which abound in Nō, also tend to universalize the *shite*'s emotion, and the result is a demonstration of depersonalized moral sensibility.

The difficult question of the very real shape-changing or transformation that occurs in a large number of the plays is yet another intensification of the shift from objective exposition to a subjective revelation or self-realization which characterizes Nō. The overt disguise of the *shite* as a humble countryman in his first appearance is discarded and he reappears resplendent in his former glory to re-enact the nature of his original experience. In those plays which introduce ghosts or other supernatural figures who ultimately reveal their proper identities, the imaginative level of dream or visionary action is rendered absolutely concrete and real, but at the expense of an awkward break in the lyrical flow. Even though every technique of Nō drama insists on anti-realism, an interruption in the lyrical progression of the play is damaging, especially when the convention of the entr'acte is so opposed to the quality of lyrical effect within the play itself. The break *(ai)* in the flow of action is filled in with a brief performance by Kyōgen players, and the most common is a narrative entr'acte *(katari-ai)* in which another version of the play's action and background is recited in vernacular. The *ai-kyōgen* opens and closes this recital in dialogue with the *waki* who remains on stage throughout. The division of a

play into two scenes is an organic consideration, however,
and there are a number of plays which avoid the difficulty
altogether, certainly with no loss of effectiveness. In
fact, the most realistic presentations have a very forceful
aspect and import, not because of any inherently dramatic
conflict or situation, but through their unbroken unity of
lyrical concentration. Even among apparition and ghost
plays, where the revelation of the *shite*'s true identity
and condition is normal, there are a number which tend to
reduce the distraction of a complete break in action. The
protagonist may retire into or behind a stage property,
alter his dress, and change masks without complete loss
of musical continuity and dramatic tension. He may even
change on stage in full sight of the audience with the
help of a *kōken* (overseer or understudy) who sits at the
back of the stage.

No drama has often been dismissed in the west as slight
and insignificant; above all as intellectually soft, and the
misconception has been perpetuated because of two important
factors: the first is that the powerful and resonant force
of inherent cultural values or attitudes which evoke an immediate response to familiar subject matter and aesthetic
practice is lost on the alien reader; the second is that
commentators have ignored, or been ignorant of, the accomplishment of musical construction, rhetorical texture and
stylized choreography as complements to the dramatic poem.
The original translation of a modern Nō on a Christian theme
which follows - one of several now performed in Japan - may
help to overcome the first of these difficulties and to provide a possible point of comparison with examples of western
assimilation from the Nō. For some years *Fukkatsu no
Kirisuto* (The Resurrected Christ) has figured as an annual
Easter production in Tokyo and was written as a reconciliation between traditional aesthetic forms and the alien
faith of Christian converts. The text is as typical an
example of the god play, or *kami Nō*, as one could wish.
It is essentially a miracle play, the projection of momentary harmony between or intersection of, the temporal and
supernatural worlds, an archetype of universal order. By
its very nature, however, the god play has less appeal for
a western audience than any other type of Nō drama. It
offers no human situation to be entered into sympathetically,
other than the awe and excitement of the miraculous encounter
itself. Even more so than other types of Nō, it is a ritual

of emotional recreation rather than the imitation of an action, and depends more heavily on choreographic and musical
composition as paradigms of the emotion to be evoked because
so much less immediate sympathy is aroused by the action
than, for example, by the tragic death of a youthful warrio
the thwarted love of a beautiful woman, or the pathetic derangement of a mind unbalanced by an excess of emotional in
volvement.

   In being fitted to a traditional Nō structure, the
historico-legendary incident of Christ's resurrection is
refocused into a moving pattern that recedes from the objective reality of the women who visit the tomb on the thir
day to the imaginatively perceived demonstration of His div
inity. In this particular play the cumulative effect of th
narrative episodes and abstract meditations is the presenta
tion of a depersonalized spiritual sensibility which is com
municated to and apprehended by the audience. Familiarity
with the Biblical account and cultural overtones of the
event are not to be discounted in the play's ultimate effec
tiveness, and the recurring quotations and images from the
Bible are encouraged by Nō tradition. In fact, the play
has considerable literary merit. In the original it is
classically ornamented with allusions and quotations from
Japanese culture as well, but these devices become submerge
in translation. The unity of its lyric mood and the elegan
of its poetry make up no small part of the play's literary
success. Oddly enough, there is little about the text, as
it stands, that could not have evolved directly from the
early Medieval trope known as the 'Quem quaeritis', a chora
dramatization of the Christian Message at Easter mass in
which European liturgical drama was born. The trope originally took the form of a dialogue between the three Marys
and the Angel at the tomb.

   Quem quaeritis in sepulchre, O Christicolae?

   Iesum Nazarenum crucifixum, O caelicolae.

   Non est hic, surrexit sicut praedixerat.

   Ite, nuntiate quia surrexit de sepulchro.

                                    Resurrexi.[9]

In structure there are several irregularities that
should be mentioned, but for the most part these are required by the subject matter. *Fukkatsu no Kirisuto* is unusual in that there is no *waki* (interlocutor) independent
of the incident on which the ritual is based, and that role
is filled by *shite tsure* (companions or followers of the
shite). Precedent for such substitution was set during
a late and experimental period of development in Nō drama
and in the present instance *tsure* are required in order to
remain faithful to the Biblical account. Another eccentri-
city is the delayed entrance of the *shite* which allows for
the speech of the angel with the heightening of dramatic
tension in its choral introduction and the beauty of the
tsure's meditation on the presence of Christ. From this
point onwards, the structure is remarkably regular for a
play of one act, and one should note how the *kuse* subsec-
tion is foreshortened and slides easily into the *kyū* section
with its major dance sequence. The direction *noru* indicates the excitement and pounding speed of *o-nori* rhythm.
Notation of pitch levels (high and low) and tone scale
(strong and weak) is given throughout, but only those lyric
forms whose style of delivery is different from the normal
pattern are noted. For example, the second lyric of the
play would normally be *nanori*, but since it is a woman's
utai it is delivered as *sashi*. The next lyric would normally be *michi-yuki*, but *mondai* is a normal substitution
and here it is more suitable for dramatic as well as musical reasons. The stage directions that I jotted down some
years ago during a memorable performance by Mr. Hōshō Kurō,
a co-author of the piece, have been incorporated as an aid
to the reader in visualizing the action. In the present
case they are used as a substitute for the line-drawings
conventionally printed in the margins of Japanese editions
which serve both to outline the choreography and correlate
stage movement with the text. The play requires something
less than an hour for performance.

Fukkatsu no Kirisuto   (The Resurrected Christ)

by: Hōshō Kurō
Muto Tomiō

Translated by Ōtsuka Fumio

H. Hoivels
Yoshida Tadao

Edited by Richard Taylor

Kidō Kyudei

Source: Luke 24: 1-9

Cast:

       Shite   Jesus Christ
 First Tsure   Mary Magdalen
Second Tsure   Mary, the mother of James

Action: before the tomb at daybreak

After the musicians and chorus are seated, a vine-topped and curtained bamboo frame which represents the sepulchre is placed in the centre of the stage. The masked and wimpled tsure in single-coloured robes enter: Mary Magdalen carrying a container of holy oil for anointing the body, and Mary, the mother of James, a single lily.

Tsure   *(In unison)*
  (Weak)   As the light broke,
                  We woke from our dream,
                  Impelled to seek
                  The resting place of our Master.

First Tsure   I am a woman of Galilee,
  (Sashi)   Searching in the shadow
                  Of this mountain
                  For the tomb of our Lord.

  (Mondai)   It is the first day of the week
                  And, carrying sweet spices,
                  We hurry to the tomb before sun-rise.

Second Tsure   I too, go there with you.

First Tsure   Come, this way!
                  This is indeed strange;
                  The massive stone that sealed
                  The entrance of the tomb
                  Is now thrown down.

Second Tsure   Can this be the work
                  Of the recent earthquakes?

First Tsure   My heart pounds!

They hurry towards the tomb and station themselves a little before and to the right of the structure.

Chorus   A sudden beam of light
 (Strong &   Radiates from heaven.
  High)   Clad in incandescent white,
                  A heavenly messenger appears.
                  Frightened and awed,
                  The women sink to the ground.

Angel   *Voice from chorus or covered frame.*
 (High)   Why do you look
                  For the living among the dead?
                  He is risen; He is not here:
                  Behold the place
                  Where they laid Him.

The women rise. Mary Magdalen crosses to the bridgeway and stands by the first pine.

First Tsure   Bleak is our path
 (Weak &   Without Him; and yet,
  Low)   His feet bathed in tears
                  And dried in long black hair,
                  The lingering scent of ointment,
                  The sweet and noble face,
                  The merciful smile:
                  All are still fresh
                  In mind, though gone.

                  Without measure
                  Is the grace and favour of God:
                  He came to remove

The pain of the sick,
And bring salvation
To the suffering;
Eventually bearing
The sins of the world,
And doing penance for them.

Tsure   *(In unison) Mary returns to her former place.*
  (High)   O yearning unsurpassed!

Chorus   Beyond all this, what is it
                    That has come to pass?
                    The tomb of the Lord has been opened.

                    Praying that he might appear,
                    They throw themselves to the ground
                    Choked with sobs.
                    They throw themselves to the ground
                    Choked with sobs.

Tsure   *(In unison)*
                    How saddened we are
                    At the telling of it.

Shite   *From behind curtain, altogether off-stage.*
                    What sounds are these
                    From in front of the tomb?

*He enters swiftly down the bridgeway and retreats to
the third pine, wearing a white dancing over-robe and
stiff divided trousers of white and silver brocade, with
a sensitive, yet compelling mask, a golden crown and a
black wig of unbound hair flowing loosely over the
shoulders. The intensity of the moment is prolonged
by a pause and heightened by the use of the stick-drum.
The figure proceeds to the second pine, postures slowly
and speaks, facing the audience.*

(Sashi –   The mind of God,
Strong &   Generous and merciful,
High)   Waiting neither
                     For scent nor flower,*
                     Has overcome death.

*   Conventional offerings at the altars of the dead.

I am resurrected,
Through the power of God,
And have proven Myself
The Redeemer.

*Entering on the stage proper, He speaks to
the women who have retreated before Him.*

Women, why do you weep?
For whom are you looking?

First Tsure   Is this the guardian of the tomb
(Weak &   Seen by the dim light of dawn?
High)   Where is the body of our Lord?

Shite   Mary!
(Strong &
High)

Tsure   *(In unison)*
(High)   Master! Master!
                  How deeply we have missed you!

Chorus   Saying this, they rush to Him,
(Strong &   Longing to touch Him,
High)   But they are driven back
                  Before His glory.
                  Overcome with awe, they sink
                  To the ground at His feet.

Shite   Mary, do not touch Me.
(Strong &
High)

Chorus   Stand up, make haste; return
(High)   To the brethren and tell them
                  That they too may know.

Shite   I am My Father
(Weak)   And the Father of Mankind.

Chorus   My God
(High)   And the God of mankind.

Shite
   (Noru –
   High)
	I am raised
	To the feet of God, My Father.

Chorus *(Strong)*	How strange this is! A wonderful light prevails, Suffusing both heaven and earth! The dignity And grandeur of the City of God Is revealed. He dances.
Shite *Finishing the dance.* *(Strong)*	Peace be with you. Divine grace be given unto you.

Chorus
   (Weak &
   High)
	He is truly resurrected.
	He is truly resurrected.
	He is proved to be the son of God.
	
	Father and Son
	In the name of the Spirit
	Are given unto the world
	At each baptism.
	
	Let there be glory
	To God in heaven,
	And for us on earth,
	Peace!
	
	Hymns to God are swelling.
	Hymns to God are swelling.
	In the purple mist
	Filled with clean perfume
	God is returned to heaven.

The shite exits swiftly along the bridgeway, pausing
to gesture transcendently; a voluminous sleeve thrown
up and allowed to billow down over the head.

   Fukkatsu no Kirisuto not only provides us with an
accessible and characteristic example of the god play, but
it also offers a point of reference for later comparison
with Yeats's *Resurrection*, especially from the point of

view of lyric construction. The one aspect of Nō which cannot be demonstrated from this text, nor from any translation available to either Pound or Yeats is the importance of rhetorical texture in mediating between the mimetic reality of the performance and the subjective impression of the audience's perception. Literary style joins with musical patterning to 'open' the mind of the spectator through aural awareness, just as dance and mime 'open' the mind through visual awareness. In achieving the required elegance and restrained suggestiveness of literary style, Zeami advises: 'Those who desire to enter upon this art should not concern themselves with other arts, save for poetry which should be studied as much as possible, as it is one of the most important adornments of this aesthetic ennen' (longevity-bringing performance).[10] Richness of language and calculated density of rhetorical texture often contrast with the general austerity of Nō and constitute a major technique for conveying maximum meaning economically. A characteristic feature of the text is the richness of allusion and quotation which underlines a dependence on legend and prior literature. Profuse ornamentation is reserved for significant passages where relevant associations help to project the desired mood or emotion. Historical as well as literary allusion is common, and quotation is primarily from the anthologies of poetry compiled at court between the tenth and fifteenth centuries. The importance of pre-existent literature in Nō as in other art forms of the period has been ascribed to the patronage of an ascendent military class which was bent on acquiring the cultural authority of the sophisticated aristocracy it replaced.[11] It is perhaps more likely that aesthetic values and preoccupations determined the extent of indulgence in neoclassicism: 'Old literary passages, old poems, and even writings of one's own which strike the hearer as familiar, are suitable for Nō.'[12] Anything which is too deep is not readily understood. Yeats did learn to rely on myth and folklore, even on writings of his own, but his obtrusive symbolism has always been a stumbling block.

Among the familiar materials incorporated into a Nō text are quotations and expressions from classical Chinese verse which are held to lend grandeur and forcefulness, as well as those from ancient Japanese poetry which bring grace and elegance. Phrasing from religious scripture is

also used for its connotations of dignity, reverence and
mystery, and like other allusions and quotations, is chosen for its relevance and familiarity. Allusions and quotations also extend the range of associations and overtones
through the relevant juxtapositioning of different periods
of time with the present. Plot incidents themselves are
either taken from existing literature or from legend, and
the original language of a story is used so long as it is
of a sufficiently elegant literary style. A Nō play may
be little more than a skilful mosaic of earlier material,
but there is room for much originality in selection and
re-organization. The borrowing ensures the immediate involvement of an audience, while the embellishing of poetic
text and the blending of mime and music provide a representation which will move the spectator. The object of performance is to suspend reason and transcend the mundane
world by refining and purifying both action and character
until they approach universality and represent ideal truth
and beauty. The incident itself is of no real consequence,
and the emotional connotations and associations of the
ritual must be present from the beginning in order that
the performance mediate directly between the action represented and the apprehension of the spectator. After taking
a suitable subject for a new play: 'One builds up the
three forms of introduction, development, and climax into
five sections, and then gathering together the words and
adding the music, writes the piece out.'[13]
    The language of Nō is archaic and rich in both formal
conventions and devices. Style is not very important in
characterization, but much emphasis is placed on decorum,
elevation and refined good taste, even when common people
are represented. Honorific speech-patterns of antique
court usage are extensively used; for example, declarative
sentences always end with the formula, *sōrō*, commands with
sōraye, and questions with *sōrōya*. Such extra-grammatical
syntax is very common, along with liberal inversion and
weighted vocabulary. Entire lines or distiches are often
repeated as an effective means of prolonging emotion, and
this oblique and arbitrary language of formal elegance
tends to lend dignity to even the simplest statement or
idea. The very nature of the Japanese language, both ancient and modern, with its involved flexional structure
makes it possible to suggest tone and mood with almost
minute precision and delicacy, and to define states of

mind in close detail. The lyric poet has at hand a ready
tool for the expression of conjecture and imagination; his
modes of thought are already characterized by general suggestiveness, free association of images and symbolic expression. The syllabary with its basic unit made up of a
combined consonant and vowel, or a single unattached vowel,
provides a high incidence of spontaneous assonance and
alliteration which has become conventionalized, and certain
sounds are immediately associated with definite moods and
tones. With such a ready-made device the poet can count
on the automatic establishment of atmosphere, in addition
to sound images which echo from line to line and suggest
continuity, while consecutive verses are intricately linked by subtle associations of mood and atmosphere. The
makura-kotoba (pillow word) is a characteristic kind of
word-play in Nō texts and consists of a conventional epi-
thet which is often founded in an assonential or alliter-
ative echo which helps the modifier hold attention to the
noun or concept qualified. The figure generally occurs
at the beginning of a line and 'pillows' the meaning of
the entire poetic line. *Makura-kotoba* are often applied
to place names and have an ennobling function as in
tamamokaru (where the gem-seaweed is cut) which might appear before the name of a bay or coastal town. Their sense
may derive from a direct association of images as in
nubatama mo (black as the leopard-flower) which might be
applied to the word night, for example, while some have no
sense content at all, being merely sound metaphors. Still
others depend for meaning on complex associations of ideas
such as *akitsu shima* (island of the dragonfly) which qualifies the province of Yamato and refers to the similarity
between the circle of the insect's body and the ring of
mountains that encloses the plain of Yamato.

    Another effect of the close syllabic nature of the
Japanese language is the marked possibility of punning
which is brought into much prominence by the tendency of
literary style to suggestiveness through supra-positioning
of disparate images. Several of the most effective and
widely used literary devices are founded in this phenome-
non of language.

    The restricted number of possible sounds had inevitably
meant that there are many homonyms in the language, and

countless words contain within themselves other words
or parts of words of quite unrelated meaning, for
example the word *shiranami*, meaning 'white waves', or
the wake behind a boat, might suggest to a Japanese
the word *shiranu*, meaning 'unknown', or *namida*, meaning
'tears'. Thus we have blended into one another three
ideas: 'unknown', 'white waves', 'tears'. One can
easily see how from a combination of such images a poem
could grow - a boat sails for an unknown destination
over the white waves, a lady watches the wake of her
lover's boat in tears.[14]

Such a variety of homonyms and multiplicity of word association gave rise to one of the most distinctive rhetorical
devices of Nō, the *kake-kotoba* (pivot word). The device is
more common to Nō than to other forms of classical poetry
and consists of two phrases, or images, hinged together on
the pivot of a single pun. The separate phrases provide
different lexical fields, and the pivot word is rightly
construed on different levels in each. The intention of
the technique is to shift the sense of the image abruptly
and to superimpose upon it a new and different image. The
first phrase often has no logical ending; the second, no
beginning, and the effect is one of surrealistic dissolution
and transformation of thought pattern. *Kake-kotoba* is characteristic of the tendency in Japanese language to comparison and interplay of word associations, and it is particularly suited to Nō in its potential for transformation and
ability to manipulate levels, and even the direction, of
thought movement. However difficult such word play may be
to translate, it is not always impossible, and the device
is so fundamental to the lyric communication that each instance should be pointed out and explained in notes when an
equivalent cannot be found in a foreign language. Ezra Pound
succeeded in carrying over the figure into English on at least
one occasion; in *Nishikigi* the chorus takes over the narratic
of the *shite* who is disguised as a local person and speaks of
the ill-fated lovers whose graves are nearby:

These bodies, having no weft,
Even now are not come together.
Truly a shameful story,
A tale to bring shame on the gods.

> Names of love,
> Now for a little *spell*,
> For a faint charm only,
> For a charm as slight as the binding together
> Of pine-flakes in Iwashiro,
> And for saying a wish over them about sunset,
> We return, and return to our lodging.
> The evening sun leaves a shadow.[15]

The shifting, turning thought patterns of the protagonist and the floating, free associations of his reverie
are further enriched and reinforced by complex currents of
images, *engo* (related words) which run through long passages and tend to unify them. *Engo* are particularly notable
in the reflective meditations of the *shite* and serve to
order the other figures of the passage, often raising them
collectively to the level of symbol. *Kigo* (season words)
generally figure in such image patterns and lend a further
set of conventionalized overtones derived from the cycle
of nature. Reference to cherry blossoms, cicadas, harvest
moons, or cold winter rain hardly require commentary, but
other kinds of seasonal activity may not carry overtones
of meaning for the non-Japanese reader. In *Kinuta* (The
Fulling Board) for example, the homely sound of cloth being
beaten smooth is closely identified with the chill stillness
of autumn evenings and comes to represent the emotional
plight of the protagonist whose husband has been absent for
several years. At the distant sound of fulling, the Lady
is reminded of an old Chinese tale in which a faithful wife
communicated mystically with her husband who was held cap-
tive by barbarians thousands of miles away. Although beneath her station, a board is brought for her, and she pounds
out her obsessive love and loneliness; the insistent beat
of the fulling block comes to represent both her longing
and her resentment, while the images of her interior monologue - wind-tossed pines, amorous cries of stags from distant mountains, the magnified sound of a water-clock
(contained in lines from a Chinese poem), a fable of lovers
condemned to meet but once a year - mount to a lyric
crescendo and subside into the single all-embracing image
from which they sprang.

> On evenings such as this
> Sounds of beating cloth,

Soughings of the night wind,
Women's sobs and insects' chirpings,
All mix and mingle.
Dew-drops and tears fall and fall,
Drip-drop! Drip-drop!
No longer can we tell
Sounds of the beating of the cloth.[16]

By association and repetition, the profusion of images
and rhetorical figures focuses the attention of the audience
on the intensity of emotion experienced, and the densest pat
terns of evocative imagery occur during the *kuse* section, th
subjective and lyrical climax of the piece. With so great a
emphasis on imagistic construction, even the rough translations of Nō texts in the notebooks of Ernest Fenollosa must
have seemed to Ezra Pound an absolute confirmation of his ow
ideas and poetic practice. Both Pound and Yeats recognized
the unifying function of a central image as a principal mean
of indicating and intensifying human feelings through the cu
ulative effect of extended associations. In his early plays
Yeats had experimented with different sorts of images in relation to naturalistic plays, but he never managed to integrate literary figures with theatrical images of action and
interaction. The dance of the Fairy Child in *The Land of
Heart's Desire*, the Angel and Butterfly of *The Hour-Glass*,
Cuchulain fighting the sea as well as the opposition of Blin
Man and Fool in *On Baile's Strand* were all successful stage
images to one extent or another, but unrelated to reinforcin
patterns of literary figures. On the other hand, the elaborate alchemical figures of *The Shadowy Waters* lacked subs-
tantiation in the stage image of Forgael and Dectora's quest
because that action held little or no meaning for the audience. Yeats was generally more successful with mythic material where very real human passion was involved, yet in
Deirdre the literary figures of jewels and hunting nets as
well as the stage images of brazier and chess board acted
as commentators on the action rather than correlatives for
the emotion or idea beyond the action. The use of stage
images as literary figures in *The Unicorn* (coach) and in
The Green Helmet (helmet and encounter with Red Man) was
not entirely satisfactory, but certainly prefigures Yeats's
later development of symbolic design in the dance plays.
Unity of image as Yeats came to understand it from

the Fenollosa translations, was not a question of integrating rhetorical or literary texture and visible stage images,
but rather a concentration and intensification of all expressive elements through repetition and variation which
makes of the central stage image a correlative or symbol
for the ideal or heroic norm that is the play's theme.
Yeats had used a one-act structure almost exclusively in
his earlier work, but Nō gave him a model for merging the
identity and experience of the protagonist with that of the
audience through the mediation of a narrator and receding
levels of subjective reality. As for the other aspects of
Nō form, there are none that Yeats had not already discovered and experimented with to one extent or another; for
example, lyric unity, varied verse forms, choral interven-
tions, songs, chanting, density of language devices, localized action, and mythic subject-matter. In the plays for
dancers these techniques are again utilized, but now recreated and uniformly subordinated to an effective withdrawal from the real world of the audience and to the
establishment of a subjective reality in which the imaginative action of the drama is played out and resolved. The
impasse for Yeats had always been a failure of dramatic form
and theatrical presentation in rendering an imagined reality.

As Pound had commented in *'Noh' or Accomplishment*, Nō
is a complete art in which poetry is assisted by music, mime
and dance in expressing intense emotion, but neither Pound
nor Yeats had much specific understanding of the ways in
which music, mime or dance actually fleshed out a Nō performance. Indeed, Yeats had experimented with statuesque
posing and measured or stylized stage movement much earlier
than 1914, and however akin to the technique of Nō acting his
own practice was, there is no evidence of influence or assimilation from that quarter. Acting technique in Nō drama
is directed towards imitating reality without reproducing
it; the actor stands outside the role, but does not show the
audience an attitude towards it as would be the case in
caricature. The actions of a given character are imitated
through movement of the whole body rather than facial expression, but not reproduced exactly; the actor gives only
a stylized, yet extremely precise, indication of those actions. The discrepancy between the performance and the
action imitated serves to involve the spectator in the completion of the ideal action suggested and in the recognition
of its significance. The movement of the actor is both a

plastic counterpart of the dialogue and, in itself, an independent element of sense imagery, an impressionist fragment of human experience which reveals the inner life of that experience and its essential nature. The distortion or stylization of outward forms discloses inner feeling by forcing the involvement of the spectator's imagination. The process is perhaps best analysed in terms of the late-nineteenth century doctrine of *Einfühlung* (empathy):

> Anything is beautiful. . .that draws us into its being.
> Thus Souriau says 'We have only one way of imagining
> things from the inside, and that is, putting ourselves
> inside them.' Bergson declares that the spectator must
> become actor. Lotze asserts that we accomplish the feat:
> 'We project ourselves into the forms of a tree, identi-
> fying our life with that of the slender shoots that swell
> and stretch forth, feeling in our souls the delight of the
> branches that drop and poise delicately in mid-air.'[17]

Such a relationship between image and reality in art was common enough in the west after the turn of the present century, and Isadora Duncan noted in her autobiography:

> At that villa in Abbazia there was a palm-tree before our
> windows. It was the first time I had seen a palm-tree
> growing in a temperate climate. I used to notice its
> leaves trembling in the early morning breeze, and from
> them I created in my dance that light fluttering of the
> arms, hands, and fingers which has been so much abused by
> my imitators; for they forget to go to the original source
> and contemplate the movements of the palm-tree, to receive
> them inwardly before giving them outwardly.[18]

One also thinks of Brecht's theory of acting for epic theatre. Eric Bentley's comment on Helene Weigel in the Brecht-Engel production of *Mother Courage* at Berlin is especially relevant to the art of *monomane*:

> To a perceptible degree, Miss Weigel stands outside the
> role and in a sense does not even look like Mother
> Courage. She is cool, relaxed, and ironical. Yet with
> great precision of movement and intonation she imitates
> exactly what Mother Courage was like. The art and
> beauty of the performance bring home to us the awful

sadness and relevance of Mother Courage's career more
convincingly and, for me, more movingly than the Stanislavsky method would be likely to do.[19]

In the miming of Nō each movement and posture of both
body and voice is analysed and carefully worked out in relation to the characterization and aesthetic effect desired;
every movement of a performance is precisely fixed in time
and space.   Imitation is normally confined to the general
aspects of an action because the exact representation of
details will, in most cases, preclude suggestive beauty from
the presentation and may even result in actual ugliness or
coarseness.   All physical movements are stylized and suggestive, sculptured and restrained; they approach the condition of dance, introduce elegance and ritual to the action,
and intimate ideality.   The movements themselves are slow
and powerful, never so fluid as to become ordinary dancing,
and a basic posture or attitude of body is common to them
all: the feet are aligned and the knees bent, while the
trunk is carried rigidly, chest forward, chin back, and elbows held in with hands resting along the upper thigh, palms
inward.   In this position the body is perfectly balanced and
easily controlled, giving the outward appearance of serenity
and immobility while visibly containing the dynamic potential for movement.   The slightest variation of posture is
extremely effective; for example, movement with the feet
apart suggests a strong or forceful character, while a
woman is mimed with feet close together, hips and knees
tightly controlled and the trunk flexible.   The physical
balance and posture of a performer is fundamental to his
interpretation of a role as well as a measure of his artistic accomplishment.   Forward motion is accomplished by
sliding the feet along the highly polished stage in the
mitten-like and closely-fitted white socks of polished cot-
ton *(tabi)* which are still a part of the national costume.
The heels never leave the floor, and in order to preserve
balance the foot is arched up from the floor as the body-
weight is shifted for the next 'step'.   The visual impact
of this kind of movement is powerful.   Since the bent knees
take up the bobbing motion of normal walking and the mechanical motion of the legs is hidden in the voluminous
robes, the heroic figure seems to glide and sweep over the
stage, uncannily freed from resistance, deliberate and

graceful as a gull over the sea. It is as though the
physical laws of the temporal world were suspended, and
the effect of a sudden gliding run after a near-static
posturing or complete immobility can be stunning.

Acting technique in Nō is not limited to external
imitation alone, and the performer also concentrates on
internal processes. The actor must identify himself with
the reality he imitates, rather than bring that reality
within the subjective sphere of his own personality. He
suppresses his ego to prevent the intrusion of personal
elements in a performance which transfigures nature into
an artistic or ideal equivalent. Something of the same
depersonalization was also introduced into European dramatic tradition through the anti-illusionist methods of
Paul Fort (1872-1960) who founded the Théâtre d'Art (Paris
1890) in an attempt to restore lyricism and imagination to
the theatre. In order to free the stage from every vestige
of realism, even the actor was to be abstracted. Fort tried
eliminating movement and gesture altogether, others tried
masks of abstract design, and Maurice Maeterlinck, who wrote
for the Théâtre d'Art under Fort, and later under Lugné-Poë,
created characters who either symbolized aspects of an inner
life or instruments of hidden forces, and advocated playing
them with mechanical, stylized movements in imitation of
puppets. Still later in England, Edward Gordon Craig deman-
ded that the actor be banished altogether and predicted the
coming of the Über-Marionette; in Russia, Meyerhold developed the theory of Bio-Mechanics and Stanislavsky experimented with inner identification of actor and character through
both realistic and stylized outward forms. The suppression
of selfhood is certainly fundamental to the art of Nō, and
an example of such controlling inner-realization of character is the device of 'motionless action' which holds that
the moments of the actor's greatest effort in communicating
his inner identification with the role occurs during intervals of perfect immobility which punctuate the flow of movement in performance. A pose is struck and held for endless
minutes in the effort to balance mental and physical action.
The creation of quietude in movement and movement in quietude is held to be the essence of restraint and refinement.
At these moments the identification of the spectator's mind
with that of the performer through the sharing of imaginative
experience is as intense and ideal as that during dance
itself. If technique does not obtrude, the presence of the

performer will appear larger than life, as on the occasion
of Eleonora Duse's performance in *The Second Mrs. Tanqueray*
(London, 1899).

> At the end of the third act, where Mrs. Tanqueray is
> driven to the wall by her enemies and, overcome with
> ennui, resolves to commit suicide, there was a moment
> when Duse stood quite still, alone on the stage. Sud-
> denly, without any special outward movement, she seemed
> to grow and grow until her head appeared to touch the
> roof of the theatre, like the moment when Demeter app-
> eared before the house of Metaneira and disclosed her-
> self as a Goddess. In that supreme gesture Duse was no
> longer the second Mrs. Tanqueray, but some wonderful
> goddess of all ages, and her growth before the eyes of
> the audience into that divine presence was one of the
> greatest artistic achievements I have ever witnessed.[20]

Yet further confirmation of Yeats's earlier experiments
with distancing techniques is found in the use of traditional
Nō masks, costumes, stage design, and lighting. A performer is said to become the living embodiment of the character he sets himself out to represent when he assumes a mask:
his entire body and spirit take on the character of the role
as though the mask had a life-force of its own. Of course,
it is difficult to believe that the performer is wholly separated from his performance, and one assumes that each actor
gives any single mask a different life of its own. The real
importance of the mask is in suggesting ideality, the eternal or universal type rather than the individual character.
Through the use of masks and other forms of abstracted or
suggested representation, the actual is ennobled and transfigured. No attempt is made to disguise either the masculin-
ity of the actor, or the fact of the mask, and some of the
masks are obviously much smaller than the faces of the performers. In roles of beautiful young women and goddesses,
for example, it is normal to have bearded jowls and throats
made massive by the strain of vocal technique in full view
beneath the stylized carving. Only the principal actor of
a play *(shite)*, his followers or companions *(tsure)*, and
sometimes a secondary character *(tomo)* required by the plot
wear masks; the dramatic foil or interlucutor *(waki)* and his
followers or companions *(tsure)* are never masked. A number
of *shite* roles are normally performed without masks,

particularly those of men in their prime, but even in these
cases there is no effort to make use of facial expression
in acting. The face is fixed in as natural an expression
as possible, unaffected and frank, but with the intensity
and blank potential of a mask. The masks themselves are
neutral in expression and highly stylized rather than realistic, those of beautiful women are almost impassive and,
like the others, have great potential for expressiveness.
The carriage of the actor's head is largely responsible for
the changing expression of a mask during performance; it is
a matter of the subtle play of light and shadow across the
smooth planes of lacquered wood. The inherent life-force
of a mask is a function of its conception and sculptural
design; potential is realized through manipulation by the
performer and the imagination of the spectator. The actor
establishes the mask's expression by the carriage of his
body and also by the intensity of inner concentration and
projection of passion, while the spectator responds to the
unspecified potential of the mask and allows his imagination to be led by sympathetic participation in the experience of the character. However the feat is accomplished,
it remains that masks do seem to come alive during performance and suggest a thrilling transcendence of temporal limitations.

Nō costumes are not accurate period pieces, but are
theatrical in their eclecticism and synthesis of styles.
In colour, texture and design they range from the sober to
the sumptuous; in shape and outline they are voluminous,
lending the characters heroic size and grandeur, but they
are well balanced and calculated to give a sculptural effect to the body. There is little attempt at realism in
costuming; dress is chosen according to the particular kind
of beauty the play is to create. Zeami held that no characterization could be successful if the costume were ugly,
and that this was especially true in the case of female
figures whose fundamental feature is costuming.[21]

> The mask and costume used by an actor in a particular
> role reveal almost as much about his interpretation of
> the part as his singing and dancing. The mask and wig
> give him the face of his choice, the voluminous robes,
> all but blotting out the outlines of his own figure,
> give him the shape prescribed by aesthetic ideals, and
> the most glorious colours ever used to adorn the human
> form surround him in beauty.[22]

The figure of the protagonist is calculated to dominate the projecting, platform stage at the back of which the musicians are seated on the floor with the chorus similarly disposed along the right-hand side. At the left a long, narrow projection leads to the off-stage area which is curtained from view, and provides the only means of entrance and exit for performers. The gallery is called a bridge *(hashigakari)* because it joins the real world of the off-stage area with the symbolic or ideal world of the stage proper, and serves as an important playing area itself. Both gallery and stage are beautifully finished in polished *hinoki*, a resonant, burnished cypress, as are the rear walls and the ornamental roofs which have been retained from an earlier outdoor design. There is no decoration to mar the architectural purity of the scene, except for a stylized representation of an ancient pine tree, associated with Shinto ritual, painted on the rear wall of the stage, and a few branches of bamboo painted on the narrow wall to the right of it. House lights burn normally throughout the performance and lend yet another accent to the unreality of the presentation. In modern times both gallery and stage are flooded by even brighter light from beneath the ornamental roofs, refocusing attention on the richly costumed and masked protagonist whose figure provides a perfect foil to the characteristic restraint of movement and to the austerity of both scene and stage properties.

There is no use of scenery as such, and the locale of action is imaginatively evoked through the poetry of the text as it is in Elizabethan drama. Some stage properties, however, may be required to stimulate the imagination of the audience or to emphasize some important physical aspect of the scene throughout its progress; such items as boats, coaches, tombs, wells and trees are actually represented on the stage. The properties are generally abstracted representations of real objects rather than symbols, although symbols may be used, as in *Aoi no ue*, for example, where a spread *kimono* indicates the sick-bed of Prince Genji's wife. All properties, however, operate on the principle that they must be elegant in themselves and simplified to the point of suggesting the object without introducing the vulgarity of realism or attracting unwanted attention to themselves. Most of them are light frames of wood or bamboo, bound with strips of cloth and allowed on stage only for the duration of their actual use. They are carried on and off in full

sight of the audience because only what is absolutely necessary is shown, and only for long enough to make a necessary
point.

Costume accessories, which may also be regarded as
stage properties, follow the same rule of economy. Warriors
generally carry swords or halberds, and demented or frenzied
characters often have branches of leaves or flowers to
accentuate by contrast their state of mind. A folding fan,
however, is the most common accessory, but all are particularly useful in extending or emphasizing movement and en-
hancing the sculptural posturing of the performer. As a
stage property, a fan may be a substitute for another object: a sword, pen, or winecup, handled so as to suggest
a flight of birds or *kimono* sleeves billowed by a breeze.
There are also conventions requiring a fan in association
with patterns of bodily movement which indicate various
ideas such as sleep, invitation, or affection, a waterfall
or wind blowing down a hillside, and still others featuring
fans which have no inherent meaning whatever, apart from
their own grace and expressiveness. In the same way the
flowing sleeves of a costume can also be an accessory to
the action: they may be spread and floated on the air to
give the effect of a ship under sail or of a bird in flight;
they may be used to create a perfectly abstract and meaning-
less beauty; or, thrown up on one arm, suddenly, at the end
of a climactic dance sequence and allowed to billow down
over the head of the performer, they may express an ecstasy
of feeling, sublimity or apotheosis.

It is difficult to estimate the specific effect on
Yeats of production method as outlined in the Fenollosa
manuscripts. As seen above in the text of *Ikuta Atsumori*,
Fenollosa's marginal notes render a rather complete stage
picture and every aspect of Nō production is certainly in
harmony with Yeats's published views and his dramatic practice before 1913. The removal of performance from stage
proper to drawing room or studio floor is an original conception, but may well have been suggested by the knowledge
that men of position and culture in Japan had Nō stages in
their own houses. The effect of Yeats's adaptation in the
plays for dancers is to give prominence to the objective
presentation of significant images over and above the subjective narration inherent in the literary form. At any
rate, Yeats had access to more explicit detail on the
staging of Nō plays than has been generally suspected, and

the importance of such knowledge with reference to mime and
dance cannot be overestimated. The most problematic experiment in Yeats's development as a dramatist was the substitution of dance for the normal dramatic climax and resolution
of a conflict-oriented plot.

In Nō the idea of conflict is subordinated to the
quality and intensity of feeling that is aroused, and the
subjective narration of the protagonist is designed to
suggest a considered reaction to the experience, while the
dances embody an idealized image of both the experience
itself and the reaction. When poetry alone ceases to be
effective as an expression of intense emotion, the protagonist dances, projecting feeling beyond logic and conscious
communication. Dances *(mai)* occur at the climactic moments
of a presentation, reflecting the particular idea or quality
of the entire piece, even where dances are obvious interpo-
lations in the plot. In *Hagoromo*, for example, the moon-
maiden offers to entertain the fisherman with a dance as
a gesture of thanks for the return of the stolen robe.
Mai epitomises the character of the text by transmuting an
expressive vocabulary of physical movement into a symbolic
utterance which evokes the theme of the play better than a
purely literal presentation, and avoids vulgar realism. The
dances are carried out with great solemnity and economy of
movement; the more spiritual the presentation, the fewer
and simpler the movements. The smallest gesture is enough
to call up a force of feeling already present in the context with powerful effect. The rhythms of bodily movement
in dancing, as in mime, derive from the quick or slow,
forceful or gentle placing of the feet in patterns of three,
five, or seven steps along a line. The eloquent gestures
and impressive posturing of the performer are harmonious
in effect and create sculptural images which slowly shift
and fuse into one another. The stylized patterns of movement are a form of dignified pantomime in which the occasional stamping of the feet *(ashibyoshi)* in time with the
rhythm of accompanying drums and the standard meter of
Japanese verse, not only adds to the cumulative musical
effect, but also stresses an extreme of emotional experience.

A major distinction is made in the classification of
dances between true forms which are executed in time to
instrumental music, and dance-like forms which are performed

in time to the chanting of a lyric poem. It is possible
to integrate the two in a single dance, but generally true
mai is purely image creating and concentrates on the beauty
of movement itself, while *mai*-like forms are more realis-
tically representational and involve a rhythmic miming of
the narration. Of true *mai* there are at least ten distinguishable forms which range in character from grave and
powerful presentations suitable for gods and warriors
through graceful and delicate forms performed by female
deities and the spirits of beautiful women to brief and
animated dances used as finale or concluding pieces. *Mai*-
like forms are used to evoke various scenes of warriors in
combat, as well as violent agitation or emotion arising
from the dramatic situation, and the exorcising of evil
spirits. In addition there are a number of special forms
associated with particular plays; some of them are true
mai and others *mai*-like. Apart from these special cases,
however, the generalized forms accommodate the expression
of ideas or emotions necessary to any given Nō and lend
form and character to the performance. (For specific details see Appendix).

Individual dances are made up of both abstract or non-
meaningful patterns, conventionalized figures, associated
with meaning, and broadly realistic movement. There are a
number of set figures or patterns of movement *(kata)* which
make up the vocabulary of Nō dancing, and these are selected and combined to assist in expressing the character and
mood of a given dance. The set figures range from patterns
that are merely graceful and beautiful in themselves to
those conventionally associated with a specific emotion or
an arbitrary image such as looking at the moon, mist drifting, or flower petals falling. Yet another category of
set figures includes stylized indications of mimetic action
such as sitting down, sleeping and weeping. A dance sequence, however, is a great deal more than an extension of
mime where a step backward, for example, may express dis-
couragement, a step forward affirmation or decision. The
more abstract forms of true *mai* utilize set figures that
concentrate on images and ideas, and they objectify states
of being already established by the text, rather than real
action. In plays where the dramatic situation is either
slight or uncomplicated, the dance may carry a considerable
weight of significance, and in the case of another category
of plays, even constitutes a *raison d'être*. The dance of

the wine-spirits in both *Shōjō* and *Sogi* is just such a
spectacular performance, and in one of the several existing versions seven such spirits dance out their graceful
and delicate steps from wave-crest to wave-crest as they
come joyfully from the water. The music and rhythm of
this dance is sprightly and gay, and the poetry suggests
images of wine cups garnished with white chrysanthemum
petals and comparisons of the wind in river reeds to the
sound of flutes, the waves upon the shore to little drums.

It is only in the more realistic *mai*-like forms that
mime is extended into dance. In *Fugito*, for example, the
protagonist is seen recreating the movements of his drowned
body being dashed against rocks, a perpetual punishment
and expiation for his obsession with revenge during life.
There is a whole category of plays in which the main character performs the dance-like mime of armed combat as a
recreation of its soul's torment in the *Asura* world, where
warriors who have died in battle are condemned to eternal
warfare against a supernatural enemy. There are in fact
two forms of violent dancing which are used in the recounting of real exploits on the battlefields of this world,
as shown in *Ikuta Atsumori* or *Tamura*. The mimetic aspect
of Nō dancing may approach a level of considerable sophis-
tication, however, as in *Tadanori*, where the *shite* dances
out a double mime, at times recreating the exploits of the
great warrior-poet of the Heike, Tadanori, and at others
indicating the emotional state of the enemy warrior who,
on reading the poem attached to his quiver, discovers the
identity of Tadanori's corpse on the battlefield. The
indication through dance of exterior action and interior
states of being are equally possible in Nō, and Yeats was
fully aware of the range of possibilities through the production notes of Ernest Fenollosa. His later practice in
the plays for dancers shows just how well he understood
the use of choreography in lyric construction and the importance of the Japanese texts he had encountered.

In addition to the Fenollosa translations, it has
always been assumed that Yeats was directly influenced by
the young Japanese dancer, Itō Michio (1893-1961) who created choreography for, and performed in, *At the Hawk's Well*.
Itō's influence on Yeats was considerable in at least one
sense; without a trained dancer, Yeats's initial experiment
with dance drama would have remained unrealized, and, being
Japanese, Itō lent an aura of authenticity to the first of

the plays inspired by Nō drama. Although based upon traditional Japanese forms, Itō's dance vocabulary was certainly
muted and modified by modern European idiom. He had trained
at the Mizuki Dancing School, Tokyo, and in 1911 travelled
to Paris where he studied for three years at the Dalcroze
School of Dancing which emphasized self-expression and the
spontaneous liberation of creative imagination through the
free rhythmic movement of the body. Emile Jacques-Dalcroze
(1865-1950) had developed the system of music education
known as Eurhythmics, which continued the work begun by
Francois Delsarte (1811-71) towards the evolution of modern
dance idiom. Itō Michio learned to dance in the freely
creative modern manner to which he adapted forms derived
from Oriental motifs and developed a personal style that
was both harmonious and rhythmical. From the very beginning he was interested in the expressive nature of dance
movement, but his views on art and dance are incompatible
with those of Nō tradition.[23] Indeed, it is clear that
Itō knew little or nothing about Nō in any case: his considered recollection of experiences in London are recorded
in an autobiography, *Utsukushi naru Kyoshitsu* (A Room for
those Who Wish to Become Beautiful) (Tokyo 1956):

> Advertised as a Japanese dancer, I had to produce a
> Japanesque atmosphere. All the dances I danced were
> original. A shōjō (the tippling elf) dance and a fox
> dance were among them. Sometimes I danced in *eboshi*
> (a high black headgear worn by nobles in court dress
> which is fastened with a purple cord around their chin)
> and *nagabakama* (a trailing, divided skirt for men's
> formal wear in court). After the performance at the
> Coliseum Theatre . . . I had a rest for about a fort-
> night, when Ezra Pound, an American poet and friend of
> mine, came to see me, and asked me to help him with
> his work. What he was engaged in was the work of fin-
> ishing the manuscripts of Professor Fenollosa. Professor
> Fenollosa had cherished a plan to publish a book on the
> Japanese Noh after he had studied Noh for seven years
> in Japan under Minoru Umewaka (one of the leading Noh
> actors). Unfortunately, however, he died before he
> could realize his plan, and Pound undertook to carry on
> his unfinished work.

'Just a moment,' I interrupted him. 'In my childhood,
I often went to see Noh plays with my uncle, who was
extremely fond of them. And my opinion is that nothing
is more dull and tedious than Noh. I could never be
your assistant'. 'You know better about Noh than I,'
answered Pound, 'I want your help badly.'

Helping with the work was a surprising experience to
me. Fenollosa's translation of the word 'Noh' was
'accomplishment'. I was told that the word 'Noh' was
derived from the Japanese 'tannō', which means skill
or mastery. In addition to that, an analogy between
Greek tragedy and the Japanese Noh was pointed out to
me. The Japanese Noh makes skilful use of masks,
choruses, and percussion instruments. In this point
it resembles the Greek tragedy, but it is by no means
an imitation of it. This was a unique view and no
Japanese had offered one like it before. Thus, I was
taught to see Noh from an entirely new point of view
by Professor Fenollosa's treatise written in English.[24]

The choreography that Itō created for *At the Hawk's Well* was
certainly not Japanesque. I happened to be in Tokyo in
December 1962 when the Itō Dance Institute mounted a performance of the Yeats play in memory of their founder, who
had died the year before. Itō's pupil and successor recreated the role of the Well's Guardian as it was first
performed in 1916. The dramatic effect of so realistic
and modernist an approach is wildly different from that of
a Nō performance. *At the Hawk's Well* has also been translated and adapted for the traditional Nō stage, and the
photographs reproduced by Oshima Shotarō in *W. B. Yeats
and Japan* amply demonstrate the disparate tempers of the
two production methods.[25] Besides supplying cultural background, identifying proper names, and reading occasional
ideographs, Itō could offer little real help to either
Pound or Yeats in their study of Nō. However, Pound did
have at least one other informant: 'Since Tami Koumé was
killed in that earthquake I have had no one to explain the
obscure passages or fill up the enormous gaps of my ignor-
ance.'[26] It was Itō Michio who had introduced this com-
patriot to Pound and Yeats:

In those days Pound told me that he was engaged in editing a book of Noh plays which had been translated by
Fenollosa. One of my uncles Matsumura had a passion
for the Noh performance and had a Noh theatre in his own
house, at Honjo in Tokyo. I was too accustomed to attending Noh plays with this uncle. I gained the idea
that Noh was extremely dull, and in fact told Pound
that it was very uninteresting. However, together with
my friends, Nijūichi Kayano, dramatist, and Taminosuke
Kumé, painter, I visited Pound and Yeats. Both poets
still wanted to hear a Noh recitation. And so Kayano
and Kumé gave a recitation of Noh. To Yeats the feeling
between Noh and the new symbolic drama was exceedingly
strong.[27]

There can be no doubt that Yeats had some small experience
of Nō. but we cannot tell of what the 'recitation' consis-
ted. Passages from a formal text *(utai)* are normally chanted from a seated position, but individual dance sequences
(shimai) might also be performed as part of a recitation.
With characteristic extravagance Pound wrote to James Joyce
(13 October 1915): 'Michio Itow is going to give some performances of Noh dancing in proper costume, next week. That
is all that's on in the 'awt-woild'. Proper japanese daimio
dress reconstructed by Du Lac and Ricketts, etc. very
precious.'[28] There is no certainty that the two references
allude to one and the same occasion, but Yeats has given an
amazingly accurate description of Nō dancing in *Certain
Noble Plays of Japan* which must have been based on authentic
performances rather than Itō's westernized dance style.

I have lately studied certain of these dances, with
Japanese players, and notice that their ideal of beauty,
unlike that of Greece and like that of pictures from
Japan and China, make them pause at moments of muscular
tension. The interest is not in the human form but in
the rhythm to which it moves, and the triumph of their
art is to express the rhythm in its intensity. There
are few swaying movements of arms and body such as make
the beauty of our dancing. They move from the hip,
keeping constantly the upper part of their body still,
and seem to associate with every gesture or pose some
definite thought. They cross the stage with a sliding
movement, and one gets the impression not of undulation
but of continuous straight lines.[29]

Perhaps more than any other factor, the expressive
rhythm to which both characters and language move constitutes the vital link between Yeats's preoccupation with
lyric drama and the tradition of Nō:

Take anything you will - theatre or speech or a man's
body - and develop its emotional expressiveness, and
you at once increase its powers of suggestion and
take away from its power of mimicry or of stating facts.
The body begins to take poses or even move in a dance ...
Speech becomes rhythmical, full of suggestion, and as
this change takes place we begin to possess, instead
of the real world of the mimics, solitudes and wilder-
nesses peopled by divinities and daimons, vast senti-
ments, the desires of the heart cast forth into forms,
mythological beings, a frenzied parturition.[30]

In addition to a unity of image in which poetry is
assisted by music, mime and dance, Nō reaches out towards
ideality in the tradition of symbolist method or that of
E. M. Forster's 'Prophecy', as outlined in *Aspects of the
Novel*, and the practice of D. H. Lawrence in *The Rainbow*.
Nō is designed to open the ear and the eye of the mind by
the concentration and intensification of images and rhythms.

The musical element of Nō appeals to the ear and the
posturing appeals to the eye of the audience. Everything in Nō has its own style, based upon the meaning
of the words, for it is language by which the profound
meaning is conveyed. Song is the substance of Nō and
elegant carriage is its expression. So, for the action
to come from the song is order, and to have the song
come from the action is disorder. As in anything, an
orderly procedure is to be desired, and the opposite is
wrong. So a *shite* must try to act according to the musical phrases. This is the way to combine song and action.[31]

What we see as contradictions in life exist only because we
are bound by the concepts of space and time, but in art
those limitations are transcended; all contradictions resolve themselves and represent truth.

Among those who witness Nō plays, the connoisseurs see
with their minds, while the untutored see with their
eyes. What the mind sees is the essence; what the eyes
see is the performance. That is why beginners, seeing
only the performance, imitate it. They imitate without
knowing the principles behind the performance. There
are, however, reasons why the performance should not
be imitated. Those who understand the Nō see it with
their mind and therefore imitate its essence.[32]

Another formulation often encountered recommends:

Forget the theatre and look at the Nō.

Forget the Nō and look at the actor.

Forget the actor and look at the idea (or spirit).

Forget the idea and you will understand the Nō.[33]

Hegel and the neo-Platonists, for example, also held
that 'the Beautiful is essentially the Spiritual making
itself known sensually, presenting itself in sensuous concrete existence.'[34] In reversing the order, the form of
a Nō performance might be compared to a map, a concentration of the features of a real place, reduced in scale and
translated into signs. It is not impossible to imagine
such a map being enlarged until it eventually merges with
the actual place itself. The point, however, is that Nō
is not an overcharged symbol, but that it adequately projects beauty and harmony as manifestations of the senses,
and produces a finite image which becomes identified with
an ideal or archetypal experience. The very nature and
practice of Nō is Impressionistic in that the sensuous
materials of art constitute the sole reality, and anti-
realistic techniques not only atomize human experience in
order to demonstrate its essential quality, but also direct
one's attention away from the meaninglessness of temporal
reality and towards some larger significance. Ultimately,
Nō is an exaltation of the spirit, but it is also a substantial evocation of ecstasy and in practice approaches
Symbolism: image and idea coincide. The distinction between form and matter is obliterated: 'Meaning reaches us
through ways not distinctly traceable by the understanding',
as Walter Pater maintained of those perfected art forms

which approached the condition of music.[35] T. S. Eliot
makes a more perceptive assertion in 'Burnt Norton':

> Words move, music moves
> Only in time; but that which is only living
> Can only die. Words, after speech, reach
> Into the silence. Only by the form, the pattern
> Can words or music reach
> The stillness, as a Chinese jar still
> Moves perpetually in its stillness.[36]

However imperfectly or incompletely understood, the
attraction of Nō for Yeats must have been very strong indeed. His own preoccupations with an heroic or spiritual
ideal, a mystical/occult world-view, and the possibility
of symbolic expression find their exact counterparts in
the Japanese form. More importantly, however, Nō offered
an end to his search for an adequate dramatic form and an
objective production method.

4.

W.B.Yeats: Plays for Dancers

Poetic form: an action which convinces not so
much by its resemblance to our life outside the
theatre as by the unity and expressiveness of
its design.[1]

Between 1915 and 1921 Yeats wrote four plays for
dancers and experimented with comedy after the fashion of
Japanese Kyōgen. Each of the dance dramas was modelled
fairly closely on a Japanese original, and a detailed comparison of Yeats's plays with their prototypes reveals a
great deal about the degree of his assimilation from the
Nō, his reliance on other sources, and his development in
controlling subject matter and dramatic form. Many of the
techniques and devices which he had worked out in his earlier experiments are also carried over into the plays for
dancers, but their relative similarity to the methods of
Nō should not confuse us as to their independent origin.
Yeats's dance plays are often said to be imitations, or
even recreations, of classical Japanese drama, and their
peculiarities have often been ascribed to a supposed deri-
vation from Nō when, in fact, their preciousness is more
a product of outdated subject matter, esoteric world-view,
and experimental production method. Yeats's apprehension
of the Nō through Ezra Pound and the Fenollosa manuscripts
did act as a catalyst in his development towards an expressive form of modern drama, yet efforts to understand the
dance plays with reference to Nō drama alone will provide
but few insights into their unique nature and achievement.

Influences from the Nō are easily traced in Yeats's plays,
but influences from other sources are of equal importance
in assessing the ultimate value and relative success of
the plays for dancers.

The real failure of the dance dramas lies in the fact
that their subject matter had even less relevance to the
lives and sensibilities of his audience than the earlier
plays. As World War I put an end to the lingering vestiges
of Victorian Romanticism, Yeats went on recreating ideal
worlds of heroes from a legendary past whose actions sym-
bolised an arcane scheme of universal order. Whether or
not Yeats's ideas did have some relevance to the circumstances of the time, it remains that even then the dance
plays must have seemed baffling anachronisms. 'Conflict
must have meaning in the audience's experience before it
can be made articulate by the dramatist and receive from
the audience the response which the dramatist's art requires.'[2] Yeats experimented with some of the most advanced
theatre techniques and aesthetic structures of his day, but
the worlds he created, however beautiful and effective, had
little apparent relationship with either modern needs or
outlook. The heroic mode alone need not have spelled disaster for the dance plays, but the supernatural and psychic
preoccupations which again and again came to the fore are
essentially esoteric and private, certainly antithetical to
the spirit of the time and unsuitable in the public theatre.
Romantic metaphysics and an occult world-view are reasonably
acceptable in lyric poetry, but rarely achieve validity on
the stage. Sean O'Casey was quick to recognize an essential
insubstantiality in Yeats's dance drama and its lack of relationship to life, both in subject matter and in production
method. In his amusing account of a drawing-room production
of *At the Hawk's Well* given at Yeats's house in Merrion
Square, he wrote: 'A play poetical to be worthy of the
theatre must be able to withstand the terror of Ta Ra Ra
Boom Dee Ay, as a blue sky, or an apple tree in bloom,
withstands any ugliness around or beneath them.'[3] The
trouble with Yeats's dance plays was that in addition to
an almost obsolete heroic apparatus and an altogether outdated occultism, his production method was highly stylized
and aggressively anti-illusionist. However well-suited to
his subject matter and theatrical aims, the non-realistic
and expressive staging of the dance dramas was not yet acceptable to the theatre-going public and proved to be still

another stumbling block to the reception of his work. When
used in conjunction with acknowledgeable images of man's
condition in the contemporary world, the very same dramatic
techniques have come to be the triumph of Beckett, Dürrenmat
Ionesco and Pinter. It is not so much that Yeats was pre-
mature in his production method, but that in using such experimental techniques to express outmoded material, his worl
appeared to be exotic and incomprehensible. The knowledge
that he had written the plays for dancers under the influence of the Japanese Nō tended to confuse the issue still
further in that it has been convenient to explain away a
number of serious critical questions by asserting that such
elements were borrowed directly from the Nō, rather than to
attempt a complete analysis and evaluation of the plays and
of the various influences upon them. There is no doubt that
Yeats was indeed influenced by the Japanese Nō. The extent
of that influence, however, can only be measured through a
detailed comparison of each dance play with its Japanese
model.

At the Hawk's Well has generally been considered an
original creation, but the text of a Fenollosa translation
that Ezra Pound omitted from *'Noh' or Accomplishment* bears
a striking resemblance to the first of Yeats's dance plays.
The *kami Nō, Yōrō* (The Sustenance of Age) was written by
Motokiyō Zeami (1363-1443), master performer and theoretician, who is believed to have perfected the essential form
of Nō drama as we know it today. The rough Fenollosa translation, as it stands, compares well with the far more scholarly version of Gaston Renondeau and the more recent English
translation by Shimazaki Chifumi.[4] The text was undoubtedly
rejected by Pound because of its inherent limitations. The
god play has much less appeal for a conventional western audience than any other type of Nō, and not a single example
was included in the Fenollosa-Pound edition. *Kami Nō* presents no human situation to be entered into sympathetically,
other than the awe and excitement of the miraculous encounter itself - the projection of momentary harmony between, or
intersection of the natural and supernatural world as an
archetype of universal order. The god play depends more com
pletely than any other type on choreography and musical composition as paradigms of the emotion to be evoked, and much
less sympathy is aroused than in the presentation of tragic
death, thwarted love, or pathetic derangement.

Yōrō

(name of the waterfall in Mino)

by Motokiyō

Cast:
    1st Shite   a father
        Tsure   his son
        Waki   an imperial messenger
    2nd Shite   God of Mt. Temple

Scene: in Mino

Waki *(sings)*	Winds are calm - All the leaves and branches are quiet. (reign is prosperous)
(Kotoba)	I am a subject to the Emperor Yuriaku. Someone told him that a wonderful fountain is in this province of Motosu in Mino. So I received his order to see it quickly. So I am now making haste to Motosu.
(Michiyuki)	It is peaceful - the land is wealthy, and the people are rich. There are roads everywhere. The gates of the passes are opened. Passing the way of Mino which I heard far in the country I came to the fall of Yōrō.
Shite & Tsure	How the water is clear! Under the shades of the pines: in the mountain of Mino! Which pines have passed so many years!
Tsure	The hill of age who is familiar to me -
Together	How quiet are our hearts to pass!
Shite	My old friends were already awakened from their dream of the world (or dead), and I passed the flower time of less and more.

S. & Tsure   My heart longs for the moon of a thatched
                  house; and my body floats like the frost
                  on a wooden bridge. Though the clouds
                  of white head gather now, the water of
                  the fall which consoles age will make
                  clear my heart. (Yōrō = yō = feeding and
                  consoling - rō = age).

(Sing)   Is this the custom in the deep valley of
                  far-off mountains? However I dip the
                  water, it is not extinguished. In the
                  house of Chosei (long living) is the gate
                  which will not become old (this refers to
                  the gates of some Chinese temple Choseiden,
                  and Furōmon).
                  But here, living in this mountain, under
                  the shade of a pine tree, and using the
                  water of the fountain as medicine, and
                  prolonging our age, how hopeful are we,
                  how happy our prospects!

Waki   I have something to ask of the old man
                  there.

Shite   You mean me? What's the matter?

Waki   Are you the father and the son of whom
                  I heard so much?

Shite   Yes, We are a father and a son.

Waki   I am the imperial messenger.

Shite   O how thankful! To receive the words of
                  the Emperor whom I see far up in the sky,
                  with this wretched body, how thankful it
                  is! We are father and son.

Waki   Someone told the Emperor that a wonderful
                  fountain pours from Motosu. He ordered
                  me to go quickly and see it. So tell me
                  in detail why it is called Yōrō.

Shite	Yes. This is my son. In the morning in the evening, he goes to the mountain, and takes fuel, and feeds me. Once being weary of mt. road, he dipped this water in his hand and drank it, but strangely his heart was quite refreshed, and he recovered.
Tsure	Thinking the medicine water of the house of Sennin will be such, I went home dipping the water and carrying it, and gave to the father and mother.
Shite	We drank it, and unconsciously we forgot our age.
Tsure	From that it was not difficult to get up so early in the morning.
Together	It was not so solitary even when we were awakened from dreams in the night. Some vigour and courage came to us: and as this true clear water consoles our age unceasingly, it is called the Fall of Yōrō.
Waki	Indeed! How grateful! I think there is some special place in this river where the water of medicine pours out.
Shite	Look. It is the fountain of water from the rock. A little on this side from the basin below.
Waki	Then is this the fountain. So saying he approached and looked at it. He found it was very clear.
Shite	The small pebbles becoming rocks having coverings of moss.
Waki	The happy example which continues to a thousand generations -

Shite	I see here in this medicine of waters.
Waki	Truly this!
Shite	Consoles the age.
Chorus	If it consoles (invigorates) age, then it will be the best medicine to the people of ripe age. And their lives will not end, forever. O how happy is this fountain! Indeed, as this of the reign which is clear on the upper Emperor part of the gem (source) water, so even we who are in the very end (mouth) of the stream (people) can live happily.
(Kuru)	Indeed as the island of Yomogi (Horai) is very far in this age, though we search it, how can we find such example? The medicine of Life, water upon water, it is quite inexhaustible.
Shite	Though the course of water which flows is not extinguished, but it is not the water of the old! (Famous quotation from Kamo no Chomei's Hōjōki).
Chorus	The bubbles which float on this stream they disappear and they come again. O how clear is this colour.
Shite	Specially this is of the moment of summer. Unparalleled.
Chorus	And who found this happy sign, to make water as medicine? We will dip the water! We will dip the water! The bamboo leaves of a jar will glow in shade (ehikuyo-sake). The Tekika (flowers of ashi = reed) beside the hedge dips the autumn of the forest leaves. (obscure in origin) The pleasure of 7 sages of Shin as the play of Ryuhakurin (he was one of the 7 sages, who made a famous essay on

> plays of sake) all are in this water,
> O dip! O dip! This medicine. I will
> offer to you the cup floating on the
> winding water (kiokusin = narrow stream
> (palace garden), on the feast called
> Kiokusin en) will strike against a rock
> and will be very slow (to drink)! So
> I will dip it with my hands, and through
> the whole night I will dip the moon.

Chorus *(Rongi)*	Who was invigorated? By the water and the deep mountain.
Shite.	We hear that it was by virtue of water that Hoso by the vigour of dew of the chrysanthemum lived for *700* years.
Chorus	Indeed, while I dipped the water of kiku in that very short space, (hearing it was a medicine) (kiku = hear Tsuyu no ma = little space) (double play of double meaning).
Shite	We passed a thousand years.
Chorus	Heaven and Earth opened, and even the grass and plants -
Shite	Blossomed and bore fruit.
Chorus	Season after season.
Shite	Only by the blessing of rain and dew.
Chorus	By nursing the old man which is like the dew and rain, the parents of flowers were invigorated. And I became familiar to this water. My sleeves were torn, and the shadow of my hands dipping the water is clearly seen in this mountain well. As to think this a medicine, so my figure of old age seems to me as young water. O how happy!

Waki	O how wonderful, this water! I will go back to my lord quickly and tell him.
Shite	(That young water is the water of the New Year). The old man felt very grateful for these blessings.
Waki	The imperial messenger fell in tears. How wonderful that I met such a thing!
(Sings)	As he did not finish this saying - strange! A light gleaming from heaven, the thunder of falls became quiet, music was heard, and flowers rained. It was not thought a common thing.
Second Shite	O how grateful! As the custom of the peaceful reign, the mountains, the river, the grass, and the peasants are calm. Winds on every 5th day and rain on every 10th day. The shining sun is lovely in the sky and the fountain of medicine of that green water will not fail. O how grateful are men!
Chorus	Even I who guard this reign, where the water is inextinguishable -
Shite	I am the God of the Temple of this mountain. (Kami and Buddha are the same).
Chorus	Or you may call me Yorin (willow) Kuanon Bosatsu.
Shite	The God Kami
Chorus	The Buddha Hotoke
Shite	These are only separation of names.
Chorus	And are the voice of means to save the people.

Shite	The storm of the mt., the water of the valley -
Chorus	The sound goes in harmony. The sound of music makes clear the heart of the falls. O the Shadow of many heavens!
Shite	The green of the pine tree seems to have passed 1000 years.
Chorus	The clear, clear well of the mt.
Shite	The water flows and flows, and the waves are calm. The lord of the peaceful reign is the ship -
Chorus	The lord is the ship, the subject is the water. The water will make the ship float. The subject looks up and reverences the lord. Such a reign will be eternal. Led by the lord of gem water, the subject on the lower part becomes clear too. O a good reign! O a good reign! I will repeat this, as the waves on the full basin come back.

The recurring association of Emperor and Sun God in
Yōrō may well have suggested the semi-divine origin of
Cuchulain, while the very plot outline of the Japanese
play could not help but attract Yeats through the perenn-
iality of its central myth. The miraculous waters of regeneration are an obvious point of contact between the
natural and supernatural worlds, a means through which
man transcends human limitations and renews his spirit.
The venerable pine which figures in the scene is also a
fixture of Nō performance, as Yeats well knew, being symbolically represented on the rear wall of every stage:
'But here, living in this mountain, under the shade of a
pine tree, and using the water of the fountain as medicine,
and prolonging our age, how hopeful are we, how happy our
prospects.' The Celtic counterpart of the miraculous
spring is also obvious in the myth of Connla's Well, over-

hung with the berries of nine rowan trees (hazels in some
versions), and it was associated in Yeats's mind with the
symbolism of Well and Tree (regeneration, wisdom and poetic
inspiration) which he had admired in Morris's medieval ro-
mances, *The Well at the World's End* and *The Water of the
Wondrous Isles*. On the other hand, Yeats's vision of the
human condition as found in *At the Hawk's Well* is a great
deal more bleak than in any of the presumed sources. Instead of a ritual presentation in celebration of order in
the universe and harmony between supernatural and temporal
powers, the myth is inverted. The Trees are stripped: the
Well is dry and guarded against trespass. The Young Man
overreaches himself in threatening the unity of godhead,
and his heroic aspirations are thwarted. Cuchulain storms
the mountain to gain the miraculous waters, but is seduced
from his purpose by the supernatural Guardian of the Well.
While under the enchantment of the goddess who possesses
the Guardian, the waters trickle forth and his chance to
assume supernatural power is lost. He goes off in renewed
pursuit of victory over the supernatural, but our awareness
of his fall from undivided being and of the inevitable limitation of his human nature constitute tragedy. Even the
setting appears to be an inversion of that in the Japanese
original. On his way to the pine-covered mountains of Mino,
the Imperial Messenger passes through a peaceful and pros-
perous land, while the opening of *At the Hawk's Well* insists
on a barren mountain landscape, windswept and barbarous;
a rough and desolate spot. The miraculous presence of the
supernatural in *Yōrō* is characterised by a strange light
gleaming from heaven, the suspension of the fall's thunder,
music filling the air and flowers raining down, while for
Yeats it is accompanied by war cries and the clash of arms,
swords beaten upon shields. Oddly enough, Yeats's vision
of modern man is not so very far removed from that of
T. S. Eliot and the new poetry of the period, but his insistence on heroic and supernatural images as focus or measure
or modern man's alienation and degradation obscures the
similarity.

  At the Hawk's Well follows the general outline of
Zeami's dramatic construction fairly closely, and brilliantl
overcomes the technical problem of infusing the action with
dramatic tension which in the original Nō had been provoked
by orchestrating rhythmic patterns of movement, music, and

density of rhetorical texture. *Yōrō* is unusual in that the
shite of part one is an actual mortal and not a supernatural
figure in disguise who is later revealed, but Yeats's play
differs from traditional Nō, which recreates the emotional
quality of an incident or experience through the ritualized
induction of the spectator's imagination, in that the dance
drama depends on realistic stage action and on Renaissance
conventions of character conflict. It is true that the
'eye of the mind' speech of the Musicians calls on the spectator to recreate the scene in his imagination, but the action itself is then played out objectively and directly
rather than having its quality or nature suggested by the
privileged narration of an intermediate consciousness.
Realistic action is not unknown in Nō tradition, although
it is of late and decadent development, but the idea of
sub-plot or secondary conflict, let alone plotting itself,
is certainly alien. Besides the active conflict between
godhead and man which forms the basic antithesis in Yeats's
inversion of *Yōrō*, there is also conflict between types of
men. Instead of retaining a secondary character, who acts
only as an interlocutor and remains outside the central incident while serving as a kind of catalyst for the recreation
of action, Yeats divided the dramatic function of the role
between the Old Man and the Youth, who are suggested by the
Father and Son of *Yōrō*, and set them in opposition to one
another. They share a common purpose, but differ drasti-
cally in temper: the timid Old Man has given in to the limitations of his human condition and withers as he lies in
wait for the miraculous waters, warming himself by the meagre
fire he barely manages to maintain. The impulsive Young Man,
on the other hand, seizes the moment to control his own fate
and mounts an heroic assault against godhead itself, his
avowed object being nothing less than to hood the Hawk, to
grow immortal.

> Some burn damp faggots, others may consume
> The entire combustible world in one small room
> As though dried straw.[5]

Stripped of his original function as deuteragonist
in *Yōrō*, the figure of the Imperial Messenger is recast in
Yeats's conception of the play as the agent of deity, the
Guardian of the Well. Significantly enough, Yokomichi
Mario's adaptation of Yeats's play for performance on the

Nō stage assigns the role of protagonist to the Old Man, and that of deuteragonist to the Young Man, and reduces the Well's Guardian to the status of companion or follower.[6] So radical a reinterpretation according to Japanese conventions of propriety demonstrates how far Yeats had moved from traditional character relationships in Nō; yet, in discussing the progress of the manuscript versions, Curtis Bradford has shown that Yeats did suppress an overt particularization of his characters in favour of the more depersonalized descriptions, Old Man and Young Man, which tend to universalize the action by directing attention to its allegorical possibilities.[7] In the same way, the mute and mysterious Guardian of the Well provides a persistent and vividly concrete reminder of the supernatural presence against which the lesser opposition of Old Man and Young Man plays itself out. The success of the device in heightening tensions is fully realized in that dramatic moment when the brooding figure is possessed by Deity and reveals itself as the Hawk, dancing out its seductive beauty and rapaciousness.

Dame Ninette de Valois very kindly described to me the Hawk's dance as she performed the role under Yeats's direction and in Itō's original costume for the second revival of *At the Hawk's Well* (Abbey Theatre, 22 July 1933). She danced barefoot in the modern style then known as abstract expressionism, and the choreography was created to express the emotional content of the mask through stylized forms. Both movement and maintained emotion were determined by the fact of the Hawk's hood, and the dance progressed from an evocation of brooding power, through suggestive seduction, to the violent ecstasy of a wild bird. Dame Ninette's conception of the role is certainly much closer to Itō's than to the classical choreography of Nō.

Yeats did follow the precedence of Nō tradition, however, in conceiving of the climactic dance as a ritualizing force, a stylized projection of transcendent passion which shifts interest from objective plot development to a perception of universal relationships or conditions. In *Yōrō* the revelation of deity is direct, godhead dances, but in *At the Hawk's Well* a significant displacement intervenes: the Guardian of the Well is possessed by deity and dances, and the hero who looks into the unmoistened eye of the Hawk is seduced from the object of his quest. His desire

is frustrated and his ultimate degradation confirmed, while
the already fallen man who evades confrontation with the
supernatural, perseveres in withering self-despite. The
dance itself reflects the essential ambiguity of the supernatural world, as does the image of the Hawk, and concentrates on the projection of creative power, violence and
sexuality as analogues of the universal relationship between godhead and man. The attraction and antagonism of
pure spirit is seen to be responsible for man's fall from
the ideal of undivided being, and the opposition of spirit
and nature, as that between the ideal human condition and
man's fallen state, is not so much resolved by the action
of the play as it is placed in balanced perspective. Pity
is aroused by the futility of man's exertions and the inevitability of his fall; there is both grandeur and mockery
in the Young Man's final assertion of heroic identity:
'He comes! Cuchulain, son of Sualtim, comes!'[8]

Another feature of Nō which Yeats borrowed directly
from his Japanese model was the removal of the hero from
the stage at a crucial moment in the ritual. Practical
necessity requires the break in action on a Nō stage as
the actor must change costume before returning to reveal
himself in a former condition and glory which sharply contrasts with his first appearance. Following the Well's
Guardian as if in a dream and after the waters of regeneration have gone unnoticed, Cuchulain's gratuitous exit and
almost immediate return is perhaps the least satisfactory
element of the play. It unnecessarily complicates the action and undermines the sense of heroic vigour with which
he later undertakes the pursuit of Aoife. Rather than
possess the supernatural through either the agency of the
water or intercourse with the Guardian who in turn is possessed by deity, the Young Man is merely seduced and thwarted.
The idea of the enchantment, a spell cast upon him while
the Guardian dances, may well imply a formulation of the
instinctive life, as does the cry of 'witchcraft' in the
earlier play, *On Baile's Strand*, but there is little point
in making the hero wander from the stage in vague pursuit
of the Hawk Woman only to amble back and report that she
has disappeared. The irresistible power and attraction of
the supernatural is established through her dance and should
suffice to document his rapt state. On the other hand his
withdrawal from the stage may have been intended as a means
of focusing attention on the contrasting imagery of the

Musician's speech:

> He might have lived at his ease,
> An old dog's head on his knees,
> Among his children and friends.[9]

Rather than accomplish the suspension of time, the rhythm
of the action and its emotional concentration are fragmen-
ted by the interruption, and the necessary climax is never
achieved. Cuchulain might better begin to mime his enchantment as the Guardian disappears and the chorus intervenes with its contrasting vision; while the Young Man
comes to himself, the Old Man should discover the delusion
and cry out his despair. The unifying factor in the scene
should be the dramatic figure of the Young Man. The fact
that the miraculous waters run unheeded before the Woman
of the Shidhe vanishes places the emphasis rightly on the
weakness of his human condition, while the tension between
Cuchulain's will to control the supernatural and his limitations as a man is later re-emphasized by his heroic exit
in pursuit of Aoife, the incarnation of the Ideal in the
physical world in which we are reminded again that the
quest for self-fulfilment inevitably ends in self-destruction
The intervention of the Musicians at the moment of the
Guardian's possession by the goddess is another remarkable
instance of assimilation. As in Nō, the dynamic addition
of massed voices is enormously effective in raising the
level of tension, and Yeats also uses the device to narrate
the dance and offer commentary which would not be appropriate to any of the characters. The role of the chorus as
mediator between the dramatic action and an invited audience
is altogether original, and, as in *Deirdre*, the Musicians
are associated with a supernatural order from the very beginning. *At the Hawk's Well* opens with richly textured
lyric verses delivered by the seemingly omniscient and mysterious chorus who set the scene and accomplish the induction of the audience into the imagined reality of the action.
Their song is further emphasized by the ritual unfolding
and folding of a cloth. Instead of a gradual withdrawal
from actuality, as in Nō, we are introduced immediately
into another level of reality which is underlined by the
counterpoint of their freer and ornamented lyricism with
the more austere and objective formality of the longer

pentameters used by the characters themselves. The sudden
intervention of the chorus as the Guardian of the Well
dances is particularly effective because it re-introduces
their more freely musical and heightened speech with all
its connotations of the supernatural world and closely
follows the practice of Nō where the chorus functions
mainly as an extension of characterization or an external
commentator substituted for the single actor at the climax
of his emotional experience.

The nature of the verse spoken by the main characters
is another instance of Yeats's divergence from the Japanese
original. The poetry is elevating, even distancing in its
formal aspect, but the language is actually discursive and
purposeful rather than discontinuous and imagistic. Unlike
the homogenous texture of monologue in Nō, Yeats's speeches
establish dramatic conflict and give substance to the underlying assumption that works and not faith is central to
spiritual development. Imagery and tone reflect the contrasting views of Old Man and Young Man while the basic
verse form they share is set against that of the Musicians.
The unity of lyric effect that had given the original version of *The Shadowy Waters* its rhapsodic character has now
been replaced by suitably active and dramatic verse forms.
Whereas Yeats's plays for dancers have been considered
static and undramatic, comparison with a Japanese model
tends to emphasize an essentially dynamic quality.

Perhaps one of the most important factors in establishing an effective dramatic reality for *At the Hawk's
Well* is the ultimate reliance on a known myth cycle. If
the Young Man had not been identified as Cuchulain and his
quest associated with the pursuit of Aoife, the action of
the play would have been sunk in that insubstantial and
amorphous past which pervades many of the less successful
early plays. Because of the legend, however, the figure of
Cuchulain has an objective presence and force which is independent of Yeats's artistic creation. As subject matter
for drama, his quest is immediately acceptable to an audience
whereas that of Dectora and Forgael is not. Yeats was
aware that Nō drama depends upon the authority of ancient
legend and literature, but he had already discovered for
himself the effectiveness of national myth in *Cathleen ni
Houlihan*, *On Baile's Strand*, and *Deirdre*. In any case, his
use of Celtic myth in *At the Hawk's Well* does help to objectify his themes and the encounter with Nō may have

encouraged him to consider a cycle of Cuchulain plays:
At the Hawk's Well, *The Green Helmet* and *On Baile's Strand*
do form a very closely-knit trilogy.

Another factor in establishing a much-needed dramatic
reality and expressing the more abstract conflict between
Youth and Age, as well as the Individual and Ideal, is the
question of setting. Yeats was certainly aware that Nō
relies on established associations of legendary actions
with specific locales, and that a known geographical location both serves to lend objective reality to the ritual
enactment, and to provide a characteristic setting for the
action of each play. Yeats seems to follow the example of
the Fenollosa texts in the opening of *At the Hawk's Well*
for, unlike his earlier plays, this begins with the careful
evocation of place; a barren and windswept mountain landscape. Although the exact location is not specified, the
scene is recognizably the coast of Scotland where Aoife
leads her warlike troop, and Cuchulain identifies himself
to the Old Man who has never heard his name: 'It is not
unknown. / I have an ancient house beyond the sea.'[10] For
the moment the actual world of the theatre audience and
the heroic world of the dramatic action coincide; disbelief
at any rate, is suspended and the stage production accepted
as a valid dramatic reality.

While the action and setting encourage imaginative
participation, the production method distances or distorts
that reality through selective stylization. The action and
dramatic conflict are recognizably naturalistic, but the
fictional world of the play is repeatedly distinguished from
the real world of the spectator. For example, the chorus
of Musicians who set the scene mediate between the audience
and the action, but their artificiality emphasizes the distinction between levels. Yeats's rejection of a conventional
stage in favour of a bare space before a wall in drawing-
room or studio is also an essential aspect of his anti-
illusionism. Rather than a privileged narration which dev-
elops into a mimed presentation, Yeats's dance plays are
dramatic throughout, but the action is not to be taken as
mere imitation of an actual occurrence. All association
with theatrical illusionism is avoided and the performance
achieves the ambiguous quality of a bardic recitation in
which the poet, often with the aid of music, narrates, en-
acts and comments upon his material. As early as 1906,
Yeats had written perceptively of epic narration, and one

can see that the distancing effect of drawing-room performance is not solely attributable to influence from the
Japanese Nō.[11]

Of course, Yeats also knew that aristocratic audiences,
private theatres and bare stages are a normal part of Nō
tradition, and that performances are usually held in full
daylight, even outdoors, and without the illusionist
tyranny of a darkened auditorium. One should recall, however, that as quoted above, he had earlier advocated 'an
even, shadowless light, like that of noon, and it may be
that a light reflected out of mirrors will give us what
we need.' (1904) In any case, the strangeness of the
costumed characters and ritualistic action of *At the
Hawk's Well* was to be further heightened in production by
using lighting that was neither more nor less artificial
than that normally found in a drawing-room or studio. Instead of spectators being drawn into the fictional world of
the stage, the fictional characters and action are thrust
into the real world of the audience. When produced according to Yeats's scheme, *At the Hawk's Well* is amazingly
forceful and effective. As soon as the action is removed
from the immediate world of the audience, however, by the
artificiality of stage or proscenium, theatrical lighting,
or eerie music, it becomes little more than an embarrassing
and fantastic charade.

In the same way, the secondary level of meaning which
the dramatic situation indicates is also emphasized through
stylization. Abstract stage properties such as Tree and
Well act as independent images, almost personages, and
suggest a significance beyond realistic representation.
The square of brilliant blue cloth upon the floor which
represents the miraculous yet inaccessible waters of the
Well was probably inspired by the folded *kimono* which indicates the Lady Aoi's sick-bed in *Aoi no ue*, but the visual
impact of its paradoxical promise in the face of certain
disillusionment is a completely original stroke; the presence of the supernatural waters is both asserted and denied.
Similarly, the depersonalization of characters renders them
representative types and focuses attention on the universal
rather than the particular. The figures take on symbolic
overtones while masks insist on the presence of archetypes
rather than realistic characters in action. Stylized movement and gesture further differentiates symbolic action

from the merely naturalistic, and dance translates emotion
into a concrete image where words alone fail. The dramatic
power of the Hawk's dance, for example, is eminently theatrical and effective, suggestive of unspecified rather
than definitive meaning, and provides a symbolic climax
to the structured rhythms of the literary text. Music and
heightened lyric speeches are used to frame the action and
establish the fiction of an ideal world, as well as to
accent the climactic dance, while the actual language of
the dialogue returns to a stylized simplicity and matter-
of-factness which encourages the sympathy of the audience.
Conventional exposition and extended plot development are
avoided; only the passionate climax of the myth-creating
incident is shown and the recognizably realistic action
constitutes the image of a dynamic field of forces, a
paradigm of universal order. The aesthetic and moral orders
are shown to coincide.

In arriving at the successful fusion of realistic conflict, symbolic design, and stylized presentation that
characterize the plays for dancers, the Japanese Nō provided both a catalyst and confirmation of the experiments
completed before 1910. Yeats wrote in August 1917: 'I
have written since "The Hawk's Well" a new Noh play called
"The Dreaming of the Bones" which I think is better. The
form suits me better than any other. I like its mixture
of lyric and dialogue and its brief intensity.'[12] The
form he had evolved was perfectly adapted to his perennial
themes and imagery: the limitations of the human condition,
the ideal of heroic action and the transcendence of the
spiritual world as projected through images of physical
violence, sexuality and artistic creation. The form was
so successful, in fact, that it found its way into almost
all of Yeats's later plays to one degree or other.

Before *At the Hawk's Well* had been published, Yeats
was already at work on a second dance play, a far more complex and perhaps less successful conception which again
took for its subject an incident from the life of Cuchulain.
Its action is explicitly linked to that of *On Baile's
Strand*, for the play begins just after the hero's body has
been rescued from the sea. In his encounter with Fand,
Cuchulain also recognizes her as the Spirit possessing the
Woman of the Shidhe in *At the Hawk's Well*, who had frustrated his quest for the supernatural waters. In *The Only*

Jealousy of Emer, however, the action is only indirectly
focused upon Cuchulain, and it is Emer, heroine and true
image of her husband's fulfilment, who suffers defeat at
the hands of the supernatural, while the once reckless
Cuchulain, now intimidated by experience, is left to find
solace in the illusion of youth and physical beauty.

As early as January 1900, Yeats had recorded the
following in a diary:

> A couple of nights ago I got a new poetical thought in
> half dream or wholly dream. I would write a poem I
> had long thought of about the man who left Aebhen of
> Draglen to die at Clontarf and put in it all the bitter
> feeling one has sometimes about Ireland. The life of
> fairy would be my lyric life. I thought of doing
> Cuchulain and Fand in the same way, of making some new
> vision of Maeve cause the need of waking him from his
> magical sleep.[13]

The basic action of *The Only Jealousy of Emer* was already
in his mind long before Yeats was introduced to the Japanese Nō, but the mythic intention of the Cuchulain cycle of
plays, as well as the outline of action, owes something to
its influence. The initial source of impetus, however, is
the early Irish romance, *Serglige Conculaind* (The Sick-Bed
of Cuchulain), the latter part of which is also known as
'The Jealousy of Emer'. Yeats was primarily interested in
the action of the latter half of the fragment although he
does retain important details from the earlier section
which relates the cause of Cuchulain's sickness and recounts
Leabhar-na h-Uidhri's journey to Fairyland in search of a
proffered cure. It is difficult to summarize the plot of
the original with any degree of exactitude since more than
one version exists, and details differ. Scholarly translations were available to Yeats,[14] as well as the conflated
account of Lady Gregory in *Cuchulain of Muirthemne*.

The story begins with the vain attempts of Cuchulain to
net two beautiful birds mysteriously linked together by a
golden chain. Wearied and depressed, the hero leant against
a rock and slept. He dreamt of two women, one dressed in
green and the other in crimson, who struck him in turn with
a horse switch until he felt near death. He remained insensible for nearly a year, whereupon a mysterious messenger

appeared and announced that a cure for his enchanted sleep
was at hand. A journey to the land of the Shidhe disclo-
sed that Fand, the discarded wife of Manannan, desired
Cuchulain for herself, and on reviving from his sick-bed,
he took her as his wife. Emer's jealousy was then aroused
as it had never been by a mere mortal, and she came to the
trysting place with her handmaidens in order to attack
Fand. Cuchulain protected her, but after much debate inclined towards Emer; the Sigerson summary continues:

> Now Manannan had become aware of Fand's danger and he
> sped thither from the east. 'He was in their presence,
> and no one perceived him but Fand alone.' The sight of
> him filled her with terror. She thought the spirit-
> spouse, who had abandoned her, now came to increase her
> humiliation, but he had magnanimously come to protect
> her. She sang her lost estate. 'Even if to-day he
> were nobly constant, my mind loves not jealousy: aff-
> ection is a subtle thing. It makes its way, without
> labour.' Manannan saluted her, and bade her choose
> between them. She avowed her preference for Cuchulain,
> but he had forsaken her, and so she would return with
> Manannan who had no queen. Cuchulain (to whom Manannan
> was invisible) asked Laeg what had happened, and when
> it was made clear to him, he ran distraught, without
> food or drink, among the mountains, and so remained for
> long.[15]

Druids calmed Cuchulain with magic incantations and admin-
istered draughts of forgetfulness to both him and Emer;
'Manannan shook his cloak between Fand and Cuchulain so
that they should never meet again.'[16]

The plot of the romance turns on a symmetrical scheme
of parallelism and inversion. Rejected by Manannan, Fand
intervenes in the natural order by enchanting Cuchulain
and wins him to herself. Emer's jealousy brings about a
confrontation and Cuchulain returns to his first love.
Manannan intervenes to preserve Fand from humiliation and
offers reconciliation with her while Fand rises above the
jealousy of Emer and accepts his magnanimous gesture. Natural order is reasserted; intercourse between the mortal
and immortal worlds is rounded off with demonstrations of
heroic character and conduct, and the hero is cut off from
the world of the Shidhe. In Yeats's version Eithne Inguba,

who figures only briefly in the first part of the original
tale, is introduced into the significant action of the
play. It is she who calls forth the possessing spirit and
it is upon her breast that Cuchulain ultimately seeks com-
fort. In Yeats's play it is Emer rather than Fand who demonstrates her heroic magnanimity in conquering jealousy,
but she does go on to suffer defeat at the moment of her
apparent victory because of the malignant jealousy that
exists in the supernatural world. The order of things is
reversed in Yeats's reworking of the old Irish material;
Emer becomes a tragic heroine after the fashion of Deirdre,
and Cuchulain the tragic victim of inexorable fate. Direct
contact with the supernatural is shown once again to bring
about the hero's downfall, and at the same time the theme
of personal jealousy and intrigue is satirized as in *The
Green Helmet*. Life among the Shidhe did become Yeats's
lyric life, but *The Only Jealousy of Emer* doesn't exactly
bristle with all the bitter feeling that he sometimes had
about Ireland. Instead, the scheme of characters and action tends to indicate a far more universal and philosophical conception, especially in selecting Bricriu rather than
Manannan as the demon who possesses the Figure of Cuchulain
and offers Emer a choice between her husband's life and his
love, thus rousing the hero from his magic sleep. In fact,
the god of discord had first been set in opposition to
Cuchulain when assimilating 'The Feast of Bricriu' and
other legends into the plot structure of *The Green Helmet*;
Bricriu of the Shidhe was then submerged in the figure of
the Red Man or demon of destruction, antiself to Cuchulain,
the Green Man of nature. When working out the plot of *The
Only Jealousy of Emer*, Yeats had originally found it difficult to decide on the agency of Cuchulain's awakening and
in March 1916 he wrote to Lady Gregory: 'Who should it be -
Cuchulain's grandfather, or some god or devil or woman?'[17]
The device actually employed is far more exciting and imaginative than the 'new vision of Maeve' proposed in 1910.
Instead of introducing Bricriu as an independent personage,
Yeats chooses to identify the trickster god closely with
Cuchulain through the direct possession of Cuchulain's
body. On stage the only distinction between the deamonic
Bricriu and Cuchulain is the former's withered arm and dis-
torted mask, details that accentuate their antithetical yet
related natures. The two spirits, however diverse, inhabit
the same body, and their relationship is confirmed by Bricriu

as soon as he has formally introduced himself:

> I show my face, and everything he loves
> Must fly.[18]

Yeats's insistence on a changeling and the direct revelation of a separate, supernatural world is hardly attributable to the old Irish romance, and particularly in the
case of plot structure and character relationships, a more
probable influence is the Japanese Nō, *Aoi no ue*. The Oriental model is a very simple ritual of spirit possession
and exorcism in which a vengeful ghost is the personification of an emotion so intense that it has become an autonomous agent. Conventional methods having failed, a sorceress attempts to divine whether the spirit threatening the
life of the Lady Aoi is that of a dead or a living person.
The figure of a love-lorn and beautiful noble woman manifests itself, giving a fictitious identity and remaining
invisible to all but the sorceress. She announces her
love for Prince Genji and her bitterness that his attentions have returned to his faithful wife, the Lady Aoi.
As her emotion mounts, she attacks the sick-bed, then rushes
out in a frenzy of passion. In the second scene a priest
conjures up and subdues the phantom, the incarnate jealousy
of the Lady Rokujō, now manifest in its true form with demonic, horned mask and hammer-headed staff. (For more complete details see p.73)

The association of Cuchulain with the Lady Aoi is not
so far-fetched an idea as might appear, especially when one
considers the close parallel between Cuchulain and Prince
Genji, husband to the Lady Aoi and object of jealousy in
Aoi no ue. As a culture hero of classical Japanese literature and particularly in his legendary love affairs, not
to mention his long-suffering wife's faithfulness, Genji
is very much a counterpart to Cuchulain as Aoi is to Emer.
The sick-bed is central to both plays as a symbol of conflict between the temporal and spiritual world and both
Aoi and Cuchulain function as mere occasions for the action
that takes place around them. Aoi is not even presented on
stage, and the Figure of Cuchulain is possessed by Bricriu
for most of the time, leaving the hero only a few speeches
delivered by his Ghost and a single line in his own person
at the end of the play.

More significantly, perhaps, the plot outline is nearly

identical in the two plays, and both open with the conjuring of a possessing spirit. In *Aoi no ue*, a *mikko* is asked to summon forth the demonic spirit endangering the life of the Lady Aoi. The apparition attacks Aoi on her sick-bed and rushes out. In *The Only Jealousy of Emer* Eithne Inguba is called upon to revive the living spirit of the bewitched Cuchulain, but discovers the changeling instead, who has possessed the inanimate body, and the exorcist herself runs from the scene. In the second scene of *Aoi no ue* a priest conjures the possessing spirit of Jealousy, and as she reveals her demonic nature in a dance, subdues her through prayers. In the second scene of *The Only Jealousy of Emer* the daemon, Bricriu, reveals Fand's seduction of Cuchulain's Ghost, and because of his own passion, breaks Cuchulain's enchantment by playing on Emer's jealousy. Cuchulain is saved from Fand's irresistible attraction which is represented in dance, but in returning him to the temporal world, her choice delivers him to the embrace of her mortal rival.

Fenollosa's rough draft was neither clear nor precise on a number of important points, and Pound was misled into some distortion of the dramatic situation and confusion of the character roles. In defending his reading of the text there are several illuminating comments which underline the relationship between the Japanese original and Yeats's dance play. For example:

> The ambiguities of certain early parts of the play seem mainly due to the fact that the 'Princess Rokujo', the concrete figure on the stage, is a phantom or image of Awoi no Uye's own jealousy. That is to say, Awoi is tormented by her own passion, and this passion obsesses her first in the form of a personal apparition of Rokujo, then in demonic form.[19]

Although there is no explicit indication in the play that Eithne Inguba and Fand are manifestations of Emer's jealousy, the relationship somehow rings true, and the suggestion of complementary natures between the spirit possessing the Guardian in *At the Hawk's Well* and Aoife is further substantiated. Pound's apprehension of the demon's existence in *Aoi no ue* is even more relevant to an understanding of *The Only Jealousy of Emer*:

The second confusion is the relation of the two apparitions. It seems difficult to make it clear that the
'hannya' has been cast out of the ghostly personality,
and that it had been, in a way, the motive force in the
ghost's actions. And again we cannot make it too clear
that the ghost is not actually a separate soul, but
only a manifestation made possible through Awoi and her
passion of jealousy. At least with this interpretation
the play seems moderately coherent and lucid.[20]

If Fand is the daemon cast out of Eithne Inguba and both
emanate from Emer's unity of being, then the same relationship holds for Bricriu and the Ghost of Cuchulain who are
explicit manifestations of Cuchulain. Yeats later offered
a very lucid account of just such a scheme of relationships:
'When my instructors see woman as man's goal and limit,
rather than as mother, they symbolize her as *Mask* and *Body
of Fate*, object of desire and object of thought, the one
a perpetual rediscovery of what the other destroys . . .
and they set this double opposite in perpetual opposition
to *Will* and *Creative Mind*.'[21] As a destructive and austere
idealization, Fand does represent an object of imaginative
desire, while the warm and passionate Eithne Inguba (and
Aoife) is the object of physical longing. In the same way
Bricriu (and Old Man) represents ruthless and destructive
activity in reaching the goal while the Ghost of Cuchulain
(and Young Man) is a figure of spontaneous heroism and
direct apprehension of the Ideal. The complex relationship
between Emer and Cuchulain is extended and schematized symbolically: Fand (Mask), Eithne Inguba (Body of Fate),
Bricriu as Figure of Cuchulain (Will) and Ghost of Cuchulain
(Creative Mind). Pound's final attempt to justify his interpretation of *Aoi no ue* is equally applicable to *The
Only Jealousy of Emer* and may well have been influenced by
Yeats himself:

I do not know whether I can make the matter more plain
or summarize it otherwise than by saying that the whole
play is a dramatization, or externalization, of Awoi's
jealousy. The passion makes her subject to the demon-
possession. The demon first comes in a disguised and
beautiful form. The prayer of the exorcist forces him
first to appear in his true shape, and then to retreat.
But the 'disguised and beautiful form' is not a mere

abstract sheet of matter. It is a sort of personal or
living mask, having a ghost-life of its own; it is at
once a shell of the princess, and a form, which is
strengthened or made palpable by the passion of Awoi.[22]

The extraordinary achievement of Yeats's play is in delineating and balancing the passion of both hero and heroine;
in extending the themes of sexual and spiritual conflict
to project a complete philosophical system, a perception
of human psychology and of order in the universe. Using
the plot structure and character relationships of *Aoi no
ue*, Yeats was able to rework the basic action of the old
Irish romance and to include the belief system he had for-
ged in 'Swedenborg, Mediums, and Desolate Places', (1914)
and *Per Amica Silentia Lunae* (1918).
     Whether or not the play is read with an eye to biog-
raphy (Fand: Maude Gonne; Eithne Inguba: Isseult; and
Emer: Georgie Yeats), or as an allegory on aesthetic pro-
cessess with Cuchulain representing artistic imagination,
the surface action constitutes a tragedy of the human condition, the triumph of Fate over Mask and of Will over
Creative Mind. Instead of forfeiting Cuchulain to Fand,
Emer loses him to Eithne Inguba, while Cuchulain is caught
between conflicting desires; those of his Ghost which are
thwarted, and those of his Figure (Bricriu) which succeed.
The subject of the play is the life experience of the hero,
his relationship with the inherent forces of his own psychology and of a circumambient universe; its action chron-
icles a further stage in the individual fall from the ideal
of undivided being. The original version of the play had
followed the Irish legend in showing the Ghost of Cuchulain
breaking through enchantment and choosing Emer over Fand,
while the final revision shows Cuchulain inescapably en-
thralled despite his momentary recollection of Emer's
faithful love. Still more emphasis is thus placed on
Emer's renunciation, and the defeat of personal fulfilment
in this life.
     Unlike the Japanese Nō, the action of *The Only Jeal-
ousy of Emer* is highly plot-oriented; even more so than was
the case in *At the Hawk's Well*. The surface action is perfectly intelligible while the symbolic underpinnings are
indeed obscure. At first, the attention of the audience
is fixed on a very realistic situation, and the opening

dialogue between Emer and Eithne Inguba leads us to expect a continuing pattern of logical plot progression as had been conventional in European drama. Emer's heroic magnanimity gives way to the direct intervention of the supernatural in Bricriu's possession of Cuchulain's body, and with the vision of action in the spirit world the play slides into a markedly anti-realistic dimension. A heightened intensity is certainly achieved through the contrasting verse forms of the two scenes, the freely varied pentameters of the basic dramatic action are successfully played against the irregularly rhymed, octasyllabic couplets of the play within the play. Mounting tension is adequately registered as the action courses towards its climax. In production the effect is far more telling than one might expect, and instead of Unity of Lyric Effect, we have further experiment in poetic composition, a patterning of verse forms as structural device.

In content and subject matter the two scenes are inversions of one another, and echoes such as Fand's jealous recriminations to Cuchulain contrast directly with Emer's earlier objectivity in confronting Eithne Inguba whose kiss bespeaks physical passion and life while that of Fand suggests the opposite. The attempt to depersonalize and abstract the characters into representative types through naming alone is not very successful, however, and attention remains focused on the dramatic immediacy of the action in both scenes as an outcome of realistic cause and effect rather than a ritual recreation of what had already taken place. The structural design of Nō is adhered to while its imagistic and anti-illusionistic method is replaced by a more conventional realism.

Even the occasion of the illusionist change of masks behind the partially drawn curtains of the sick-bed which marks the possession of Cuchulain's body by the changeling is an invitation to naturalistic realism that severely limits the archetypal significance of the apparition. The rhythm of action is broken by an awkward artificiality while the act of transformation could have been capitalized upon by using a stick-mask, quickly and obviously assumed as well as easily discarded. The presence of a very real, curtained bed suggests a conventional proscenium stage rather than the radical production method of drawing-room performance that had been evolved for *At the Hawk's Well*. The sick-bed itself could have been represented symbolically as in *Aoi no*

ue and extreme stylization of performance played off against
the heavy realism of the literary text. In the same way
Cuchulain's hesitation and final submission to Fand would
have been much more vividly 'real' if mimed in response to
the goddess's metallic posturing and further substantiated
by the chorus of Musicians. The actual dialogue between
the Woman of the Shidhe and the Ghost of Cuchulain is rather
embarrassing in any case, and her dance is relegated to the
minor purpose of enthralling the phantom rather than expressing the emotional climax of the scene. If the play had
followed Nō tradition as closely as *At the Hawk's Well*, the
dance would have been Emer's and a central feature of the
action.

Otherwise, the dramatic form is based on that of the
earlier dance play, especially in its use of a formal chorus.
The more or less realistic surface action is differentiated
from the actual world of the audience by the frame of a
lyrical induction and closing ceremony. In establishing the
dominant imagery, a suitable mood of poetic intensity is
created through the contrast of simple and natural verse
with arcane subject matter, while surface realism is insisted upon in the speech which summons up the concrete details
of setting and dramatic circumstances. The recitation erupts
into song at the end, restating the ornamental imagery of
sea bird and shell which at first seems to be associated with
Eithne Inguba and Emer, but in fact corresponds with Eithne
Inguba and Fand. The relevance of these images is justified
by the action of the play, but the audience must look for
their significance rather than be assisted by them in understanding the action. In any case, the imagery affects neither stage presentation nor dramatic tension and appears far
more literary in character than theatrical. Recurrences of
the figures is limited and the closing lyrics of the play
substitute parallel images altogether, a living heart and
lifeless statues. Unity of Image, if it exists at all, is
found in the scheme of character relationships and not in
the superficial symbolism of sea bird and shell.

In all, *The Only Jealousy of Emer* falls short of Yeats's
earlier achievement in *At the Hawk's Well*. A balance between symbolic meaning and surface reality has not been struck,
but the play is a very powerful conception for all its com-
plexities, and the symbolic design of character relationships now multiplied by two is not only an advance on the
scheme of Old Man, Young Man, and Guardian of the Well, but

it is also a feature that occurs again and again in subsequent plays.

The Cat and the Moon, which was begun in 1917, bears a marked resemblance to *The Only Jealousy of Emer*, especially in its relationship to Nō tradition and concern with Yeats's private philosophy. The play was meant to be patterned after Japanese Kyōgen (playful words), but Yeats had little detailed knowledge of the genre. Rather than imitating either Kyōgen or absurdist satyr plays such as Jarry's *Ubu roi*, *The Cat and the Moon* explores the possibility of comic inversion in animating serious subject matter.

The conception of symbolic characters, Blind Man (Body) and Lame Man (Soul), is certainly as closely related to earlier schemes which had matured in *On Baile's Strand*, Blind Man - Conchubar (Reason) and Fool - Cuchulain (Intuition), as to parallel figures in *At the Hawk's Well*, Old Man and Young Man. I suspect that the original purpose of the play was to complete the Cuchulain cycle and provide a comic interlude between the action of *On Baile's Strand* and *The Only Jealousy of Emer*, just as the early curtain-raiser, *The Green Helmet*, conveniently fell between *At the Hawk's Well* and *On Baile's Strand*. The two plays do share a boisterousness of comic invention and seriousness of underlying theme, and both aim at demonstrating a similar quality or aspect of the heroic spirit, as well as contrasting sharply in outcome with the plays that follow them. Another possible source or confirmation of the symbolism is found in the legend of 'Cruachan'. According to Lady Gregory, Nera, who had entered the Hill of the Shidhe, saw a Blind Man with a Lame Man upon his back making their way each day to a Well to see if the King's Crown were still safely hidden there. On asking why they, rather than anyone else, should be given the task, he was told that the King himself has blinded the one and lamed the other.[23]

The central action of *The Cat and the Moon* is taken from Synge's source for *The Well of the Saints*; that is, *Moralité de l'aveugle et du boiteau* by André de La Vigne. In the original the afflicted pair are cured by sacred relics carried in a passing procession; the blind man is delighted, while the cripple curses the saint for destroying an easy life. Synge uses the blind beggars, Martin and Mary Doul, to contrast a life of charity and imaginative reality with the corrupting and sordid assumptions of

bourgeois reality; the play ends with a refusal to be
cured a second time and the resumption of a happier life
in the imagination. In Yeats's version the Blind Man
chooses his sight and exclusion from Beatific Vision,
while the Lame Man chooses to be blessed and transcends
the limitations of the temporal world. The latter sees
the supernatural figure who has blessed him and dances out
a benediction with the Saint upon his back. The whole is
enacted before the symbol of Tree and Well, and constitutes
both an inversion of Cuchulain's quest in *At the Hawk's
Well* and also a modernization. The Celtic gods and heroes
give way to Christianity and peasant superstition, while
the ideal world is reduced to that of common tramps and
beggars, but with a corresponding affirmation of joy, spontaneity and fulfilment for the individual.

Themes from his developing vision of philosophy and
history are introduced into the play as elaborate and arcane jokes, but carry their full weight of meaning regardless of the comic conception. The arrival at St Colman's
Well is counted out as one thousand steps, the units of
a *Magnus Annus*, for example, and Yeats tells us in a note
that the Saint upon the Lame Man's back represents a transcendent stage in the universal cycle of spiritual development, which, in turn, is symbolized by the eternal waxing
and waning of the moon. However comic and joyful the presentation, travesty of the ideas themselves is avoided, nor
is there conscious parody of the authentic form he had created for the dance plays. Both the climactic dance of mock-
heroic battle and the ritual obeisance to the four cardinal
directions which introduces the Lame Man's dance of beati-
tude are well conceived as comic projections within the
context of the play's surface reality, rather than being
absurdist parodies of Fand's earlier mime.

As in *The Green Helmet*, the essential unity of *The
Cat and the Moon* is founded in the perennial appeal of a
mythic or folkloristic conception, but the action is not
modelled on any particular Japanese text, although the
single Kyōgen translation among Fenollosa's papers was
Kikazu Zatō in which a blind man and a deaf man play tricks
on one another based upon their infirmities. *The Cat and
the Moon* follows the outline of the earlier dance plays very
closely and with excellent effect. There is a hint of the
Nō travel song in the opening section of the play, and a
sense of place is created very concretely through lyrical

description, lending credibility to the whole. The one concession to the requirements of the subject matter is the unvaried prose and peasant dialect used throughout. Besides encompassing the action, the lyrics sung by Musicians also introduce the singular metaphor of the cat who represents man, and mirrors in his eyes the progressive changes of the moon, his opposite and object of desire. It is possible that Yeats found confirmation for his symbolism of the moon' phases in the dance performed by the heavenly maiden in *Hagoromo*, which represents the motions of the twenty-eight maidens of the moon. The use of the Musician's voice to suggest the presence of the invisible Saint is undoubtedly inspired by Nō tradition as is the expressive quality of the dances performed by the Blind Man and the Lame Man which serve as images of their experience.

As in *The Only Jealousy of Emer*, the subject of *The Cat and the Moon* is the inner conflict which defeats the self-fulfilment of the individual, but rather than an heroic example as in *At the Hawk's Well*, the comedy suggests something of the multiplicity involved in the universal cycle by projecting the progress of both body and soul as archetypal and anti-heroic figures. Although the symbolism is arcane, it is almost immediately intelligible and certainly familiar from the earlier plays. What baffles expectation, however, is the suppression of plot and concentration on a simple dramatic encounter. Instead of a conventional play, Yeats gives us a structured happening, 'a mere mouthful of sweet air'. More or less unencumbered by cause and effect relationships between the motives and actions of characters, Yeats has created a dance drama that faithfully follows Nō tradition. Very simply, there is a journey to a special place, an encounter with the supernatural, and a transformation is enacted. No subject or meaning other than the nature and quality of that transformation is at stake, and the means of objectifying the theme is largely poetic. The absurdist dialogue throughout is a sure indication that significance lies elsewhere, and as the action approaches climax, one sees that visual and verbal images combine with patterns of movement and sound to stimulate the imagination of the audience and ensure its direct participation in the experience. Indeed, questions of morality or elaborate interpretation are irrelevant. As with Nō, the play is what matters, and the important achievement of *The Cat and the Moon* is found in its freedom of invention outside the accepted notions of dramatic form. Together with *The Green Helmet*, the play looks forward to further experiments with suprapositioning of discontinuous scenes and visual images as well as providing a model for the treatment of themes for which no convenient myth or legend could be found.

Yeats's treatment of theme in *The Cat and the Moon* also recommended itself to *The Player Queen*, which had remained unfinished since 1907-8, and in both he explored more fully the antiself of his own temperament and art. Written in the mock-heroic mode, *The Player Queen* approaches farce and, like Kyōgen, encourages amused detachment from trivial and ignoble action, but its primary purpose is to explore human frailty and the degradation of the human condition. The comic conception finally transcends itself through the intervention of a higher rationality, a characteristic Yeatsian twist: Decima comes to reconcile the antinomies of Harlot and Queen, an apotheosis of self which gives the action point and meaning. *The Player Queen* follows the experiments of *The Unicorn from the Stars* and *The Green Helmet*, where comic inversion was used to animate more serious subject matter, but here, for the first time, the comedy provides the form and outline of the drama, not merely an accent or texture.

Once the dramatic situation and literary symbolism are established, the action of *The Player Queen* is rooted in a surface realism of logical motivation and characterization, while comic irrationality lies in terms of the discrepancy between actuality and desire. Una, the Queen, is unsuited to her state and plays the Saint. Decima's fate is to play Noah's Wife, but she aspires to the role of Queen, and Septimus, cast as Noah, apes the role of Poet, idealizing Decima and embracing Nona. The antinomies of spiritual life and physical being which are brilliantly represented in the images of unicorn and donkey are resolved in an exchange of roles. The ambiguous apotheosis of being which transforms woman into ideal image is celebrated while the artist's heroic quest for identification with that ideal is unequivocally frustrated. In choosing to live wholly in the spirit, Una gives up her role as Queen, and Decima finds fulfilment in its assumption. Deprived of the object of his desire (Decima idealized), Septimus is relegated to the natural love of Nona. In brief, Una (Octema) - Nona-Decima are images of completed personalities who have overcome the accident of their human limitations on one level or another, while their inter-relationship with Septimus (comic figure of poet, lover and hero) suggests an eternal order of forces which animates human conduct. The essential distinction between the action of *The Player Queen* and that of *The Only Jealousy of Emer* is that Decima overcomes the limitations of her human condition while Emer is tragically defeated by them. For all their superficial differences, the two plays appear to be versions of the same archetypal schem the tension between temporal and spiritual being. In *The Player Queen* the achievement of life in the spirit is rendered acceptable to a modern audience through a vision of comic inconsequence, whereas the same idea appears embarrassing in a heroic vision such as *The Shadowy Waters*.

Unlike *At the Hawk's Well*, in which mythic character and action constitute a single, dynamic image of universal force, and an acceptable level of surface reality is integrated with archetypal significance, *The Player Queen* suffers from the need to establish and justify both its immediate dramatic situation and ultimate symbolism. In the absence of a mythic or legendary plot with established characters, action and meaning, the first scene is devoted to setting up the opposition of age versus youth, and vulgar control of temporal affairs versus aristocratic aspiration to idealism. The images of black tower and diurnal cycle from dawn to noon are perhaps too literary and esoteric for the theatre, while the unicorn (spirit), donkey-beggar (poet), Adam (lover) and Noah (hero) are well justified and readily understood. The result however is an induction scene that accounts for one third of the dialogue, an imbalance of exposition and main action which obscures the focus of interest. A chorus of townsmen could provide the necessary background information and imagery while the actual scene might open with Septimus, raving drunk in the throne-room, and so condense the action to a more effective brief intensity. In the same way the anti-climactic and rhetorical ending suggests that action and symbolic design are not perfectly integrated. There should be no need for elaborate rationalisation after the annunciation of the donkey; the players might better dance before Queen and Prime Minister, circling around Septimus and Nona who mime their relationship to one another.

In construction as well as conception, one sees an essential relationship between *The Player Queen* and the

plays for dancers, especially in the unity and intensity
of the central scene, framed as it is by induction and epilogue. While employing the comic inversion he believed
was characteristic of Kyōgen, Yeats actually followed the
form of his earlier assimilations from Nō, but vestiges
of its origin in the period prior to 1910 predominate;
for example, the depersonalization of characters, supernatural intervention, indefinite location in time and
place, stylized setting, patterns of verbal or literary
images and songs performed by the main characters - '"He
went away" my mother sang', 'Put off that mask of burning
gold', and 'Shall I fancy beast or fowl'.

The use of players dressed as birds and beasts from
Noah's Ark is an excellent example of Yeats's growing
success with visual images for theatre, but the dance
they perform certainly does not derive from Nō tradition.
The first two plays for dancers do follow their Japanese
models in that they build towards dances which express
the emotional state or character of the dancer, but the
wheeling of the birds and beasts in *The Player Queen* is
more directly related to Elizabethan round-dances, images
of order and reconciliation with which Shakespeare ends
several of his comedies. However well conceived and successful the play might be, it offered no new direction or
technique for the handling of dramatic form and presentation, but it did demonstrate the application of a method
evolved in *The Cat and the Moon* to older and unfinished
material.

The Dreaming of the Bones, on the other hand, written
at about the same time as *The Cat and the Moon* and earlier
than the final version of *The Player Queen*, represents a
far more successful attempt to balance the double vision
of degradation from the ideal and the affirmation of temporal existence by returning to the more chaste and anti-
illusionistic construction of *At the Hawk's Well*. As
pointed out some years ago by F.A.C. Wilson, the basic
structure of the play was inspired by *Nishikigi*, and *The
Dreaming of the Bones* does follow the plot outline of the
Japanese model, but the central image and situation are
just as closely related to Yeats's early story, 'Hanrahan's
Vision' (1897) in which the ghosts of Diarmuid and
Dervorgilla appear to the poet Hanrahan and seek forgiveness in the mist atop Ben Bulben. *Nishikigi* falls into the
category of 'Possession piece', and it is one of those

plays generally based on a ghost story in which the souls
of the dead are bound to earth by some particularly intense human passion. The ritual opens with a priest and
his companions on a pilgrimage to a distant northern province. A man and a woman of the place enter and call attention to the accessories they carry which are symbols of
unrequited love. The *nishikigi* (decorated sticks) of the
title are tokens of courtship which a man leaves before a
maiden's gate each day until she accepts his suit. If
after a thousand days she still has not received him, he
must admit defeat. The grave of just such a rejected suitor is pointed out nearby as both the man and woman vanish.
After the interval they come forward as though in a dream
or vision and reenact their past, seeking repentance and
release from their attachment to life, which, in fact, is
granted them. They pledge their love and the mime finishes
with a lively dance of joy before the poetic vision dissolves. (For more complete details see pp.72-3)

In writing *The Dreaming of the Bones* Yeats transposed
the action to modern Ireland and replaced the stock figure
of the conventional priest with the more dramatic character
of the Young Man who is escaping the consequences of his
participation in the Easter Rising of 1916. The scene is
set in Clare-Galway where he meets a Stranger and a
Young Girl of the place who offer to guide him to his
rendezvous and introduce the themes of national hatred toward the British and the passionate remorse of the dead.
A journey over the top of the mountain to the sea is undertaken and the second scene consists of a dialogue which re-
hearses the motives and actions of the past as they bear
upon the present circumstances of all three characters,
leading inevitably to the revelation of the pair's identity.
Diarmuid and Dervorgilla seek forgiveness in order that they
may escape the consequences of their passion, but however
poignantly they present their plight, or however sympathetically the Young Man views their all-too-human transgression
the cumulative effect of its actual consequences makes it
impossible to forgive them. They dance out their anguish
and longing before the vision dissolves. In its general
outline the action is exactly that of *Nishikigi*, especially
in the concentration of symbolism and circumstances before
the trip to the tomb and the recreation of the lovers'
original relationship in the second scene. The protagonists
of the Japanese play are forgiven, however, and their rep-

etition of the action redeems them from remorse. The vivid
imagery of desolation across the land, the death and destruction occasioned by the Easter Rising itself, and the
bitterness and hatred that have resulted historically from
their alliance with the Norman against Dervorgilla's husband, render their remorse implacable.

In both mood and method *The Dreaming of the Bones* follows the practice of Nō drama much more closely than any of
the other dance plays, yet wholly within the dramatic form
first evolved for *At the Hawk's Well*: lyric induction and
epilogue, archetypal characters, surface conflict, symbolic
relationship of images, and culminating dance. The dramatic
irony of the supernatural figures who speak of themselves
so impersonally and the sustained air of mystery which
surrounds them, are directly related to the practice of
Nō, while the dynamic effect of the choral narration and
lyric commentary that underscores the first stages of the
ritualized journey are perhaps taken from the Fenollosa-
Pound text of *Kayoi Komachi:*

Chorus
(announcing the action and change of scene)

So he went out of his little cottage in the temple en-
closure.
He went to Ichihara and prayed.[24]

Both through stylized movement and the recitation of
the chorus, emphasis is focused on recreating the journey
in imagination rather than on verisimilitude, and the episode achieves the force of a minor climax which marks the
end of the play's first scene. The description of the
journey is transformed into a concrete image of the fact
itself by the accompanying circuits of the stage, and an
imaginative impression is created of a spiral path in a
Dantesque mountain valley that is filled with darkness.
The metaphor of the stone wine cup filled with fantastic
and passionate dreams which recurs in the songs of the
Musicians[25] confirms the occult importance of the over-
ingenious figure, while the verses constitute a Nō-like
mediation on the arcane principle of 'dreaming back', not
itself a central theme, but merely an assumption or given
condition of that fictional world. The Musicians narrate
the actual ascent as a symbolic movement from a temporal

state through death and on to a condition of pure spirit:
from shallow well and burial ground, past grassy fields and
ragged thorn-trees, to a place among the stones above the
ash and well beyond the cries of the tomb-nested owl which
figures in each of the three speeches. The complementary
songs concentrate on a spiritual ascent through images of
the fear and loneliness of bitter-sweet night, the pride
of a rascal heart remembering and remembering, and the cry
of dreaming bones that release calamity while the antithetical image of the Red Cock of March figures in each of the
three sections. The dawn-crowing of the Cock represents the
annunciation of a new cycle, the fullness of time in conceiving its own opposite.

　　After so lyrical and striking a passage the dramatic
dialogue of the three characters reasserts reasonableness
and the relation of Ireland's present troubles to those
of the past is rehearsed. The question of forgiving
Diarmuid and Dervorgilla is raised against the contrast
between their subjective and mysterious speeches and the
objective and matter-of-fact style used by the Young Man.
Once forgiveness is denied, the action again moves from
one level of reality to another, and the stylization of
musical accompaniment and another circuit of the stage indicates the party's progress to the rim of the mountain
where the longing and despair of the ghosts is mimed in
the twilight of the coming dawn. The dance is narrated
by the Young Man who finally perceives the identity of
the pair, and their unregenerating tragedy is sharply
contrasted with his unrelenting purpose and uprightness.
The Young Man is inevitably associated with Cuchulain as
a modern culture hero, and the Easter Rising is now seen
as the reversal of the treachery that brought the Norman
to Ireland. The consequences of that original sin are
spent as a new, heroic era in Irish history is brought into
being. The symmetry and counterpoint of character, incident and aesthetic devices constitute a symbolic design
which in fact reconciles the spectator to the forgiveness
denied by the Young Man. A successful dramatic image is
created and a poetic vision of universal necessity is projected in both personal and historical terms:

　　For nothing can be sole or whole
　　That has not been rent.[26]

One cannot help but admire the almost perfect construction of *The Dreaming of the Bones*, its clarity and
brief intensity. Beyond the superficial plot outline of
Nishikigi and the use of stylization in both the journey
up the mountain and the mimetic dance, the achievement is
undeniably Yeats's. Much of the play's strength, however,
is found in the immediacy of its action and the historical
authority of its subject matter. Unlike the earlier dance
plays, *The Dreaming of the Bones* has a natural link with
the real world of the audience and encourages their participation. Its success in terms of Yeats's development as
a dramatist is in the precision with which the surface
reality coincides with symbolic meaning and the boldness
with which a drama of image, atmosphere and idea is expressed through lyrical patterning, rather than naturalistic plot sequences.

The last of Yeats's finished experiments with dance
drama took for subject the crucifixion of Christ, the
culture hero of a primary era and a figure of some historical authority for his audience. Although the character of
Christ is antithetical to that of Cuchulain, the two heroes
do complement one another and share their miraculous conceptions by human mothers through the mysterious agency of
supernatural consorts. Each in turn was claimed as son by
a mortal father. While Cuchulain often represents man's
ultimate fall from undivided being, Christ, as the counter-
symbol, represents the resumption of man's innate spirituality, the realization of his anterior divinity. *Calvary*
is not merely a recreation of the crucifixion, however, but
a qualification of the nature of Christ's sacrifice in the
context of a larger view of individual necessity and universal order. Oscar Wilde's 'The Doer of Good' (1894) is
certainly one of the major sources for *Calvary*,[27] and the
central idea had already been formulated by the hero of
Yeats's early short story, 'The Tables of the Law' (1897):
'I am not among those for whom Christ died, and this is
why I must be hidden. I have a leprosy that even eternity
cannot cure. I have seen the whole, and how can I come
again to believe that a part is the whole? I have lost my
soul because I have looked out of the eyes of the angels.'[28]
As a dramatic ritual, the play is by far the boldest and
most interesting experiment in the new dance form, and
Yeats assimilated various elements from the Nō in writing
it, particularly from the play *Kakitsubata*, which he

appears to have used as a model.

Kakitsubata is a very delicate evocation of elegance and lyric beauty in which the Spirit of Water Iris first appears disguised as a local maiden who sings of the famous flowers that the *waki* has come to admire. She recites a poem by Narihira, a lover of women and incarnation of music and art, and recalls his attachment for that very place. In the second half the girl is revealed as a great lady, the beloved of Narihira in a time long past, and finally as the Spirit of the Flowers. The dance she performs actually suggests his presence as she recounts the story of his life and laments his passing as the end of a golden age. (For more complete details see pp.70-1)

Aware of the fragmentary condition of the Fenollosa text and the play's illusive character, Ezra Pound added a closing note to the translation which emphasizes the essential relationship of the play to the conception of *Calvary:*

> The spirit manifests itself in that particular iris marsh because Narihira in passing that place centuries before had thought of her . . . The Muses were 'the Daughters of Memory'. It is by memory that this spirit appears, she is able or 'bound' because of the passing thought of these iris. That is to say, they, as well as the first shadowy and then bright apparition, are the outer veils of her being. Beauty is the road to salvation, and her apparition 'to win people to the Lord' or 'to enlighten these people' is part of the ritual, that is to say, she demonstrates the 'immortality of the soul' or the 'permanence or endurance of the individual personality' by her apparition - first, as a simple girl of the locality; secondly, in the ancient splendours. At least that is the general meaning of the play so far as I understand it.[29]

In the basic conception of *Calvary* the Flower Spirit is replaced by the figure of Christ, who relives his passion in imagination and projects in his mind the troubling, antithetical figures that plague his thought and bind his spirit to its purgatorial recreations. The apparitions in *Kakitsubata* are transposed in *Calvary* as Lazarus, Judas and the Roman Soldiers who cumulatively occasion Christ's cry of intellectual despair: 'My Father, why hast Thou

forsaken me?'[30] All three are manifestations or facets of
a unified human experience, and none have objective existence in the play outside the protagonist's dream. As in
Nō, every aspect of perception in the ritual recreation
is filtered and focused through the figure of Christ; and
even the chorus of Musicians which acts as deuteragonist
cannot be said to have an independent understanding of the
central event. The actual personages involved, however,
possess unquestioned validity and familiarity in western
culture; so much so in fact that their symbolic nature
and relationship within the play have often proved disconcerting to critics. Yeats's version of the Christian mystery is anything but orthodox, and his view of Christ is
fundamental to an understanding of the play. As early as
1897, Yeats wrote 'The historical Christ was indeed no
more than the supreme symbol of the artistic imagination
in which, with every passion wrought to perfect beauty by
art and poetry, we shall live, when the body has passed
away for the last time.'[31] Still later he maintained:

> We say of Him because His sacrifice was voluntary that
> He was love itself, and yet that part of Him which made
> Christendom was not love but pity, and not pity for in-
> tellectual despair, though the man in Him, being *anti-
> thetical* like His age, knew it in the Garden, but *pri-
> mary* pity, that for the common lot, man's death, seeing
> that He raised Lazarus, sickness, seeing that He healed
> many, sin, seeing that He died.[32]

The figure of Christ is presented not in its dual nature
as both man and god, but as man alone, and the surface action concentrates on the despair he suffered when confronted by the limited effectiveness of his pity for the common
lot. On a more esoteric level we have another representation of double opposition, but this time without the element of sexual conflict so fundamental to *The Only Jealousy of Emer*: Christ (Mask), The Roman Soldiers (Body of
Fate), Lazarus (Will), and Judas (Creative Mind). Another
convenient scheme for exploring the relationship of characters is found in Peter Ure's reading of the obscure
aphorism from *The Resurrection*, 'God and man die each
other's life, live each other's death':[33]

1. God dies man's life, or life-in-death: the dead
    God is like a live man (Christ).

2. God lives man's death, or death-in-life: the
    eternal God becomes a man, and dies. (The Roman
    Soldiers).

3. Man dies God's life, or life-in-death: the dead
    man is like a living God; he cannot die, or can-
    not find the death appropriate to man (Lazarus).

4. Man lives God's death, or death-in-life: the
    living man endeavours to live like an immortal,
    spiritual creature, to 'ascend to Heaven', or to
    be, like the resurrected Christ, 'a phantom with
    a beating heart'. In this way man diminishes his
    humanity, and the self no longer claims, 'as by a
    soldier's right / A charter to commit the crime
    once more'(Judas).[34]

The separate encounters or images are excellently conceived and brilliantly unified, both thematically and
structurally. The shock value of the ingratitude displayed
by Lazarus, who objects to the chance (God's choice) inherent in his unlooked-for resurrection on the fourth day,
amply keys the audience to a heretical reinterpretation
of the Christian myth. Lazarus had found perfect peace
and fortuitous obliteration of self-hood in death; through
Christ's pity he was dragged unwillingly to the light 'as
boys drag out / A rabbit when they have dug its hole away',[3]
and he now claims Christ's death, not realizing that its
import is far different from his own. Christ's spontaneous
resurrection on the third day represents the self-realization
of spirituality, and antithesis to the non-being that Lazarus now seeks in vain. Christ encounters his first failure
a man who refuses participation in the spiritual quest, whose
object of desire is both plausible and exactly opposite to
his own. The episode is both complete and self-contained,
and is divided from the second scene by the artificial intervention of a choral narration and song which describes
Martha and the three Marys as figures antithetical to
Lazarus, individuals who imitate the quest. They live only
in Christ's love; deprived of it, they would fall victims
to their baser human nature. These imagined figures are

said to vanish, and we understand their flight from Christ's
thought as Judas enters. Here is a man outside Christ's
capacity to pity because he too refused the quest, he will
not serve God's choice (chance), but rivals deity in acting
independently, establishing his own identity and moral reality beyond the possible reach of God's power. Again the
encounter is complete, the aspiration humanly credible, and
Christ experiences a second failure. Instead of another
choral interlude, however, with its commentary and transitional imagery, three Roman Soldiers, the servants of
Caesar, break into the scene and so accelerate the basic
rhythm of the play. Necessity routs reflection, and circumstance moves the action to its inevitable climax. The
Soldiers reassure Christ of their total disinterest in
His passion, their pure objectivity. To them, the quest
for spiritual fulfilment is not even an option, neither do
they seek oblivion or a rival control of nature. They love
life itself, and worship natural chance which is represented by dice carved from an old sheep's thigh at Ephesus;
Christ's subjectivity and his despair at the moment of
physical death are conditions of which the Soldiers are
incapable since they expect nothing and accept all. Christ's
despair is an acknowledgement of circumstantial limitations
which prevent him from assuming universal responsibility
and of defeat in his desire to turn everyone into what he
is.

> Love is created and preserved by intellectual analysis,
> for we love only that which is unique, and it belongs
> to contemplation, not to action, for we would not change
> that which we love . . . Fragment delights in fragment
> and seeks possession, not service; whereas the Good
> Samaritan discovers himself in the likeness of another,
> covered with sores and abandoned by thieves upon the
> roadside, and in that other serves himself.[36]

In the stylized representation of the crucifixion
and the dance of the Roman Soldiers which conclude the ritual presentation, Yeats offers a unique and complex image
for contemplation and analysis. The physical degradation
of Christ's death is the necessary counterpoint to apotheosis in the spirit and the representation of the crucifixion
carries with it both its own force as the central symbol
of Christianity and the wider associations of a more

universal philosophy. In holding the cross which symbol-
izes the betrayal of Christ, Judas represents the recreation of original sin, 'non serviam', giving another turn
to the wheel of incarnation and spirituality, while the
Soldiers of Caesar circle about the static group in a cosmic dance which celebrates natural chance within a fixed
outline of order. They encompass Christ's passion and
suggest a larger fabric of universal design in which it is
but a single thread. It is strange, however, that Lazarus
should be excluded from the scene, for his particular
denial of Christ's spiritual quest is not otherwise represented. In producing the play myself, I would not be
able to resist leaving him on stage throughout, leaning on
a pilgrim's staff, his mind fixed upon nothing. However
problematical any reading of *Calvary* may be, there can be
little doubt of its success'in producing a dramatic stage
picture for drawing-room performance which is both elec-
trifying and significant. The motionless grouping of
Christ, the Cross and Judas, with Caesar's Soldiers miming
a quarrel, a throw of dice, and the ecstasy of universal
harmony is a conception of great power. Surely, it is a
far more forceful and evocative image than the dance of
Diarmuid and Dervorgilla before the motionless Young Man
in *The Dreaming of the Bones* which it closely resembles.

Of the four plays for dancers *Calvary* certainly represents the most sophisticated and extended experimentation, especially in its use of autonomous and discontinuous
scenes which are amplified and integrated through sense imagery. Like Nō, the dance plays provide a drama of aesthetic means and forms which parallels that of its subject
matter and logical processes. In addition to character,
action and stage properties which express complex relationships as concrete symbols, the use of verbal figures is
particularly successful in *Calvary*. The counterpoint of
bird (eagle, heron, and swan) and beast (rabbit and sheep)
provides a dense multiplicity of unambiguous associations
and underscores particular symbolic relationships. The
verse forms employed are carefully modulated to distinguish
stylized action from verisimilitude, and the formal, rhymed
tetrameters of the songs for unfolding and folding the
cloth give way to blank lines of greater length and cadenced musical phrasing which are punctuated for special effect by brief lyrics in terse trimeters. Even the rhythmic
patterning of action is manipulated by foreshortening or

curtailing later units such as leaving out the spoken
chorus between the apparition of Judas and that of the
Roman Soldiers, and the play tends to accelerate towards
its climax, much in the manner of Nō. Whether assimilated
from the Japanese drama or not, such dynamic control of
structural patterning and performance rhythm is amazingly
effective.

However many elements Nō tradition and Yeats's plays
for dancers have in common, actual assimilation is largely
technical. While Nō is concerned with the embodiment of
interior psychic states and subjective emotion, Yeats's
dance plays are preoccupied with a demonstration of archetypal relationships and patterns of experience in which
opposed aspects of cosmic psychology are apprehended.
Rather than the narrated meditation of Nō, Yeats developed
a symbolic drama of logical appearances in which consistency of stylization provides coherence; mask, music, dance
and the symbolic arrangement of character, incident and
image serve to discover universal order in situations that
approximate life. In the final analysis, Nō was not so
much a direct influence on Yeats as the source of a new
point of departure for continued experimentation with established themes and aesthetic concerns. The Japanese
drama did provide Yeats with prototypes for recreating his
visions and ideas directly upon the stage, and made him
aware of new possibilities for breaking with the conventions of Renaissance drama. Even though each of the four
plays was modelled on an existing Nō, none imitated the
form and substance of its original, but each freely assimilated techniques and conceptualizations to its own ends.
With *Calvary* the initial impetus of influence from the Nō
more or less exhausted itself, and the later drama tends
to experiment with themes and forms already evolved.

5.

W.B.Yeats: Later Assimilation

Art produces something beyond the form of things,
Though its importance lies in preserving the form
                                        of things:
Poetry gives us thoughts beyond the domain of art,
But is valued in that it exhibits the characteris-
                                        tics of art.[1]

Even after the publication of *Calvary*, Yeats attempted another play based on a text from the Fenollosa manuscripts, but only an outline sketch remains, and an account of the untitled piece has been published by F.A.C. Wilson as 'The Bridegroom', dated 1923.[2] The play was begun in 1918 according to Hazard Adams, who refers to a work of that date which 'has to do with a young girl, who lives as a goatherd in an old tower on a hill, and her lover, whose mother wants to block their marriage.'[3] The play is also mentioned by Brigit Bjersley, but the Wilson account is the most complete yet published, and must be taken as authoritative. Whether or not the sole source of inspiration, 'The Bridegroom' does follow the general plot of *Sumidagawa* rather closely.

The Sumida River is one of those plays which project frenzy or derangement resulting from the loss of a child or lover, and the action centres on a noble woman searching frantically for her missing son. She arrives at the river bank where a ferry man mocks her publicly because of her distracted state. She rebukes him and during the crossing he tells the story of a slave-trader who had travelled that way the year before with a tender boy who had fallen ill

and could go no further. The local people had tended him,
but he died and was buried on the further shore. The noble
woman recognizes her son from the details of the story,
laments the cruelty of fate, and proceeds to the burial
mound which she claws ineffectually with her bare hands,
hoping to see the face of her son once more. As she weeps
and prays, she hears his voice and catches a fleeting
glimpse of his ghost. (For more complete details see
pp. 71-2.)

In Yeats's plot the situation is altogether transposed;
instead of a mother/son relationship there is an uncon-
summated love interest between a boy and girl which is revealed to the audience through the agency of an old fisherman and impeded in its progress through the jealousy of the
boy's mother. After a quarrel with his mother who prays
that he may drown should he defy her, the youth plans to
row across the river to the old tower where the girl lives,
and she, half asleep and dreaming of an ideal, princely
lover, sends him away from her door and leads him to the
mistaken conclusion that she is deceiving him with another
man. In despair he throws himself into the flood and she
follows suit on discovering what has actually happened.
The old fisherman buries the lovers under two crossed
sticks, and the play ends with a manifestation of the
young girl's ghost to the boy's mother offering forgiveness
but being met with bitterness and self-justification. The
ferryman, mother and son of *Sumidagawa* have been elaborated
into the old fisherman and mother, the young girl and boy
of 'The Bridegroom' in order to accommodate Yeats's preoccupation with the conflict of Youth and Age, the double
opposition of Creative Mind and Body of Fate with Mask and
Will, and his concern for the precise nature of human love
and spiritual aspiration. Such central features as exposition through a deuteragonist, the crossing of the river,
the tragic death of the hero and the apparition of a ghost
are assimilated directly from the Japanese original, as are
other elements from such probable sources as *Romeo and
Juliet* and *Riders to the Sea*. The conception of tragedy
arising from a confusion of ideal and temporal reality
is eminently Yeatsian in its acknowledgement of ambiguity,
and points to the characteristic idea that love between
man and woman is essentially love of the ideal or archetypal presence in the beloved. The magnanimity and self-
sacrifice of the lovers raises their relationship to a

supernatural plane, while the bitter recriminations of the
boy's mother returns the action to an awareness of the degradation and limitation of the human condition. That the
play was never finished is not surprising, however, when
one considers that the dramatic situation has neither historical authority nor emblematic promise, and that essentially the same material has already found its proper
expression in the more heroic projections of *The Only
Jealousy of Emer* and *The Dreaming of the Bones*. Yeats
had not followed the form of the earlier dance plays in
the fragment as reported by Wilson, but had returned to
the episodic construction in five scenes which he had favoured previously. As a text, 'The Bridegroom' is of no
consequence whatever, but it is an interesting document
as a demonstration of the dead-end that Yeats faced when
his theme found neither an established mythic plot nor an
adequately expressive form.

Having abandoned 'The Bridegroom' Yeats turned to the
more promising idea of the resurrection of Christ as a revelation of man's divinity, a contrary vision to that of
the death of Christ as a projection of god's humanity. The
early scenarios published by Curtis Bradford provide a very
interesting link between the text of *Calvary* and the final
version of *The Resurrection*, and show that the work was
first conceived as a dance play.[4] One of the two sketches
suggests a reverse image of the structural pattern found in
Calvary; the figure of Christ is caught up in dreaming-
back and is confronted by the three Marys and two mysterious men who seem to have forfeited their divine natures
because of an excessive attachment to the human condition.
The second of the two sketches insists even more strongly
on an investigation of the nature of divinity by making
each of Christ's three encounters a meeting with a supernatural figure; Buddha, Dionysus, and Attis/Adonis, as well
as ending with the three Marys and a gesture of apotheosis.
The scheme is very well balanced and creates a valid context for examining the nature of divinity, but it also tends
to confound the assertion that Christ was the new Adam and
legislator of a revolutionary dispensation. Philosophically,
it would be almost impossible to justify the inclusion of
Buddha, and equally impossible to distinguish Christ from
the other two as anything more than just another fertility
god. The presence of so many antique divinities would

certainly alienate the sympathy of any modern audience,
and the force of the opening image of Christ's appearance
in grave clothes far outweighs the rhetorical abstraction
with which the play was to close: 'I am the life and the
way'.[5] Instead of relying on the conventional associations
of Christian tradition and an aesthetic pattern of song,
dance, poetry and music borrowed from Nō which build towards an emotional climax, Yeats favoured dramatic tension
and a paradigmatic *schema* composed of opposed character relationships.

A comparison of Yeats's earliest scenario with the
modern Japanese Nō, *Fukkatsu no Kirisuto* (The Resurrected
Christ) (see above), shows a basic parallelism of conception except for the introduction of philosophical dialogue
between Christ and his interlocutors and the weakness of
the final declaration of divinity. The Japanese version
reveals the divine nature of Christ directly and simply, in-
sisting on the mystery and wonder of the miraculous manifestation, while Yeats tends to rationalize and justify
the idea before asserting it. The second scenario further
elaborates the schematic arrangement of opposed points of
view which represent the divine Christ's Mask and Body of
Fate, Will and Creative Mind, but the central incident of
the play is still the image of dreaming-back, Christ wound
in grave clothes, which opens the action and after which
all is anticlimax. It was not until the first complete
manuscript, later revised several times and finally published as the *Adelphi* text of 1927, that Yeats introduced
'the beating heart of a phantom' as the significant revelation of Christ's divinity, and moved the climax to its
proper place at the end of the play.

In the introduction to *The Resurrection* published in
Wheels and Butterflies (1934) Yeats acknowledged the experiments of Sir William Crookes, published many years before in *Studies in Psychical Research*, as the source of the
central situation in the finished play,[6] already he had included a similar image in the Musician's song for folding
the cloth in *The Only Jealousy of Emer*:

Why does your heart beat thus?
Plain to be understood,
I have met in a man's house
A statue of solitude,
Moving there and walking;

> Its strange heart beating fast
> For all our talking.
> O still that heart at last.[7]

It may even be that Yeats was reading E. E. Fournier
D'Albe's *The Life of Sir William Crookes* (London 1923)
when the appropriateness of the image for his play struck
him. Fournier D'Albe quotes Crookes' own account of
séances with the medium Florence Cook and his experience
of the apparition known as Katie King from letters published in *The Spiritualist* (1874):

> On several occasions she took my arm when walking, and
> the impression conveyed to my mind that it was a living
> woman by my side, instead of a visitor from the other
> world, was so strong that the temptation to repeat a
> recent celebrated experiment became almost irresistible.
> Feeling however, that if I had not a spirit, I had at
> all events a *lady* close to me, I asked her permission
> to clasp her in my arms so as to be able to verify the
> interesting observations which a bold experimentalist
> has recently somewhat verbosely recorded. Permission
> was graciously given, and I accordingly did - well, as
> any gentleman would do under the circumstances.
> Mr. Volckmann will be pleased to know that I can corrob-
> orate his statement that the 'ghost' (not 'struggling'
> however) was as material a being as Miss Cook herself. [8]

So startling and transformed a dramatic image as 'the
beating heart of a phantom' required a corresponding change
in the original scenario from the divine to the human point
of view; Buddha, Dionysus and Attis/Adonis become Hebrew,
Alexandrian Greek (Egyptian) and Syrian, while the emblematic relationship of characters with reference to those of
Calvary is inevitably diluted. The effect of transposing
the characters to the human sphere was to make the drama
the most immediately accessible of Yeats's middle plays by
giving the action an appearance of natural, if not illusionistic, reality. The price paid was a corresponding reduc-
tion in symbolic significance, however, for the play fails
to deliver up any meaning beyond that of the surface action.
On the other hand, the final text is reasonably theatrical,
and given the contrary views of Christ's nature advocated
by the Greek and Hebrew and the inevitable synthesis of

the Syrian who accepts him as man and god simultaneously,
the logic of cause and effect is indisputable. The added
dimension of dramatic tension provided by allusions to
the antithetical nature of Dionysiac rituals is a brilliant
stroke and leads inescapably to the revelation of the dead
god's beating heart and his reversal of the former dispensation. The natural, but formally cadenced prose, provides
an excellent vehicle for the dramatic conception, and songs
which open, bring to a climax and close the aesthetic construction serve as indications of transcendence. Whether
or not the stage directions imply production on a proscenium stage, *The Resurrection* retains almost all the char-
acteristics of a dance play. It is true that the dance
itself is absent, but the action is intellectual and requires no physical image, while such elements are present
as the framing songs of Musicians, reliance on established
associations of myth, creation of an identifiable setting,
archetypal characters, conflict, logical plot progression,
and plot reversal (intervention of the supernatural) as
structural climax. Considering its surface clarity and
lack of symbolic depth, *The Resurrection* is perhaps the
slightest of Yeats's mature plays and marks an extreme
limit of experimentation in the balancing of revolutionary
form and traditional subject matter.

During the six years that elapsed between the inception and last major revision of *The Resurrection*, Yeats
was also at work on two other plays. *The Words Upon the
Window-Pane*, which was written and first performed in 1930,
is very closely related in theme and central situation to
Calvary and *The Resurrection*, while *Fighting the Waves* is
merely a revision of *The Only Jealousy of Emer*, which had
been inspired by purely external events. More than ten
years earlier Yeats had lost Itō Michio, the Japanese dancer who created the role of the Guardian in *At the Hawk's
Well*, and the subsequent plays for dancers remained largely
unproduced because of difficulty in finding trained performers adequate to the conception. The fact that Yeats continued to experiment with the new form attests to an un-
flagging belief in rhythmical speech, stylized movement,
and poetic composition for the creation of expressive moods
and atmospheres, but it was not until his introduction to
the work of Ninette de Valois that the means of realizing
his inspiration became available.

Yeats was also much impressed by the *avant-garde* work of Terence Gray at the Festival Theatre, Cambridge, where Ninette de Valois served as choreographic director, creating dance sequences for dramatic productions and helping regular actors to express themselves through stylized movement as well as occasionally producing independent dance programmes and *divertissements*. Gray's policy was aggressively anti-illusionistic; in a book entitled *Dance Drama* he complained: 'The basis of artistic expression has been lost sight of, and the most that is attempted or achieved is the interpretation in movement of the rhythms of musical composition.'[9] The very contemporary abstract expressionism and futurist movement that Dame Ninette used for the Chorus of Furies in *The Oresteia*, with which the Festival opened in November 1926, had demonstrated both the expressive power and uncompromising modernity of her work. In January 1927 Yeats saw the Festival production of *On Baile's Strand* as directed by Norman Marshall with special music by Florence Farr and movement arranged by Ninette de Valois. The production was particularly successful, the decor striking in various shades of grey and the symbolism of Fool/Blind Man emphasized by grotesque masks and movement confined to the forestage.

Yeats was excited by the confirmation of his own production theories and the resurgent possibility of a poetic theatre in Ireland which might withstand the persistent popularity of peasant drama and the school of Cork realists. According to Dame Ninette:

> The mind of Yeats was made up; he would have a small school of Ballet at the Abbey and I would send over a teacher. I would visit Dublin every three months and produce his *Plays for Dancers* and perform in them myself; thus, he said, the poetic drama in Ireland would live again and take its rightful place in the Nation's own Theatre, and the oblivion imposed on it by the popularity of peasant drama would become a thing of the past.[10]

With the small subsidy granted by the Irish Free State Government the directors of the National Theatre were able to remodel their buildings and to establish the Abbey School of Acting (September 1927) and the Abbey School

of Ballet (November 1927). At the same time the Peacock
Theatre, an intimate and modernized auditorium adjoining
the Abbey and designed for experimental work, was opened
(15 November 1927). Ninette de Valois did send over a
teacher and came herself for a fortnight each season with
a few students from her school to help in staging simple
dance programmes and the more elaborate plays for dancers.
By the time the more ambitious production of *Fighting the
Waves* was possible (13 August 1929), the little school
for dancers had given five public performances, and there
can be little doubt that the revision of *The Only Jealousy of Emer* was at least partially undertaken to exploit
the talent at hand. Yeats had begun writing the prose
version in 1927, presumably with Ninette de Valois and her
students in mind, but the only change from the original
actually required was to write out the voice part for The
Woman of the Shidhe; Dame Ninette was essentially a dancer and refused to speak from the stage. In fact, Yeats
took the opportunity to recast the play in prose, tight-
ening up dialogue and simplifying language wherever he
could. *The Only Jealousy of Emer*, even in its final version, had been far too complex, both texturally and structurally, and the present revision followed his discoveries
in *Calvary* and *The Resurrection* that mythic action gained
in import from basically naturalistic treatment heightened
by patterns of music and stylized movement. The charge
that Yeats turned mere librettist in *Fighting the Waves*
is altogether unfounded; the climax of action is at least
as much informed by literary construction as by music or
choreography, although the music of George Antheil may
well have obscured the literary text. In many ways the
condensation of the text and the expressive character of
the extra-literary production elements give a far more compelling version of the action than the earlier text of *The
Only Jealousy of Emer*. Certainly, the omission of Fand's
speeches was fortuitous, and the larger musical and theatrical (balletic) conceptions occasioned by his encounter
with the strong professionalism of Ninette de Valois bore
further fruit in the writing of *The King of the Great
Clock Tower*, *The Hearne's Egg*, and *The Death of Cuchulain*.
Production details for *Fighting the Waves* indicate a return to the Fenollosa-Pound edition of Nō: the wave-
patterned curtain looks back to the dominant image of

Suma Genji, and the *shite*'s sea-wave dance in that play
is a probable source for Cuchulain's mimed battle against
a *corps de ballet* representing waves. Fand's final dance
of bitter grief, the over-sized von Krop masks from the
Amsterdam production of 1922 by van Dalsum, and the exciting modern music for full orchestra by George Antheil combined to produce the kind of exultant vitality and strength
that Yeats had sought in his attempts to write Kyōgen.
Rather perceptively, Lady Gregory wrote: 'I went to Dublin
and saw *The Fighting of the Waves* - wild, beautiful, the
motion of the dancers, the rhythm of the music, the scene.
The words lost, the masks hideous - yet added to the strange
unreality. We might all have been at the bottom of the
sea.'[11]

Although written between *Fighting the Waves* and *The
King of the Great Clock Tower*, the realism of *The Words
Upon the Window-Pane* follows very closely on the dramatic
conception and execution of *The Resurrection* and looks forward to the achievement of *Purgatory*. The more straight-
forwardly naturalistic action of these three dramas distinguish them from the esoteric subject matter and musical
composition of the other late plays, but even here there is
some indication of influence and assimilation from the
Japanese Nō. As in *The Resurrection*, the central situation
of *The Words Upon the Window-Pane* is the revelation of the
supernatural as an objectively real presence imposing itself irrationally upon a mundane and circumstantial world.
Such a conception is also common to Nō, where an historical
figure of some importance often appears miraculously, reliving the torment or emotional crisis which links its
spirit to temporal existence. Even the theme of remorse
and unrequited love, as in *Kayoi Komachi* or *Nishikigi*, for
example, is close to Nō tradition, and the induction/com-
mentary provided by the *waki*-like figure of John Corbet is
equally familiar. In parallel with Yeats's developed form
for the dance plays, as much dramatic conflict and opposition as possible is incorporated; youth and age are opposed
in the central figures of John Corbet and Dr Trench, and
the *petit bourgeois* participants in the *séance* are brilliantly conceived as an ironic inversion of Swift's heroic
world. The point of the play, however, is not merely the
miraculous intervention of the supernatural as a demonstration of universal order; the drama also demonstrates
the perpetual opposition and interplay of Mask and Body of

Fate, Will and Creative Mind. The central question is
Swift's celibacy, the root of his remorse and torment. On
the one side he is beset by Vanessa, representing chance
and passion, and Stella, representing choice and reason;
on the other he refuses steadfastly to consummate his personality or beget children, both because of the personal
taint of ill-health or madness and because of the general
taint of madness in the human intellect, the degradation
and limitation of the human condition. The inclusion of
Yeats's private philosophy, however, in no way obscures
the action of the play, and the personal tragedy of
Jonathan Swift is obviously emblematic of a whole nation's
failure to consummate its potential. Images of the present
pettiness are constantly before us; coursing and shopkeep-
ing, spiritualism and evangelical uplift. The correspondence is underlined by patterns of metaphor, as when in the
age of heroes Vanessa speaks of her own body: 'O, it is
white - white as the gambler's dice - white ivory dice.
Think of the uncertainty. Perhaps a mad child - perhaps a
rascal perhaps a knave - perhaps not, Jonathan. The dice
of the intellect are loaded, but I am the common ivory
dice.'[12] Stella is characterized by the words upon the
window-pane, the heroic couplets of the Age of Reason which
are repeated at the beginning and end of the play within
the play:

> You taught how I might youth prolong
> By knowing what is right and wrong;
> How from my heart to bring supplies
> Of lustre to my fading eyes;
> How soon a beauteous mind repairs
> The loss of chang'd or falling hairs;
> How wit and virtue from within
> Can spread a smoothness o'er the skin.[13]

Even though Yeats did move away from the more decorative
use of metaphor found in his early work, the patterns of
images that occur in his middle and late plays have little
to do with an insistence on Unity of Image in Nō tradition.
In *The Words Upon the Window-Pane*, as elsewhere, Yeats
adapts the more Shakespearean method of recurring images
which reinforce characterization and the structural outline
of the drama. The formal contrast of rhymed decasyllabic
couplets and eighteenth-century diction with the naturalistic

prose and circumstances of the *séance* room is taken from
his own earlier usage, and successfully distinguishes the
antithetical action of the play within the play, as had
the irregularly rhymed octasyllabic couplets of *The Only
Jealousy of Emer*. The ironic counterpoint of the verses
taken from *The Irish Church Hymnal* is also excellently conceived, as is the bathos of Lulu's baby-talk. The orchestration of such rhythms within an ostensibly realistic
and matter-of-fact framework of experience is amazing and
succeeds in providing the play with a pervasive rhythmic
composition while avoiding the mechanical artificiality
and arbitrariness of conventional verse patterns. Stylized
movement has no proper place in *The Words Upon the Window-
Pane*, but neither was it appropriate in *The Resurrection*,
which the later work most closely resembles. On their
very different levels both dramas set out to investigate
the nature of the supernatural and every tenable position
or point of view is represented. In both cases an historical past is invoked as a dramatic contrast, paganism
versus Christianity and contemporary pettiness versus the
heroic possibility of eighteenth-century Ireland. In each,
the supernatural intervenes, radically displacing all prior
assumptions. *The Words Upon the Window-Pane* is a far richer
and more complete treatment of the subject, however, and
provides a wider symbolic context; its climax is far more
theatrical and convincing. Established cultural attitudes
towards the resurrection of Christ limit the possibilities
of that play, while the voices of Vanessa and Jonathan
Swift which come from the mouth of Mrs. Henderson are indeed uncanny, especially so after the intervention of Lulu.
John Corbet's rational explanation reassures the mind, and
we are then riveted by the force of daemonic possession
which transforms the ghostly suggestion of Swift's presence
into a dramatic fact. For the very first time Yeats succeeds in shifting the scene of the action from the stage to
the imagination of the audience, and for a single instant
we know that thought and existence are one and the same.
The mind apprehends the supernatural directly, not its mere
image as in 'the beating heart of a phantom'. Stella's
poem attests to that idea on the level of personal relationships, and Swift's fear of insanity is predicated on
the belief that thought and existence are identical. Within
the play, Yeats extends the doctrine to explain both human

personality and history, and elsewhere makes it the basis
of his artistic and philosophical theories. In much of
his work during this period the coincidence of thought and
existence is shown as being both man's triumph and his despair, the means by which he transcends his human limitation
and by which he destroys himself. Unlike *Calvary*, however,
which balances the two visions, the action of *The Words
Upon the Window-Pane* is singularly tragic, the dice of intellect are loaded and Swift's prayer: 'O God, hear the
prayer of Jonathan Swift that afflicted man, and grant that
he may leave to posterity nothing but his intellect that
came to him from Heaven'[14] is answered by an agonized *cri
de coeur*: 'Perish the day on which I was born!'[15]

    The King of the Great Clock Tower, which was begun in
1933, follows logically on the success of *The Words Upon
the Window-Pane* and represents a rather different attempt
to demonstrate the simultaneity of thought and existence.
The earlier play concentrated on the idea of dreaming-back;
that is, the translation of passionate thought into physical experience, while *The King of the Great Clock Tower*
seeks to translate the aesthetic experience of ritual drama
into the pure thought that it images. Although it was first
written in prose, the play has neither story-line nor secondary conflict which provides dramatic tension, nothing in
fact but a symbolic situation or relationship of characters,
songs and a climactic dance. As soon as it was produced
(30 July 1934), Yeats realized that decorum required the
added dimension of poetry, and he rewrote the text in blank
verse which does provide a more complete sense of aesthetic
multiplicity. The play was still unsatisfactory, however,
and, as in *The Resurrection*, its flaw arises from an over-
simplification of subject matter and composition, which results in a lack of both symbolic depth and dramatic relevance.

    However esoteric the particular interpretation, *The
King of the Great Clock Tower* is essentially a ritual presentation of cyclic renewal, not merely the death of the old
year and birth of the new, nor an analogue of artistic activity as the intersection of natural and metaphysical
states, but rather any such pattern that can be construed
from the mythic cycle of desire, death, inception and regeneration. The ritual image is the dance of destructive
womanhood with the severed head of her would-be lover, the
inevitability of impregnation and the miraculous resurrection of her mate, which derives from the fabled dance

performed by the daughter of Herodias with the head of
John the Baptist. The figure of Salome, whether in the
painting of Gustave Moreau or the drama of Oscar Wilde,
had once been a central image in Decadent art. In his
essay 'Gustave Moreau', as reprinted in *Studies in Seven
Arts*, Arthur Symons translated the following from Huysmans'
A Rebours and commented that in this criticism Moreau's art
culminates, achieves fulfilment and passes into literature:

> In the work of Gustave Moreau, conceived on no scriptural
> data, des Esseintes saw at last the realization of the
> strange, superhuman Salome that he had dreamed. She
> was no more the mere dancing-girl who, with the corrupt
> torsion of her limbs, tears a cry of desire from an old
> man; who, with her eddying breasts, her palpitating body,
> her quivering thighs, breaks the energy, melts the will
> of a king; she had become the symbolic deity of indes-
> tructible Lust, the goddess of immortal Hysteria, the
> accursed Beauty, chosen among many by the catalepsy that
> has stiffened her limbs, that has hardened her muscles;
> the monstrous, indifferent, irresponsible, irresistible,
> insensible Beast, poisoning, like Helen of old, all that
> go near her, all that look upon her, all that she touches

Nor had Wilde's decadent drama, *Salome*, drifted into oblivion
by the end of the nineteenth century; it once again came into
fashion with the revival of poetic theatre and dance drama.
A production had been scheduled at the Festival Theatre for
31 October 1927 with choreography by Ninette de Valois, but
difficulty over censorship arose at the last minute and the
performance never took place. *Salome* was performed privately
at the Festival on 2 June 1929, however, and a production
was mounted by the Gate Theatre, Dublin, at the Peacock on
12 December 1928; it was advertised as the first public performance in either Ireland or Great Britain.[17] During the
1930-1 season at the Gate Theatre, London, which was intimately associated with its Cambridge counterpart:

> Another then unknown actress who made her reputation was
> Margaret Rawlings, who acted in Wilde's *Salome* with a
> cast which also included Flora Robson, Robert Speaight,
> John Clements, Hedley Briggs and Esmond Knight. The
> dances were arranged by Ninette de Valois, settings and
> costumes were by John Armstrong, and the music was com-
> posed by Constant Lambert.[18]

That same production was brought to Cambridge for public
performance on 23 November 1931, and there can be little
doubt that all this activity played some part in the conception of *The King of the Great Clock Tower*. It is even
possible that the Festival production of *Nishikigi* in the
Fenollosa-Pound translation on 20 November 1933 had something to do with Yeats's renewal of interest in ritual
dance drama, as had the Abbey revivals of his earlier dance
plays.

     In any case we do know that Yeats wrote *The King of
the Great Clock Tower* with Ninette de Valois in mind for
the leading role, and that in construction he returned to
the basic simplicity of *At the Hawk's Well*. As in *Words
Upon the Window-Pane*, we have a defensive old man, an aggressive youth and a mysterious female figure, 'Dumb as an
image made of wood or metal,/ A screen between the living
and the dead.'[19] Although the play was written for a dancer and not an actress, a dramatic context for the dance
with severed head was required. The expected opposition
between the two male characters is suppressed, however, for
the King lacks both force of character and representative
significance, existing only for the purpose of exposition
and substituting for the Queen in dialogue with the Stroller when her speeches would have been more effectively
given by one of the attendants. At best, the presence of
the King is a distraction, the symbolism of the Clock Tower
and his prostration before the transfigured Queen an em-
barrassment. In simplifying construction to the point of
eliminating both plot interest and dramatic conflict while
relying wholly on extra-literary modes of production, Yeats
violated the delicate balance of subject matter and method
that he had evolved in the plays for dancers. The relative
success of the earlier dance plays had been a product of
condensation and compression, the assimilation of interrelated themes into a single ritual of exposition whose
objective reality and human relevance was founded in a
known mythology or cultural history and the creation of
intellectual depth through the juxtapositioning of dramatic contexts. The nineteenth-century myth of Salome offered a splendidly theatrical image, but nothing even vaguely
resembling a rational plot, and Yeats was forced to rely on
the internal logic of an alleged prophecy to justify the
dance. The introduction of the Celtic god, Aengus, and
feeble attempts at ironic inversion after the fashion of

The Cat and The Moon or *The Player Queen* seem mere breaches
of decorum and do not help the audience to recognize the
archetypal forces at work. The degraded poet/hero seeks
the semi-divine ideal, substituting his own thought for
its objective existence, and the ideal first appears as
being less than worthy of his desire. In the Queen's dance
with the Stroller's head we recognize that he lives her
death and transcends human limitation as she dies his life
and descends into the human condition, but the image is an
irrelevant gesture; what meaning can all this have for an
audience that does not accept the pre-war posture of aesthetic decadence? However theatrical the image, it lacks
significance, and the half-hearted attempt to associate
the symbolic action of the play with Celtic mythology and
the quest theme of *The Wanderings of Oisin* ultimately fails.
The alternative song for the severed head in the second
version even intensifies the effort to provide a context
or meaning for the action by calling up parallel figures
from Yeats's earlier work, but the correspondences at best
are tenuous, and the allusions more meretricious than
meaningful.

On 11 October 1934 Yeats wrote to a young friend,
Margot Ruddock:

> I am rewriting *The King of the Great Clock Tower* giving
> the Queen a speaking part, that you may act it. I have
> so arranged it that you can give place to a dancer (quite
> easy as you will both wear masks). The old version of
> the play is bad because abstract and incoherent. This
> version is poignant and simple - lyrical dialogue all
> simple.[20]

For whatever reason Yeats actually undertook the task, *A
Full Moon in March* is quite rightly acknowledged to be
far superior to its original, and one can hardly justify
the retention of the earlier version in *Collected Plays*.
The strength of the play's final revision is in the measure
of concreteness and objectivity introduced by the more
elaborate interplay of Queen and Swineherd and in the more
precise language of the whole. The Queen's impregnation
becomes a dramatic fact, for example, and something of her
character or nature is indicated. Indeed, she now bears
a more marked resemblance to the heroine of Mallarmé's
Hérodiade than to that of Wilde's *Salome*, and the relevance

of Yeats's recollection in 'The Tragic Generation' should
be kept in mind:

> I can remember the day in Fountain Court when Symons
> first read me Hérodiade's address to some Sibyl who is
> her nurse and, it may be, the moon also:
>
>> The horror of my virginity
>> Delights me, and I would envelop me
>> In the terror of my tresses, that, by night,
>> Inviolate reptile, I might feel the white
>> And glimmering radiance of thy frozen fire.[21]

The very change of title indicates a characteristic shift
of interest from the action as intersection of a temporal
and ideal world to that of inception and regeneration itself. The Queen is both the accursed beauty, monstrous,
indifferent, irresistible and insensible, and the Full
Moon of March which brings forth the child of the winter
solstice, image of cyclical renewal. The Queen becomes
an active participant in the ritual, desiring to give herself and Kingdom for a song and night of love, while the
Stroller has been recast as a simple Swineherd who desires
both lady and kingship. The dramatic conflict between the
two is immediately recognized as archetypal and is much en-
hanced by the fairy-tale setting. As in *The Cat and the
Moon*, Yeats turned to the psychological inevitability of
folklore and the traditional tale of the cruel or exasper-
ating princess who is constrained to offer herself in
marriage to any man who successfully passes a difficult
test. *A Full Moon in March* seems to follow oriental versions of this theme, and perhaps Yeats had Puccini's
Turandot (1926) in mind; the plot outlines have much in
common, especially the mellowing of the Queen's antagonism
through the steadfastness of love. The action leads naturally and inescapably to the death of the Swineherd and
the recognition of cosmic order in the Queen's dance and
Swineherd's song. As in *At the Hawk's Well*, the masked
characters are purely representative and their interrelationship constitutes the play's meaning; crown of gold and
dung of swine are complementary, for 'Love has pitched his
mansion in/The place of excrement'.[22]

  The antitheses and oppositions, so much a part of
Yeats's dramatic form and meaning, are not necessarily

derived from his knowledge of Nō, yet there is an undoubted
affinity between his usage and Nō tradition, just as there
is a familiar quality about the ready substitution of the
chorus of Attendants for the voices of the protagonists at
the moment of crisis and ecstasy. *A Full Moon in March*
is not the first occasion of this assimilation but it is a
particularly successful example of influence from the classical Japanese theatre. The initial impersonality of the
chorus which creates its own role is perhaps more Piran-
dellian and Modernist in conception, but the Attendants
still function as in the earlier dance plays; to frame and
comment on the independent reality of fictional action,
provide an induction to that reality, and add a sense of
multiplicity to both the action and musical composition.
The verse is, however, undistinguished; Yeats had readily
admitted of *The King of the Great Clock Tower*; 'I have gone
over to the enemy. I say to the musician "Lose my words
in patterns of sound as the name of God is lost in Arabian
arabesques. They are a secret between the singers, myself,
yourself. The plain fable, the plain prose of the dialogue,
Ninette de Valois' dance are there for the audience".'23
The *anima* of *A Full Moon in March* is found in its conception
and structure, the very rhythms of its production and climactic dance. By dividing the action into two scenes Yeats
has closely approximated the form of traditional Nō where
the basic narration is also separated from a scene of transfiguration by the intervention of a choral commentary and
the protagonist's withdrawal from the stage. Because every
element of the drama is subordinated to that final image
and all are closely unified, 'it comes very close to the
enactment of a movement of the sensibility.'24 Like Nō
itself, the play is a meditation, but in this case a meditation on a theme or abstract idea rather than on an emotion or state of being.

Although Yeats had returned to Pater's ideal of lyrical
unity in *A Full Moon in March*, the treatment is uncompro-
misingly modern and where Dectora drifted toward a higher
and vaguely disembodied spiritual encounter in *The Shadowy
Waters*, the Queen and Swineherd find transcendence in the
mundane phenomena of birth and death. Like *The Shadowy
Waters*, *A Full Moon in March* is a human, rather than divine,
drama: 'It condenses the myth of *The Resurrection* and reverses its perspective. No longer is the divine drama -

Virgin and Star, beating heart of Dionysus - given at the
end, a basis in the flaming heart of man. Now the Swineherd's heart itself becomes the Star.'[25] The combination
of dance drama construction, mythic plot of folklore, and
symbolist dance with severed head finally enabled Yeats to
recreate his most fundamental thought as theatrical spectacle, while his success with the material led him to attempt an even more radical design of much wider scope and
complexity in his next play.

The *Herne's Egg* was written in 1935, within a year
of *A Full Moon in March*, and it attempts to gather into a
single unity the major themes and theatrical images that
Yeats had developed over the preceding twenty years. The
basic sources for both action and symbolism have already
been well documented; the vision of continual warfare from
The Stories of Red Hanrahan and *Where There is Nothing/The
Unicorn from the Stars*, the herne as antithetical image
from *Calvary*, the substitution of eggs from an early Yeats
article, 'Bardic Ireland',[26] Congal's ignominious death
at the hands of an idiot from Samuel Ferguson's *Congal*,
and reincarnation as a donkey from Alexandra David-Neel's
With Mystics and Magicians in Tibet.[27] Secondary sources
and influences have been suggested in Spenser and Shelley,
Balzac, Blake and Swedenborg, not to mention Ovid, Plutarch
and a host of others. The play has generated considerable
controversy among critics and even given rise to a certain
amount of spleen but, in fact, it is nothing so incoherent,
esoteric, or unwholesome as has been contended. Within the
limits of the fictional world created, the story-line progresses pretty much according to the logic of cause and
effect, although there are episodes which lie outside the
plot proper and attest to the nature or quality of some
elements within that world rather than further the plot.
The surface action is at least as clear and coherent as
that of any other Yeats play written after 1915, but the
apprehension of its significance and the interpretation
of its symbolism offer difficulties which arise directly
from shifting modes of presentation, the ambiguity of
ironic inversion and arcane imagery. Instead of thematically interrelated incidents or episodes such as those of
Calvary, a unifying plot structure and internal verisimilitude have been imposed on distinctly separate but contig-
uous, symbolic actions: Congal's warfare with Aedh, his
attack on godhead (the theft of the herne's eggs and rape

of Attracta), and the degradation of his fate (ignominious
death at the hands of a Fool and rebirth as a donkey).
The resulting composition is understandably strained.

Juxtaposed with the joke about the two rich fleas who
retired and bought a dog, the ceaseless activity and perfectly balanced conflict of the heroic world which is projected in the first scene suggests an uncreative equilib-
rium, an absurd and unproductive paradise. The point made
is really independent of subsequent action and serves as
a basic condition of existence against which the rest of
the presentation is measured. It could be argued that the
scene is unnecessary to the drama and that unity of action
would be better preserved by foregoing the representation
entirely and merely alluding to the concept later, but the
mimed battle serves as a symbolic curtain raiser, just as
Cuchulain's battle with the sea had done in *Fighting the
Waves*, and also sets the action apart from the everyday
world of the audience through its stylization. The scene
is as much one of direct action as induction, but it does
accomplish the same end as the chorus of musicians in the
dance plays.

The second scene makes a new beginning, and one which
is equally startling, with the appearance of a life-sized
stuffed donkey on wheels, a device which is most probably
taken from classical Indian theatre where toy animals appear on stage and one which had already been exploited by
Brecht in the surrealist and farcical interlude, *Das
Elephantenkalb*, played in the foyer during the interval at
productions of *Mann ist Mann* (1926, 1928 and 1931). The
relation of subsequent action to the heroic battle of the
preceding scene is soon made clear; the herne's eggs sought
by Congal are required for the table of kings, and his
assault on divinity in stealing the sacred eggs is an assertion of his heroic nature. The counterplay of Congal's
association with a donkey is fairly obvious, his quest both
serious and farcical. In asserting his place in the heroic
world, Congal challenges godhead, and his fate is fixed.
Scene II also elaborates on the hero's relationship with
the supernatural through its intermediary, ideal woman, and
Scene III continues the theme. It is not until Scene IV,
however, that we find the outcome of Congal's opposition
to Aedh. Spurred on by drink and honest outrage at the
dishonour of being served a vulgar hen's egg Congal attacks
Aedh with an equally vulgar table-leg and kills him. The

perfect balance of their opposition is now broken and a new
cycle begins. Congal laments:

> I would not have had him die that way
> Or die at all, he should have been immortal.
> Our fifty battles had made us friends;
> And there are fifty more to come.
> New weapons, a new leader will be found
> And everything begin again.[28]

There is more than a hint in all this that through passion
and the intervention of the supernatural, cycles of history and personality are animated, and that the action of
the play comprehends the span of the hero's career from
zenith to nadir, from the consummation of his nature to
the ignominy of his physical death.

The hero's confrontation with the supernatural and his
ultimate degradation derive from his encounter with Attracta,
a type of Woman of the Shidhe (*At the Hawk's Well* and *The
Only Jealousy of Emer*) or Queen (*The Player Queen* and *A
Full Moon in March*). Congal sees her as a mere sexual object and repudiates her presumed relationship with the
Great Herne:

> Women thrown into despair
> By the winter of their virginity
> Take its abominable snow,
> As boys take common snow, and make
> An image of god, or bird or beast
> To feed their sensuality.[29]

Attracta believes that there is no reality but the Great
Herne, and Congal maintains that a sexual encounter with
an old campaigner, such as himself, is the only cure for
everything that woman dreams. He recommends 'Seven men
packed into a day/Or dawdled out through seven years',[30]
and having both committed sacrilege and scoffed at the
curse, he and his six followers give way to three young
girls, followers of Attracta, who enter timidly bearing
symbolic gifts. They talk of the men they will marry and
of the Great Herne, Attracta's lover, until the priestess
falls into a trance and mimes her subordination to the
divine will. The insistence on the number seven is again
intensified in Scenes IV and V, and one is reminded of the

esoteric characters in *The Player Queen*; Septimus, Octema, Nona, and Decima (Una). The fragmentation of Congal into seven and of Attracta into four is most simply explained in terms of the septenary nature of man, a concept fundamental to all mystical/occult systems in the nineteenth and twentieth centuries and elaborated from the Platonic or Pauline division of man's being into body, animal soul, and spiritual soul. Madame Blavatsky's definition of psychic principles is unusually clear:

> The Elements or original essences, the basic differentiations upon and of which all things are built up. We use the term to denote the seven individual and fundamental aspects of the One Universal Reality in Kosmos and in man. Hence also the seven aspects in their manifestation in the human being - divine, spiritual psychic, emotional, astral, psychological and simply physical.[31]

THE SEPTENARY NATURE OF MAN

Lower Quaternary (perishable)

physical body - vehicle of all other 'principles'
                    during life
vital principle - necessary to 'lower quaternary'
astral body - double, phantom body
seat of desire and passion - centre of animal man,
                              mortal versus immortal
                              entity

Upper Triad   (imperishable)

mind/intellect - link between mortality and immortal
                    essences
spiritual soul - vehicle of pure universal spirit
pure spirit - one with Absolute, as its radiation.[32]

The interpretation is also borne out to some extent in Congal's pronouncement of the rape:

> I name the seven: Congal of Tara
> Patrick, Malachi, Mike, John, James,
> And that course hulk of clay, Mathias.[33]

In battle Congal was poised in perfect balance with his
opposite. In quest of the supernatural, however, he defeated Aedh and became High King. The object of desire,
the cosmic egg, also proves to be the egg of discord. In
further pursuit of the supernatural through intercourse
with Attracta, Congal becomes the consummate hero and completed man who has realized his full spiritual potential.
It is not so much that he elevates himself through union
with her, as in the relationship of Swineherd and Queen in
A Full Moon in March, but rather that he imitates divinity
in fulfilling her physical desire, for Attracta, as her
name suggests, presides over the lower principles of animal nature. The speeches of passion and desire in Scene
II bespeak her nature, and her attendants bring gifts of
cream, butter and hen's eggs which both reinforce the idea
of generation and represent the role of Kate, Mary, and
Agnes as *astral*, *vital*, and *physical principles*. Intercourse is natural and necessary between Attracta and the
septenary nature of man because in its own being, godhead
is excluded from physical intercourse with man; a physical
manifestation or metaphor is necessary for the literal
minded, such as the miraculous gold of Danae, Leda's swan,
and the star-shot ear of the Virgin Mary. In *The Herne's
Egg* Congal, in his seven individual aspects, represents
the One Universal Reality in man while the Great Herne
represents that Reality in Kosmos. The incorporality of
the Great Herne had already been imaged in the curious
third scene where Congal and his soldiers vainly try to
stone the god who flies well within their range, before
they give up their arms altogether on entering Tara. As
in Scene I, the action is quite extraneous to the plot and
the abrupt switch to poetic suprapositioning coupled with
such esoteric symbolism is disconcerting. A valid point is
made, nevertheless: 'He is god and out of reach',[34] but
the structure and force of the play is seriously flawed.
Yeats retained the scene because of its bearing on Attracta's denial that the seven men had made love to her. Thrice
the thunder affirms the irrationality of her assertion, but
rather than being faced with an insoluble paradox, we understand that the seven men constitute the corporeal manifestation of godhead and that Attracta had known divinity,
however mistaken she may have been as to its outward form.
The central truth of the ritual drama is also clear: the

interplay of desire and fulfilment animates the universe.
Congal comments:

> We all complete a task or circle,
> Want a woman, then all goes - pff.[35]

To a certain extent, Congal is Cuchulain grown old,
the confirmed hero who has completed his task or cycle and
prepares to find release from the human condition. The
central situation of *At the Hawk's Well* is Cuchulain's
quest for the miraculous water and his frustrated pursuit
of the intermediary, the Guardian of the Well, who is possessed by the Hawk-Goddess. In the later play Congal seeks
the sacred eggs and rapes the intermediary in his septenary
being, himself the incarnation of godhead which is also
symbolized by the Great Herne. Like the Christ of *Calvary*,
Congal is the perfected hero who must experience the completed cycle of human existence to its bitter end in a
sordid death before rising again as pure spirit, at one
with the Absolute. Congal is both subjective and objective
hero, however, and the intersecting forces of his dual nature are represented by the several themes and actions of
the play. He masters physical existence as well as perfecting his higher faculties, and redeems animal nature
through intercourse with Attracta. The rhetorical question,
'Was I the woman lying there?'[36] implies a negative response; intercourse with the supernatural is transfiguring,
and Attracta has been elevated by her intimacy with godhead. Now that his task or cycle is complete, Congal
accepts the fate ordained by the laws of universal existence, without necessarily understanding those laws, and
prepares to face the consequence of his actions much as
Cuchulain had done at the end of *The Green Helmet*.
The play's final scene elaborates a third independent
image or thematic preoccupation in presenting the death of
the Hero. Although wounded by Tom the Fool who had been
offered a purse of pennies as incentive to kill the king,
Congal kills himself and cries out to the Great Herne:

> Your chosen kitchen spit has killed me,
> But killed me at my own will, not yours.[37]

In both Fool and Hero there is an echo of Judas as he appeared in *Calvary*, and the correspondence between Christ's

death and Congal's is made even more obvious. Instead of
succumbing to despair, however, Congal dies asserting his
independence of god's choice, but his victory over the
Great Herne is balanced by the identification of the Hero
as Fool and the fulfilment of Attracta's curse. It is
inevitable that Congal should die at the hands of a Fool,
whether his own or Tom's, and the Fool's role as counterpart to that of the Hero is a familiar concept from *The
Hour-Glass* and *On Baile's Strand*. The hero progresses
towards his apotheosis only when he plays the Fool, and
nothing can be so foolish, or so heroic as to challenge
godhead itself. The correspondence with the antithetical
death of Christ is also emphasized in the ritual presence
of elemental symbols derived from Celtic mythology; the
cauldron lid, cooking-pot, spit and stone that are carried
in by the Fool. Like the seamless garment of Christ for
which the Roman Soldiers cast dice, mystical/occult tradition interpreted the shield, crater, spear, and stone as
the fabric of physical creation, the four basic elements.
The esoteric symbols had figured largely in the intensely
serious poetry of Yeats's youth, and through their correspondences with the suits of the Tarot cards, they appear in
'The Death of Hanrahan' as Pleasure, Power, Courage and
Knowledge. In the stylized and comic action of *The Herne's
Egg*, on the other hand, the debased images are also used to
characterize a kind of Fool. In keeping with Yeats's ironic
inversions throughout, the humble kitchen spit, rather than
the heroic spear, serves as the instrument of the Hero's
death, but as in the earlier comedies, the farcical nature
of the situation is an integral part of the play's meaning
and in no way diminishes the force of the action. On the
contrary, chance and choice, significance and absurdity,
high seriousness and humour are all equally a part of the
universal scheme, and the comic inversions also contribute
to the aesthetic composition of the play by creating ambig-
uities and paradoxes that engage the imagination of the
audience. High-spirited nonsense lends vitality to otherwise dull and obscure material, while conscious contradictions and unresolved action add levels of intellectual
depth by suggesting the widest possible associations and
engaging the imagination of the audience to unravel a consistent interpretation. Perhaps the clearest example of
this usage is found in the circumstances of the characteristic turn Yeats gives the ending of the play. In

pronouncing the Great Herne's curse upon Congal for his
sacrilege, Attracta indicated that Congal deserved to be
reborn an animal, but out of pity she takes upon herself
the donkey-herd in order to produce a human body for Congal's
soul. The donkey-herd and priestess undertake the divine
act of creation, just as the Swineherd and Queen of *A Full
Moon in March* had done, but they are attempting to inter-
fere with choice and chance rather than celebrate the law
of universal order. There is no surprise when the braying
of a donkey interrupts them, announcing the accomplishment
of fate and reasserting natural chance as it had done in
The Player Queen. The logical assumption is that Congal
is to be reborn an ass, but the play's final speech further
qualifies the event:

> Corney. I have heard that a donkey carries its young
> Longer than any other beast,
> Thirteen months it must carry it.
>   *He laughs*
> All that trouble and nothing to show for it,
> Nothing but just another donkey.[38]

Since the thirteenth sphere or cycle usually represents a
state of pure spiritual reality outside temporal limitations,
one might well read the last two lines as irony and recognize the implication that Congal's reincarnation as a rough
beast will inaugurate another era, a new dispensation. Just
as the Hero rebels against the High King and usurps his
throne, he also assaults an antithetical image of godhead
(bird) and is himself transformed into its primary image
(beast). The seeming absurdity of human existence and universal order is exploded through the contemplation of its
exact opposite.

Certainly *The Herne's Egg* constitutes the most complex
and complete metaphor for theatre that Yeats ever attempted.
It fails for a number of reasons, particularly through obscurity of subject matter and constructional uncertainty, but
the failure is impressive. The material is neither so
thoroughly assimilated nor so clearly expressed as it might
be, but one must remember that much of Yeats's pleasure in
it was private and personal. It was written, he tells us,
'in the happier moments of a long illness that had so separated me from life that I felt irresponsible.'[39] The play'
strength and its importance in the development of modern

drama is derived from precisely that mood of gaiety and
abandon which bespeaks both an apprehension of, and delight
in, the absurdity of the human condition. The very detachment of its vision is an exact counterpart to the dispass-
ionate, cold eye Yeats would cast on both life and death,
and it is much better suited to the modern temper than his
earlier tonal range. His inversions and parodies of ideal
existence should be recognized as an important stage in the
development of anti-heroic theatre, and it is not surprising
that of all his work, *The Herne's Egg* should have been chosen for translation in the *Compagnie Madeleine Renaud
Cahiers*. Although Yeats always insisted on the existence
of meaning and purpose in the universe, regardless of the
absurdity and suffering of the human condition, his methods
of poetic composition and stage presentation have influenced
the recent flowering of the Theatre of the Absurd.

Among the more impressive achievements of *The Herne's Egg*
are the subtlety and inclusiveness of theatrical images and
the renewed excellence of the poetic texture. The evocation
of eternal conflict, aggressive sexuality, and ritual death/
rebirth are so wrought as to capture something of the intended infinity of connotations and interrelationships, while
the lyric intensity of modern speech idiom is reasserted
after the evident failure of *The King of the Great Clock
Tower* and *A Full Moon in March*. As to direct influence from
the Japanese Nō, there is little comment to be made. Attracta does sing at the climax of the action, 'When I take a
beast to my joyful breast', instead of acting out the rape,
and there are many other occasions for dance-mime and stylized gesture, but the usage is closer to western tradition
than to the Japanese in that such action is expository
rather than climactic. The play requires neither chorus nor
masks, and because of the complexity of the action and size
of cast, performance in a drawing-room or studio would be
impractical. Rather than finding its origins in the Nō
itself, *The Herne's Egg* is a further experiment with dramatic form and production method already established in *The
Cat and the Moon* and *The Player Queen*, *At the Hawk's Well*
(via *A Full Moon in March*) and *Calvary*. In the first instance, there is the comic vision of human absurdity achieved
through conscious irony, contradiction and paradox; in the
second, the symbolic design of character; and in the third,
action along with a poetic suprapositioning of image clus-
ters and episodes which leads to the rhythmic structure of
lyric composition.

The Death of Cuchulain was begun in 1938, the same
year in which *Purgatory* was written, and represents a return to the original form of the dance plays. Because of
its obvious affinities with *The Herne's Egg*, however, I
should prefer to discuss it first. Although *The Death of
Cuchulain* is based on the traditional tale of the hero's
enchantment by Queen Maeve and his end at the hands of
her troops, the action is concerned with thematic material
derived from the earlier plays for dancers. In fact, the
work might even be taken as a thorough revision of *The
Herne's Egg*, and one which loses as much in vitality and
force as it gains in clarity of construction, while the
same obscurity of symbolism obtains and beclouds its
meaning. Again, we have the familiar images of vain battle,
vain love and vain repose which had persisted in Yeats's
writing since the publication of *The Wanderings of Oisin*,
and the play divides itself into three distinct images;
Cuchulain's encounter with his mistress, the battle with
Maeve which includes his ignominious death and the dance
with his severed head. Although the separate encounters
and the theme of death recall the construction of *Calvary*,
the characters of the first scene (Eithne Inguba and Emer,
Maeve and the Morrigu) are derived from the symbolic representations of *The Only Jealousy of Emer*. Cuchulain is
now faced with alternative courses of action recommended
by Eithne Inguba and Emer, but Eithne Inguba is seen to be
under Maeve's enchantment and only released through the
intervention of the supernatural Morrigu, goddess of war.
Not knowing which report to believe, Cuchulain's instinctive choice is to engage in battle before reinforcements
arrive. Like the Queen of *A Full Moon in March* he proclaims
'I make the truth',[40] but in fact his will and ordained
fate coincide: he goes to his death.

The opening situation of the second scene reverses
the action of *At the Hawk's Well*; the ageing Cuchulain
finds momentary refuge and support at the pillar-stone by
the magical pool after receiving six mortal wounds in the
battle with the forces of Maeve, whereas the younger hero
of the earlier work had been denied regeneration and supernatural inspiration at the dry well beneath the barren
trees. Aoife appears, stating that she has come to kill
him, presumably in revenge for her son's death and her own
submission to him so many years before, but her presence

is only required in order that the past may be rehearsed and the implications of the immediate present made clear. Her complete meaninglessness as a dramatic character is accented by the woefully inadequate invention of her last speech:

> Somebody comes,
> Some countryman, and when he finds you here,
> And none to protect him, will be terrified.
> I will keep out of his sight, for I have things
> That I must ask questions on before I kill you.[41]

Rather than appearing as a stunning reversal, the Blind Man who enters and actually does kill Cuchulain is immediately recognized by the audience as the rightful agent of fate, and by contrast, the appearance of Aoife seems even more absurd and unnecessary than before. In recalling that he had stood between a Fool and the sea at Baile's Strand, the Blind Man raises associations of the conflict between prudent reason and instinctive action, the body and the spirit, which had informed *On Baile's Strand*. In *The Death of Cuchulain* the Blind Man is also associated with Judas, as was the Fool in *The Herne's Egg*; the purse offered for the head of the hero is now specifically twelve pennies, and Cuchulain, like Christ (and Congal), must die man's death in order to fulfill his cosmic *ethos*.

The final scene is indeed startling, it is also characteristic of Yeatsian method in its continuation of the action beyond the death of the hero and its ultimate reversal of audience expectation. The sibylline speech of the Morrigu is meant as a gloss on the symbolism of Cuchulain's character as well as the esoteric meaning of the action, and Emer's dance with the hero's severed head mimes her apprehension of that symbolism just as the Queen of *A Full Moon in March* danced out her recognition of miraculous regeneration. The final commentary by the chorus of street-singers, who may have been inspired by Jarry's usage in *Ubu roi*, expands the focus of our understanding and relates the mythic ritual to the wider reality of history and Irish nationalism. The appearance of the crowheaded goddess of war with a black parallelogram representing Cuchulain's head is an obvious symbol of the hero's inevitable defeat in his battle with human existence;

her utterance and the other parallelograms refer to the
elements in the septenary nature of man which had been
reflected in *The Herne's Egg* by Congal and his six followers. Cuchulain, like Congal, dies at his own hand in
the sense that the Blind Man is as much a projection of
his dual nature as is the Fool, and with that last act
Cuchulain fulfills his own destiny, completes his being and
dies in the body as a prelude to rebirth in the spirit.
The correspondences between the Morrigu's identification
of six 'men' and Madame Blavatsky's definitions are exact;
the youthful lover is the *physical body*, and the *vital
principle* in intercourse with Maeve, or the ideal and
semi-divine woman, gives birth to both *phantom double* and
the *desire* or *passion* of mortal man. The men of no account
are *intellect* and *spiritual principles* which have no bearing on the life of the body; it is only the degradation of
physical death that Cuchulain experiences.

> This head is great Cuchulain's, those other six
> Gave him six mortal wounds. This man came first,
> Youth lingered though the years ran on, that season
> A woman loves the best. Maeve's latest lover,
> This man, had given him the second wound,
> He had passed her once; these were her sons,
> Two valiant men that gave the third and fourth:
> These other men were men of no account,
> They saw that he was weakening and crept in;
> One gave him the sixth wound and one the fifth.[42]

The wounds are the progressive stages towards that death,
and in another sense, stages towards the realization of
higher faculties and rebirth. In her dance, Emer rages
against Cuchulain's progressive decline as physical man
and also celebrates the triumph of pure spirit, the consummation of being, realized by the hero, and the final
note is the apocryphal song of the bird into whose soft,
feathery shape Cuchulain's soul has returned. The mime
itself is another version of the dance performed with
severed head in both *The King of the Great Clock Tower*
and *A Full Moon in March*, but the inspiration and stylized
symbols are more probably taken directly from the Fenollosa-
Pound synopsis of *Koi no Omoni* (The Burden of Love).

From the very first the burden of love lay in the centre
front of the stage, thus 'becoming actually one of the
characters'. It was a cube done up in red and gold
brocado and tied with green cords . . . The lady sat
at the right corner, immobile, rather the lover's image
of his mistress than a living being. He sings, com-
plains, and tries several times to lift the burden, but
cannot. The court officer sits a little toward the
right-back. Shasi dies and passes out. The officer
addresses the lady, who suddenly seems to come to life.
She listens, then leaves her seat, half-kneels near the
burden, her face set silently and immovably toward it.
This is more graphic and impressive than can well be
imagined. All leave the stage save this silent figure
contemplating the burden.[43]

Whether it is conscious or not, the construction of
The Death of Cuchulain is the most Nō-like of all Yeats's
plays. The action progresses through an alternation of
narration and meditation, rising to a medial climax, and
after an interval renews itself in a brief scene of contrasting mood and tempo which is dominated by a symbolic
dance. Certainly the reliance on a known mythic cycle
and constant references to prior action which is familiar
from earlier treatment by Yeats, provides a richness of
texture that is very reminiscent of Nō and a marked improvement on the arbitrary fancy of his more recent work.
There are no masks, however, and stage directions indicate
blackouts for scene changes which not only suggest conventional stage production but also introduce an element of
illusionism which might well deny the aesthetic distance
implied in ritualized action. The scenes themselves are
not only clearly marked and cleanly juxtaposed, but they
show a distinct improvement in symbolic design over the
confusion of *The Herne's Egg*. Although still perhaps rather
fussy, the first scene is a far more accessible and intelligible projection of Cuchulain's human limitation in coming
to terms with the opposing elements of his own personality
(Will and Mask, Body of Fate and Creative Mind) than *The
Only Jealousy of Emer*, and the symbolism is very well integrated with subsequent action. Eithne Inguba and Maeve,
the natural and supernatural counterparts of physical being,
defeat Emer and the Morrigu, counterparts of spiritual
existence, who foresee Cuchulain's death. Discord and

prophecy play as much a part in this episode as they had
in delineating the inevitability of the hero's fate in
The Herne's Egg. The awkwardness of Aoife's appearance in
the second scene is really a product of Yeats's insistence
on realistic circumstance and could easily have been avoided.
Having conceived a scene which both symbolized the archetypal principle that governs man's existence and discloses
realistic motivation for Cuchulain's folly in fighting
against impossible odds, Yeats is impelled directly to the
scene of battle. There is no natural way to bring in
Aoife and the memory of her enmity towards Cuchulain as
presented in the action of *At the Hawk's Well* and *On
Baile's Strand*. A possible solution might have been to
follow the prototype of *Calvary* more closely and recast
the whole from the point of view of the dying hero tied to
the pillar-stone who relives in quasi-vision the three encounters; Aoife, Eithne Inguba and the Blind Man. The
movement from dream to reality would be particularly fe-
licitous in underlining the detachment from physical existence that characterizes the action of the play. As the
play reads, however, Cuchulain is so separated from life
and his proper self that he mistakes Eithne Inguba's action for treason, but forgives it, and cannot understand
Aoife's recreation of the past. It is interesting to note
that the added detail of her youthful desire for him and
voluntary submission in the face of his disinterest reit-
erates the central situation of *A Full Moon in March*, and
coincides with the passions and desire that Cuchulain
arouses in each of the other female figures of the play.

Following the developed form of the plays for dancers,
the choruses encapsulate the action of the piece and also
comment upon it, but they are more closely related to the
action and imagery of the drama than in any other Yeats
play. The identification of personages from the chorus
with characters was first attempted in *On Baile's Strand*,
but not repeated until the appearance of the young man
and elderly woman who sing the lyrics of the protagonists
whom they approximate in *A Full Moon in March*. In *The
Death of Cuchulain* the Old Man who delivers the prologue
is so detached from life that he no longer remembers the
name of his father and mother, and he acts as a counterpart
to Cuchulain in the refined fire of his passion which out-
lasts both physical strength and vigour of mind. The comic

spectacle of the furious Old Man whose criticism of both
modern life and naturalistic art establishes a frame of
reference for the audience, gives the play a brilliant
opening and parallels the ironic inversion of the Blind
Man who slays the hero. The Old Man of the prologue aptly
makes the point that on the present occasion the audience
'must know the old epics and Mr. Yeats' plays about them',[44]
but even though the admission applies to almost all of his
work for theatre after 1915, it does not provide much help
in understanding either action or symbolism. The plays
for dancers and those later works based upon them rarely
provide enough dramatic context to render them significant,
at least not without reference to associations and parallels
in other plays. The Blind Old Beggarman who sets out to
kill Cuchulain, for example, is yet another type of uncomprehending figure, but one whose closeness to death had not
separated him from physical existence, for he is very keen
indeed on the twelve pennies, on keeping body and soul
together. His function as the agent of Cuchulain's death
is easily recognized as an inversion of heroic order, but
the richness of the invention and of its philosophical
potential is only realized in contrast with the Blind Man's
character as he appears in *On Baile's Strand*, and with the
Fool who wounds Congal in *The Herne's Egg*. The ultimate
irony is that prudence itself, which teaches preservation
of the body, destroys the heroic world, just as the joyful
spontaneity of instinctive action accomplishes the same
end. It is altogether fitting that the Blind Man should
use the knife with which he cuts his meat to kill the hero,
just as the Fool of *The Herne's Egg* had used a kitchen spit,
for *The Death of Cuchulain* is not so much a play about the
death of the hero as it is about the death of the body, the
death of man. The Morrigu's speech in the last scene certainly confirms the point, and her *ex cathedra* commentary
does function as a kind of medial chorus. The song of the
common street singer after Cuchulain's apotheosis is elec-
trifyingly theatrical in its contrast of mood and tone, but
again the irony is only textural, and the lyrics serve a
serious purpose in relating the action of the play to the
contemporary scene in Ireland. Instead of queen and hero,
the degraded times offer harlot and beggarman as representative types and, in commenting on the loss of heroic stature, they again raise the main issue of the drama; is

physical existence the sole reality? Of course, the answer
is no; the contemplation of the actual, as in the heroic
gesture of Pearse and Connolly, recognizes the presence of
the archetype, and the heroic form in physical life is as
nothing by comparison with a carving in stone, the transience
and limitations of the physical being compared with a mon-
ument of art, an image of unageing intellect.

However successfully Yeats dealt with the problems of
subject matter and presentation in *The Death of Cuchulain*,
it remains that the doctrine is rather dry fare and the
surface action has little or no interest in its own right.
The opening and closing choruses do contribute a certain
liveliness and a wider point of view, but the ever-present
farce of *The Herne's Egg* was more effective in engaging the
imagination and arousing intellectual curiosity. As literature, on the other hand, *The Death of Cuchulain* is among
the best of Yeats's anti-realistic plays, but the merging
of naturalistic surface action and symbolist design, as in
The Words Upon the Window-Pane, had inevitably proved much
more successful with the public.

In its preoccupation with emblematic patterns of universal order centred on violent conflict and sexuality, which
link temporal to supernatural being, *Purgatory* is very closely
related to the other plays of Yeats's last phase. The surface action is immediately accessible; so much so, in fact,
that the mythic patterns represented are often overlooked,
and the conclusion is sometimes seen as a contradiction
rather than an inevitable outcome. As is always the case
in Yeats's drama, the characters are primarily particular-
izations of archetypal forces or states of being, and in
Purgatory the action opens with yet another permutation
on the symbolic design of *At the Hawk's Well*. Instead of
young hero, sterile old sage, and semi-divine woman beside
a withered tree and dry well, we have a loutish youth, degraded old tinker, and ghostly lovers in company with a
blasted tree and ruined manor house. Rather than a quest
for supernatural control of the physical universe, the Old
Man of *Purgatory* merely relives past events, but shares
with the youthful Cuchulain the heroic (foolish?) determin-
ation to influence fate; the inescapable tragedy is not so
much his as it is that of the human condition. The story
of the young gentlewoman and the common groom is an ingenious
image of the Queen-Swineherd relationship which represents

the primordial attraction that animates the universe, and
is equally valid as an explanation of historical and national
development. Another aspect of that central myth is shown,
however, and instead of the miraculous resurrection of the
hero, we have the degradation of spiritual being: 'A song -
the night of love / An ignorant forest and the dung of
swine'.45 The Old Man is 'just another donkey', born of
the natural attraction between a well-born girl and a
stable hand, but with no higher faculty tempering their
purely physical desire. The girl's choice mirrors that
of Queen rather than Aoife and approximates that of Cuchulain in both *The Only Jealousy of Emer* and *The Death of
Cuchulain*. In the context of destroying an aristocratic
tradition of refinement and taste as symbolized by the
great house, the action also becomes a paradigm for the
loss of heroic values and the present vulgarity in contemporary Ireland. At the age of sixteen the Old Man had
murdered his father who drunkenly burned down the house,
in retaliation for the insults and indignities suffered
by himself and his mother, and the event is an inversion
of the revenge Aoife's son sought in his heroic fight with
Cuchulain. In characteristic fashion the intervention of
the supernatural precipitates crisis, and the vision of his
mother's ghost reliving her passion induces the Old Man to
murder his loutish son in order to end the consequences of
her act. Again the circumstances of *On Baile's Strand* are
rehearsed in a diminished and inverted form; unknowingly
Cuchulain put an end to his own line and so to heroic tradition, while the Old Man's conscious effort to end the consequences of human frailty prove futile. The conventional
horror of murdering both one's father and son is, in Yeats's
mind, belittled by the horror of man's incarnate state, the
inevitable defeat of both hero and beggarman in the struggle
with human existence. Even the white ivory dice of the
body are loaded, and the Old Man's prayer echoes the anguish
of Jonathan Swift in *The Words Upon the Window-Pane:*

                              O God,
Release my mother's soul from its dream!
Mankind can do no more. Appease
The misery of the living and the remorse of the dead.46

    The ghostly apparition of the lovers' night is directly
assimilated from *Nishikigi*, rather than coming by way of

The Dreaming of the Bones: the description of the grave-
mound as seen by the travelling priests in the Fenollosa-
Pound translation is much to the point:

> Strange, what seemed so very old a cave
> Is all glittering-bright within,
> Like the flicker of fire,
> It is like the inside of a house,
> They are setting up a loom,
> And heaping up charm-sticks, No
> The hangings are out of old time.
> Is it illusion, illusion?[47]

The lovers in *Nishikigi*, however, are ultimately freed from
their remorse and their futile recreation of the past, but
such can never be the case in Yeats's bleak vision of human
existence with neither heroic nor spiritual aspiration.
Apart from the ghost scene itself, there are no other direct
influences from the Nō, but to assume that this particular
drama is solely derived from earlier assimilations of the
dance plays is to exaggerate the case somewhat. A comparison of *Purgatory* with Lord Dunsany's *The Glittering Gate*
(1909), for example, reveals its close kinship to the early
peasant drama which had inaugurated the Abbey Theatre, even
to the point of construction and absurdist content, but it
is true that in *Purgatory* Yeats did incorporate echoes of
imagery and thematic treatment from much of his work after
1915. In addition to those already mentioned there are also
repetitions such as the exclamation of the Boy on seeing the
ghost of his grandfather: 'A dead, living, murdered man!'[48]
which recalls the recognition of the irrational in *The
Resurrection*; 'The heart of a phantom is beating!'[49] Echoes
of *The Herne's Egg* and *The Death of Cuchulain*, not to mention
their antecedents, are present in the bag of money over
which the Boy and Old Man quarrel, as well as in the jack-
knife which the protagonist used to cut his dinner and to
murder both father and son. In fact, the only original
image invented for *Purgatory* is the 'cold, sweet, glisten-
ing light'[50] that bathes the riven tree and represents the
ideal; a purified state of ultimate detachment from human
passion such as that suggested in the death of Congal and
Cuchulain. As in *The Dreaming of the Bones*, however, the
consequences of the original wrong persist, and until they
dissipate themselves naturally and in the fullness of time.
the remorse of the dead cannot be appeased.

Critics have acclaimed *Purgatory* for its amazing compression and clean outline, but one suspects that much of
its appeal, like that of *On Baile's Strand*, *The Resurrection*, or *Words Upon the Window-Pane* lies in its immediate
accessibility and recourse to the naturalistic techniques
of Renaissance forms. The real strength of *Purgatory*, on
the other hand, lies in its unobtrusive poetic quality, the
harmony of realistic subject matter and symbolist design
within a lyrical composition of undoubted concentration and
power. To some extent I have already tried to suggest something of the balance between surface reality and symbolist
readings, while its lyrical composition is also a feature
with close affinities to Yeats's earlier assimilations from
the Nō. In keeping with his essentially naturalistic
plot Yeats dispensed with anti-illusionistic techniques
such as chorus, song, mask, and mime or dance. Instead of
contrasting voice patterns, he unified the action with a
freely varied verse form in iambic tetrameters which is
admirably suited to the terse, sharp idiom of modern speech.
The most remarkable feature of this very natural verse form
is its ability to reflect emotional intensification as the
rising dramatic action moves through contrast and reversal
to its inevitable climax. More than in any of the preceding plays the verse of *Purgatory* acts as an organizing
principle for the various symbols and character relationships, focusing attention on aesthetic movement and image
pattern rather than on surface action and character motivation. The image of the riven tree and ruined house, the
conflict between Old Man and Boy (past and present) is juxtaposed with the dumb show of the ghostly apparition, and
a higher reality is imagined in the transfigured tree, even
though human action cannot affect it and fate must work itself out. The irrational apparition and the degradation
of the human condition themselves constitute a mythic pattern of wonder, ecstasy and woe which informs the essential
cycle and movement of the whole.

The words with which Ronald Peacock assessed the
achievement of Hugo von Hofmannsthal are curiously relevant
to Yeats's later plays and particularly to *Purgatory*:

His sense of the collaboration of the arts in the theatre
is more than aesthetic discrimination. It is a profound
sense of ritual, cult, liturgy and festival, which have
always, both in primitive and enlightened religions,

used the various arts in combination to one end. The
unity of his whole conception of a composite art depends
on his consciousness of the ritualistic foundations of
the theatre, of the festivals of popular and religious
life, of the theatre as the conscious stylization of
the natural drama of life lived between the human and
the divine. The discovery of theatre is the discovery
of the deepest continuities in human life, the discovery
of symbols that express total human community.[51]

The success of Yeats's symbolic designs lay in the refash-
ioning of traditional images and creating dynamic *personae*
that adequately expressed the inward drama of man's physical and spiritual nature.

Take anything you will - theatre as speech or a man's
body - and develop its emotional expressiveness, and
you at once increase its power of suggestion and take
away from its power of mimicry or of stating facts.
The body begins to take poses or even moves in a dance . .
Speech becomes rhythmical, full of suggestion, and as
this change takes place we begin to possess, instead
of the real world of the mimics, solitudes and wilder-
nesses peopled by divinities and daimons, vast senti-
ments, the desires of the heart cast forth into forms,
mythological being, a frenzied parturition.[52]

It is an accepted commonplace of criticism to say that
Yeats developed a drama of evocation rather than exposition,
but the singular interrelationship of metaphysical conception, symbolic design and anti-illusionist staging that
animates his work is best particularized as a product of
conscious assimilation and development from the Japanese
Nō. The measure of Yeats's genius, however, is found in
the creation of an expressive and virile lyricism, a technical accomplishment which harmonizes theme, incident and
method of presentation into a rhythmic unity and calls
attention to itself in the progressive shifts from the
early work of narrative ballad meter and blank verse to
the conscious counterpoint of blank verse and brief lyrics
in the later plays. The confirmation of his genius rests
in the establishment of post-dramatic theatre, 'theatre in
which the individual recognized the evocative power of the

play, and opened himself to imaginative experience, as
distinct from the traffic of the stage.'[53]

Unfortunately, the fact that the action of Yeats's
drama takes place only in the imagination of the audience
accounts for both its artistic strength and its popular
failure. Had Yeats's aesthetic theory and actual practice
been unimpeachable, in fact, it would still remain that
his spectators lacked sympathy for his subject matter and
personal view of universal order. It is is true that
'the history of the drama is the history of interaction
between the author's imagination, the actor's skill and
the spectator's expectation', and that 'the conjunction
of all these issues from and evokes an inner drama that
is played by each of the actors and each member of the
audience',[54] then it follows that Yeats's flaw as a dramatist lay in his failure to meet the expectations of the
spectator. Even the more naturalistic plays, those which
are reasonably accessible and quite well received by
modern audiences, have never enjoyed actual popularity
because of their mystical/occult underpinnings and associations, yet the image of tramp or beggar-man as a representation of the modern predicament has recently become
a great success, and Yeats's ideal of lyrical construction
has been widely accepted and imitated. It is true that
absurdist drama has emphasized the representation of real
and contemporary human experience, but this has been accomplished through anti-illusionist staging, suprapositioning
of images, ironic inversions, and softening of the sharp
and artificial edges of verse forms to a more familiar and
comfortable poetic prose. Where Yeats evoked an inner
truth that was speculative and spiritual, contemporary
dramatists prefer to reflect a subjective reality that is
relevant and psychological.

Actually, the progress of Yeats's career as a dramatist did approach the contemporary view of man's unprotec-
ted situation in a hostile universe, and in those plays
which consider the nature of the human condition rather
than project a spiritual or heroic aspiration, we find a
growing disillusionment and despair. From an early celebration of the ideal he moved to the recognition of a re-
deeming heroism in the face of man's inevitable defeat and
finally to a definite affirmation of comic disorder as the
only meaningful gesture with which to confront the absurdity

and horror of man's existence in the flesh. Even the
tragedy of *Purgatory* is not so much personal as it is
ritualized. The turning-point in Yeats's development
as a dramatist was the discovery of the Japanese Nō,
which provided the germ of a new theoretical outlook
and technical accomplishment, made possible the full
expression of his perennial themes, and eventually led
to a new concept of theatre.

Appendix

The following notes in outline form cover a full range of technical details involved in the performance of Nō; information has been indented in descending order of importance and application.

   I.   Classification of Plays

  II.   Composition of Nō Programme

 III.   Literary and Musical Structure

  IV.   Styles of Chanting

   V.   Tone Systems

  VI.   Dance Forms

I. *CLASSIFICATION OF PLAYS*

A. By Subject-Matter

   1. *Kami Nō*: god play
      mythology, origins of shrines, etc.

   2. *Shūgen Nō*: congratulatory play
      celebration of historical event or legend

   3. *Mūgen Nō*: apparition play
      ghost or spirit relives prior experience

   4. *Genzai Nō*: realistic play
      immediate action, not recollection of incident
      portrayal of human passion and present life

B. By *Shite* Role

    1.   Shinto and Buddhist deities

    2.   Ghosts of men and women

    3.   Living men and women

    4.   Spirits of vegetative world and animals

    5.   Devils and lower spirits

C. By Quality of Emotional Experience Portrayed

    1.   *Shūgen*: joy and happiness

    2.   *Yūgen*:   refinement and elegance

    3.   *Rembo*:   love and attachment

    4.   *Aishō*:   sadness and lament

    5.   *Rengyoku*: the sublime[1]

II. *COMPOSITION OF NŌ PROGRAMME*

A. *Kami Nō (Waki Nō)*: God Play
    leisurely and dignified tempo
    mood or atmosphere of benediction or rejoicing
      force or grace may also be accented
    true *mai* style is normal (see VI. *Dance Forms*, below)
      even when *hataraki* is performed

    subdivisions:

    1. *kami-mai* of noble young god

    2. *hataraki* of fierce deity

    3. *gaku* of ugly, aged god

    4. solemn *shin no jo no mai* of aged god

    5. graceful *chū no mai* of beautiful goddess

B. *Shura-mono (Otoko-mono)*: Warrior (man) piece
    general mood best described as stirring
    normally recounts great defeat
      or tragic death of young prince or old warrior
    suffering controlled by refinement and elegance
    calculated to soften stern hearts of warrior class
    directs attention of spiritual quality of life
    kakeri is often performed

C. *Kazura-mono (Onna-mono)*: Wig (woman) piece
   said to embody the very soul of Nō
   noted for restraint, quiet elegance and lyric beauty
   celebrates love and attachment
   a preliminary dance sequence is normal
   subdivisions:

   1. *kagura* of goddess

   2. woman dancing out delicate emotions or predicament
      or a broken old woman recalling her youth

   3. female spirit figure of animist belief
      or male spirit-figure of animist belief
      Narihira, incarnation of art and protector of women
      (included because of affinity of mood)

D. *Kurui-mono*: Lunatic or mad piece
   more accurately, dramatic presentation
   human grief and lament are characteristic moods
   general atmosphere of longing or yearning, as in
     Kazure-mono
   most difficult to perform because of dual nature of role
   subdivisions:

   1. *Kurui-mono* proper:
      derangement or frenzy at loss of child or lover
      (usually a female character)
      distraction or frenzy in joy or ecstasy
      (usually a male character)

   2. *Onryo-mono (Shūnen-mono)*: possession piece
      personification of intense feeling as agent of evil
      souls of dead dominated by lingering spur of passion,
        bound to earth after death through emotional in-
        volvement

   3. *Genzai-mono*: earthly piece
      realistic presentation
        action not seen as recollection
      usually concerns warriors and battle
      kakeri and *otoko-mai* are characteristic
        tempo livelier than *shura-mono*
      often involves acrobatics
            rarely performed, except for *Ataka* and *Funa
                                                    Benkei*

E. *Kiri-Nō*: Finale or concluding play
    fast tempo and agitated in nature
    frankly gay and spectacular
    intended as indication of the sublime
    usually involves fierce demon or lesser spirit figure
    dominant dance forms are *hataraki*, *inori* and *haya-mai*
    mai-like style predominates, even for true *mai* forms,
      providing another contrast with *kami-nō*[2]

III. *LITERARY AND MUSICAL STRUCTURE*

Jo: Introduction; slow, solemn and powerful
    Entrance of *waki* (deuteragonist) and *tsure* (companions)

    Entrance music (instrumental)
    'music indicating the order of play'

A. *Shidai*: entrance speech of the *waki*
    formal announcement of subject, situation, or
      circumstance
    simple, unadorned poem of two verse lines
      delivered in Fixed-Rhythm, Higher Melodic Style
      (see IV. *Styles of Chanting*, below)
      solo, or in unison with *tsure*
      burst of music *(uchi-kiri)* marks end of first line
      both lines then delivered together
      second line repeated softly by chorus
    issei (see below) may be substituted

B. *Nanori*: self-introduction of *waki*
    statement of name, social condition and intention
    a more or less developed poetic form
    delivered in Pure-Speech style
      sung as *sashi* (see below) in female roles

C. *Michi-yuki*: travel song of *waki*
    normally a description of a journey
      may introduce other matter as well
    one of several *uta* forms
    poem of six or eight lines
      first verse may contain three distiches
    delivered in Fixed-Rhythm, Higher Melodic Style
      uchi-kiri marks first verse and mid-point

first verse may be repeated by *tsure* alone
second half may open with line of three distiches
last line is normally repeated
michi-yuki is noted for relaxed and lyric beauty
measured circuiting of stage may represent journey

   Tsuki-Zerifu: arrival of *waki*
not an essential form
delivered in Pure-Speech style

Ha: Development; lively, graceful and delicate
(Ha 1.   Introduction)
   Entrance of shite (protagonist) and *tsure*

   Entrance music (instrumental)

A. *Issei*: entrance speech of *shite*
   formal announcement, serious and weighty
   poem of two stanzas, together known as *shin no issei*
      issei proper, two verse lines
         first line may contain three distiches
      ni no ku, two lines only
      delivered in Free-Rhythm, Rich Melodic Style
         most melodious of all *utai*
         solo, or in unison with *tsure*
   shin no issei delivered from *hashigakari* (bridge)
      shite normally faces audience
      shite and *tsure* face one another for unison chant
   ni no ku divided when sung with *tsure*
      first verse delivered by *tsure*
      second in unison with *shite*
   issei occasionally assigned to *waki*
   shidai (see above) may be substituted
      delivered by *shite* or in unison with *tsure*
   yobi-kake may be substituted as well
      variant of *mondai* (see below)
      brief call from distance, part of following dialogue
      delivered in Pure-Speech style
         high pitch and with slow dragging rhythm
         from bridge or behind curtain

B. *Sashi*: prose-like introductory or transitional form
   reconciles *utai* of different conceptions and natures
      transition from *issei* to first *uta* of *shite*

            lacks clearly defined literary form
            contains allusion or quotation from ancient poetry,
                particularly if *issei* has no such figures
            delivery in simple and flexible recitative
          • melodiously sung
                tempo increases throughout
                suitable style for *utai* of *kokata* (child actor)
                nanori of female roles delivered in *sashi* form
                normally delivered from stage proper
            sashi may introduce other forms; e.g., *michi-yuki*
                modification sometimes occurs in form introduced
            may exist independently
                as extended expression of thought or feeling
                more intricate and musically satisfying if independen
                rhythmically unrestrained
            may also replace omitted forms
                e.g., *issei* and *shidai* (see above)

C. *Uta*: descriptive or lyric song of *shite*
            normally given in two parts
            sage-uta, poem of two verses
                the first line may contain three distiches
                delivered in Fixed-Rhythm, Lower Melodic Style
                normally ended with *uchi-kiri*
            age-uta, poem of six or eight lines
                the first verse may contain three distiches
                delivered in Fixed-Rhythm, Higher Melodic Style
                first verse may be marked by *uchi-kiri*
                medial *uchi-kiri* omitted
                first verse may be repeated by *tsure* alone
                last verse is normally repeated.

(*Ha* 2. Development) Exchange between *shite* and *waki*

A. *Mondai*: dialogue
            statement of feelings which motivate speaker
            free prose-like form delivered in Pure-Speech style
                subtle evocation of calm or agitation
            may include *katari* (narrative or recital)
                uniform and regular verses
                delivered in Pure-Speech style

B. *Sashi*: prose-like transitional piece (see above)
            flexible recitative

may include *kakari* 'preliminary recitative'
Fumi: reading of a letter
    not an essential form
    delivered in Free-Rhythm, Simple Melodic Style
    normally sung in *yowa* (weak) melodic mode (see V.
      Tone Systems, below)

  Kudoki: lament
    not an essential form
    delivered in Free-Rhythm, Simple Melodic Style
    normally sung in *yowa* (weak) melodic mode

C. *Uta*:   account of significant action or experience
    as above, but may be delivered by *shite* and chorus
    sage-uta, two verse lines
      Fixed-Rhythm, Lower Melodic Style
    age-uta, six or eight verse lines
      Fixed-Rhythm, Higher Melodic Style

(*Ha* 3.   Climax) Exposition by *shite* and chorus

  Ji-utai (ji-dori):   separate introduction
    not an essential form
    variation of *shidai* (see above) performed by chorus
    simple unadorned poem of two verse lines
    Fixed-Rhythm, Higher Melodic Style

A. *Kuri*:   preparation or introduction for *kuse* (see below)
    also a form or method of inflection
  opens with maxim or principle of religious doctrine
    developed through consideration of its application
  literary form is little developed
    never more than five or six lines
  performed by *shite* and chorus
    opening line delivered by *shite*
    chorus takes up chant at second line
    shite may sing a verse in the middle of the piece
  delivered in Free-Rhythm, Rich Melodic Style
    unrestricted rhythm makes *kuri* prose-like
    uses special intonational patterns and cadences
    chant is variable, but animated
  when omitted, *kuse* retains *sashi* as introduction
    preliminary *mai* may be performed with *kuri*

B. *Sashi*: introductory or transitional form (see above)
 contains statement of principle or religious doctrine
  maxim may be linked to that of *kuri*
 lacks clearly defined form
 delivered as simple and flexible recitative
  sung by *shite* in *tsuyo* (strong) melodic mode

C. *Kuse*: lyric projection of action and mood
 literary form is highly developed
  much allusion and quotation from ancient poetry
  verse forms are very irregular
 provides musical climax and focus of play
 delivered by chorus
  first and second sections
  Fixed Rhythm, Lower Melodic Style
 third section; Fixed-Rhythm, Higher Melodic Style
  first line called *ageha* (elevation)
  sung by *shite* who raises pitch level
 freest of all *utai*
  balanced by calmly insistent rhythm
 musical emphasis on rhythm rather than melody
 normally occurs before *ai* (interval between scenes)
  scene division not essential; depends on plot
 kuse may occur after *ai*
  as required by plot and musical effect

 Mai: dance normally performed to accompaniment of *kuse*
  i-guse, *shite* motionless at centre-stage during chant
   before *ai* if play is divided into scenes
  mai-guse, choreographic elaboration
   after *ai* if play is divided into scenes
  both may occur in sequence, *i-guse* first

D. *Rongi*: concluding dialogue of *shite* and chorus
 shared ritual in exposition of thought and feeling
 poems not of fixed length
 delivered in Fixed-Rhythm, Higher Melodic Style
  response form, lively and sharp
  attack is abrupt, verses overlapped
  provides musical resolution
  pace of final syllables is slackened
  rhythm prolonged
  provides induction to low, calm choral reprise
 uta may follow

Exit music for *shite* and *tsure* (instrumental)
    not an essential form
    play may not be divided into scenes

Interval *(ai)*: break in the flow of action
    permits change of costume indicating transformation
      all plays are not so divided
    entr'acte performance by *kyōgen* players
    not to be confused with Kyōgen (independent comic
      interludes) given between separate Nō of
      complete programme

A. *Katari-ai*: narrative *entr'acte*
    vernacular elucidation of action and background
    version may differ widely from that of performance
    dialogue with *waki* opens and closes recital
    passage is as regular as *katari* proper (see above)
      rarely printed or even written down
    delivered in Pure-Speech style
      faster than *katari* and at higher pitch
      musical beat and syllable coincide closely
    ai-kyōgen seated at centre-stage

B. *Tachi ai*: standing *entr'acte*
      comparatively rare
    substitutes action or business for narration
    interpolated scene unnecessary to principal action
      may have *rapport* with subject or spirit of larger
        action
    animation is useful in diverting audience attention
      shite may be changing costume and mask inside
        fragile prop
    scene may even be played with *shite* on stage
    may require *katari-ai* if minor deity is involved

  Ashirai-ai: servant role within Nō play itself
    included for dramatic purpose (e.g. *Funa Benkei*)
    furthers plot, or for contrast and relief

Kyū: Finale or conclusion; rapid and brief

A. *Machi-utai*: waiting song of *waki*
    anticipates entrance of *nochi-jite* (transformed *shite*)
    shortened version of *uta* (see above)

four or five verses
the first may contain three distiches
delivered in Fixed-Rhythm, Higher Melodic Style
uchi-kiri omitted unless of *uta* length

Entrance music of *nochi-jite* (instrumental)
'music indicating the subject of play'

Issei: introductory speech of *nochi-jite* (see above)
not an essential form
poem of five distiches and one of four
delivered in Free-Rhythm, Rich Melodic Style

B. *Waka*: accompaniment for *mai*-like dance
words refer generally to movements of dance
omitted if true *mai* is performed
in this case, dialogue precedes *mai*
poem of six or eight verses
first verse delivered by *nochi-jite* (second or
transformed *shite*)
beginning marked by momentary immobility of actor
chant taken up by chorus at second line

Mai: fast and brief performance
contrasting form and character to earlier *mai*

C. Concluding piece *(kiri)* of chorus
short free form
linked with *waka* when following that form
rhythm patterns associated with *shite* role

Nori-ji:
in plays of the supernatural, but not the ghosts of
warriors
delivered in Fixed-Rhythm *(ō-nori)*
with colourful melodic contours

Chū-nori-ji:
in plays of warriors only
delivered in Fixed-Rhythm *(chū-nori)*

Kiri:
in plays with neither supernatural figures nor warriors
delivered in Fixed-Rhythm *(hira-nori)* [3]

Exit: in character along *hashigakari* (bridge)
    musicians last: chorus exits through hatch at back
      of stage

IV. *STYLES OF CHANTING*

A. Pure-Speech Style *(kotoba)*
    figured or heightened recitation
      characteristic dip below reciting tone
      significant rise above and return to original pitch
    intonational formula repeated in each line
    follows natural intonation of verse form
    generally without instrumental accompaniment[4]

B. Free-Rhythm *(hyōshi-awazu)*
    usually sung by *shite* or *waki*

    1. Simple Melodic Style
        close to recitative
        descends from High main tone to Low or Very Low
        (see V. *Tone Systems*, below)
        employs special melodic patterns
        sometimes without instrumental accompaniment

    2. Rich Melodic Style
        predominantly High pitch
        profuse patterns of ornamentation
        instrumental accompaniment

C. Fixed-Rhythm *(hyōshi-au)*
    usually chanted by chorus

    1. Higher Melodic Style
        movement between High and Middle tones
        employs *hira-nori* rhythm
          most natural and commonly used of fixed patterns
          duration of first, fourth, & seventh syllables
            doubled
          four extra intervals (counting interstich *caesura*)
          twelve syllables of line fit sixteen beats of bar
        instrumental accompaniment

    2. Lower Melodic Style
        movement between Middle and Low tones
        employs *hira-nori* rhythm
        instrumental accompaniment

3. Special Rhythm Style
    melody suppressed
    usually reserved for concluding passage of play
    instrumental accompaniment
    either: ō-*nori* rhythm
      each syllable fitted to one beat (two half beats)
      effect of formal measure and majesty
    or: chū-*nori* rhythm
      each syllable fitted to single half-beat
      effect of excitement and tension
      pounding speed and regularity[5]

V. *TONE SYSTEMS*

A. *Tsuyo* (strong) *(recitativo)*
    intoned recitation, emphasis on rhythm
    style of stately power
    compressed tone scale; High and Low pitch only
      pitch intervals inexact and unstable
        from major second to minor third
      sforzando-like dynamics, intense *vibrato*
    accent, dynamic stress and tone colour assume importance

B. *Yowa* (weak) *(cantabile)*
    emphasis on melody
    suitable for heightened emotion
    full octave scale
      four main tones: High, Middle, Low, and Very Low
      four intermediate transitional tones
    prolongations, swings and turns are common[6]

VI. *DANCE FORMS*

A. True *Mai*: image-creating forms
    concentrating on beauty of movement
    accompanied by instrumental music

  1. Grave and powerful dances

    Kami-mai: most solemn and dignified of *mai* forms
      normally performed by youthful deity earlier
        disguised as man
      pace is very slow; *taiko* (stick-drum) may be used

Kagura: sacred performance by female deity
may be accompanied by *taiko*

Gaku: forceful and animated
variation of Bugaku (ancient court dance)
often performed by ugly and aged deity

Otoko-mai: grave and solemn dance
has pronounced or emphatic gestures and movements
usually performed by unmasked warriors
taiko is never used

2. Graceful and delicate dances

Jo no mai: slow and elegant form
usually performed by female spirit or goddess

Shin no mai: similar to *jo no mai*
more solemn and slower still
usually performed by god earlier disguised as
 an old man
may serve as introduction to *jo no mai*
taiko may be used

Chū no mai: performance of middle pace
very graceful and feminine in character
performed by young and beautiful woman or goddess

Tennyo no mai (sandan no mai): variation of *chū no mai*
performed by female spirit in role of *tsure*
taiko may be used

3. Agitated and brief dances

Ha no mai: short and relatively animated dance
sometimes added to *tennyo no mai* as finale or
 conclusion

Haya-mai: more lively and lighter in spirit
than *ha no mai*
performed at quite rapid pace
taiko may be used

Kyū no mai: short and urgent form given as climax
like *haya-mai*; rarely seen, but singularly effective

B. *Mai*-like forms:
more or less realistic representations
accompanied by chanting of poetic text

Hataraki: (jumping or leaping about)
  characterized by violent movements
  suggesting strength and power
  evokes image of warriors in combat
  forms of *hataraki* common to gods and demons

Kakeri: less violent than *hataraki*
  still suitable for staged combats of *genzai-mono*
  may include splendid acrobatics and duels *(kiri kumi*
  also effective in expressing frenzy and derangement

Tachi-mawari: similar in many ways to *kakeri*
  represents violent emotion or agitation
  rapid circuits of stage are characteristic

Iroe: graceful and restrained version of *tachi-mawari*
  slow, calm dance of *kuri* or *sashi* of *kuse* section
  normally precedes *kuse* section (see below)

Inari (prayer): stylized movements of exorcism

C. Special forms: unique performances
  associated only with individual plays
  include *mai* of both true and *mai*-like forms

Okina no mai (kami-gaku) and *Sensai no mai*
  special congratulatory pieces to Okina
  call for two extra hand-drums in orchestra

Rambyōshi: singular and astonishing performance
  represents nature of protagonist in *Dōjōji*
  uses only one small hand-drum for accompaniment

Midare: short and agitated dance of Orang-utan
  two variants exist; may be given by one or more *shit*
  peculiar to *Shōjō* and *Sogi*; *taiko* used

Shishi-mai: lion dance of *Mochizuka* and *Shakkya*
  taiko used[7]

D. *Kata*: dance postures or patterns of movement
  Shita-i: kneeling posture with one knee
  raised indicates that the character is seated

Tatsu: standing posture with chest forward
  chin and elbows back, and head erect
  hands along top of thigh, palms inward
  knees bent and feet aligned

Umpo (hakobi): basic movement or walk
   gliding on heels, which never leave floor
   arching back foot to balance body weight

Terasu (to brighten) and *Kumorasu* (to cloud)
   indicates change of expression on mask
   performer looks up slightly, mask brightens or smiles
   performer looks down slightly, mask clouds or saddens

Shiori: indicates grief, weeping or holding back tears
   open hand slowly lifted to hide eyes
   both hands used for emphasis

Sorikaeri: suggests great pain or leaping into sea
   open hands raised, palms showing
   body weight on left leg, right knee raised
   slow pivot to left, bending slightly forward
   right leg lowered on completion of turn

Munazue: expression of age or weariness
   performer leans chest on long walking stick
   gazes into distance

Sashikomi (pointing) - *Hiraki* (opening)
   marks off stages of a dance sequence
   (sashikomi)
   holding out a closed fan in the right hand
   simultaneously advancing the right foot a half step
   (hiraki)
   spreading apart extended arms
   retreating three steps backward
   (sashi-mawashi-hiraki) a variant
   turning around between *sashikomi* and *hiraki*

Ageha-ōgi: suggests looking into distance or
      removing cloak
   open fan held before face
   fan lifted over head while taking three steps
      backwards

Sayū: concluding sequence, normally follows *ageha-ōgi*
   step to left with left arm outstretched
   followed by stamp of left foot
   right arm then extended, step taken to the right

Yuken ōgi: expression of joy; sometimes purely
      decorative

open fan held to chest and lifted to right
pattern generally repeated twice.

Uchiawase (joining hands): expression of surprise
or despair
arms spread out, hands joined, body inclined
slightly forward
executed with or without open fan in right hand
describes fluttering of wings when repeated twice

Hane-ōgi (fluttering fan): indicates action such
as shooting an arrow
open fan in left hand crosses right elbow
fan quickly moved to left
describes fluttering wings or the wind when
repeated twice

Take-ōgi (shield fan): indicates shield in battle
drawn sword in right hand
open fan held out by two fingers of left hand

Kasumi no ōgi (mist fan): suggests drifting mist
also represents waterfall, wind blowing down
hillside
open fan slowly lowered
revolved to plane parallel with floor

Kumo no ōgi (cloud fan): implies gazing at clouds,
sky, or distant mountains
left hand forward, right hand folded over fan
hands drawn apart as performer looks upwards

Tsuki no ōgi (moon fan): implies looking at moon
also *Kakae-ōgi* (embracing fan)
left shoulder touched with open fan in right hand
performer looks upward, diagonally to right

Tsumani ōgi: unusual pattern, meaning varies
indicates falling blossoms in *Futari Shizuka*
lowering of fishing nets in *Akogi*
measuring the height of children in *Izutsu*

Makura no ōgi (pillow fan): represents sleeping
open fan in left hand conceals left side of face

Maneki ōgi (inviting fan): indicates beckoning
also serves as sign of affection
open fan lifted above the shoulder
turned over in 'fanning' motion
often repeated several times[8]

Notes

PREFACE

1. Peter Arnott, *The Theatres of Japan*, p.9 See Bibliography for complete details of all publications.

Chapter I. *W. B. YEATS: EARLY PLAYS*

1. W. B. Yeats, *Florence Farr, Bernard Shaw, W. B. Yeats Letters*, p.57.

2. See *Samhain* (September 1903), pp.9-10.

3. *Samhain* (December 1904), p.19.

4. Leonard Nathan, *The Tragic Drama of William Butler Yeats*, p.

5. George Lukacs in *The Theory of the Modern Stage*, ed. Eric Bentley, p.447.

6. Quoted in *The Oxford Companion to the Theatre*, ed. Phyllis Hartnoll, p.258.

7. *Samhain* (October 1902), p.4.

8. See *Samhain* (September 1903), p.35.

9. *Samhain* (December 1904), p.30.

10. *Essays and Introductions*, p.159.

11. *Ibid.*, p.243.

12. *Appreciations*, pp.211-12.

13. *Samhain*, p.10.

14. Quoted by Gerald Fay in *The Abbey Theatre*, p.92.
15. *Samhain* (December 1904), p.32.
16. *The Variorum Edition of the Plays of W. B. Yeats*, p.1291.
17. *Ibid.*, p.332.
18. In *Cuchulain of Muirthemne*, pp.1-6.
19. *Variorum Plays*, p.342.
20. David Greene and Edward Stephen, *J. M. Synge*, p.157.
21. *The Letters of W. B. Yeats*, p.55.
22. See *Variorum Plays*, pp.644-6.
23. *Samhain* (December 1904), p.30.
24. Arnold Goldman, 'The Oeuvre Takes Shape', p.221.
25. *Variorum Plays*, p.645.
26. *Ibid.*, p.1306.
27. *Ibid.*, p.391.
28. *Ibid.*, p.454

Chapter 2. *FENOLLOSA AND POUND: AGENTS OF TRANSMISSION*

1. Ezra Pound, translator, *Women of Trachis*, p.50.
2. 'Notes on the Japanese Lyric Drama', 129.
3. *'Noh' or Accomplishment*, p.120.
4. *Ibid.*, p.251.
5. Ernest Fenollosa, 'The Classical Stage of Japan', 199-231.
6. *'Noh' or Accomplishment*, p.17.
7. *Ibid.*, p.63.
8. *Ibid.*, p.220.
9. *Ibid.*, p.46.
10. *Ibid.*, p.19.
11. *Letters of Ezra Pound*, pp.30-31.
12. *Ibid.*, p.214.

13. *Ō Bei Jin no Nōgaku ken Kyū*, p.20.

14. See 'Traditions of Noh Plays', 345-68.

15. See Konishi Jin'ichi, (New Approaches to the Study of the Nō Drama), pp.4-5.

16. *Bulletin de l'Ecole Francaise d'Extrême-Orient*, 1-43, reprinted in *Le Nō* (1944).

17. See also Richard Taylor, 'The Notebooks of Ernest Fenollosa', pp.540-76.

18. Van Wyck Brooks, *Fenollosa and His Circle*, pp.2-3.

19. Lawrence Chisolm, *Fenollosa*, p.22.

20. *Ibid.*, p.42.

21. 'An Outline of Japanese Art', p.73.

22. *Ibid.*, p.277.

23. *The Mysteries of Magic*, p.xxxii.

24. *Essays and Introductions*, pp.201-2.

25. 'An Outline of Japanese Art', p.63.

26. *Ibid.*, p.63.

27. *Ibid.*, pp.68-9.

28. *Epoch of Chinese and Japanese Art*, 1, p.52.

29. *Ibid.*, 2, pp.4-6.

30. *Ibid.*, 1, p.xxvii.

31. *Imagination in Art*, p.7.

32. *Ibid.*, p.9.

33. 'The Nature of Fine Art' p.756.

34. See Earl Miner, *The Japanese Tradition in British and American Literature*, pp.66-74.

35. 'Notes on the Japanese Lyric Drama', p.130.

Chapter 3. *THE JAPANESE NŌ: ART AND ACCOMPLISHMENT*

1. Donald Keene, *Nō*, p.19.

2. Nippon Gakujutsu Shinkōkai, *Japanese Noh Drama*, 3, p.26.

3. Quoted in Ueda Makoto, *Literary and Art Theories in Japan*, p.103. For a more complete exposition see Chapter 7, 'The Making of the Comic: Toraaki on the Art of Comedy'.

4. In Beatrice Suzuki, *Nōgaku*, p.23.

5. See Patrick O'Neill, *Early Nō Drama*, p.50.

6. *Ibid.*, p.147.

7. See Minagawa Tatsuo, 'Japanese *Noh* Music', p.199.

8. See Keene, *Nō*, p.76.

9. Quoted in Edmund Chambers, *The Mediaeval Stage*, 2, p.9.

10. *'Seami Jūroku Bushū'*, p.535.

11. See Richard McKinnon, 'The Nō and Zeami', p.356.

12. Zeami as quoted in O'Neill, *Early Nō Drama*, p.98.

13. *Ibid.*, p.118.

14. Donald Keene, *Japanese Literature*, p.4.

15. *'Noh' or Accomplishment*, pp.136-7. Italics mine.

16. *Japanese Noh Drama* 3, p.125.

17. Joseph Shipley, *Trends in Literature*, p.272.

18. *My Life*, p.119.

19. *In Search of Theater*, p.158.

20. Isadora Duncan, *The Art of the Dance*, p.121.

21. See *'Seami Jūroku Bushū'*, p.546.

22. Donald Keene, *Nō*, p.74.

23. See Ōshima Shotarō, *W. B. Yeats and Japan*, p.47.

24. Quoted by Ōshima, pp.43-4.

25. The Nō adaptation was first performed at the Kita School,

Tokyo, in 1949 and was revived again in 1950 and 1952.
See John Mills, 'W. B. Yeats and Noh', p.500.

26. Letter to Katsue Kitasono dated 24 May 1936 in *Letters of Ezra Pound*, p.282.

27. Quoted by Ōshima, p.180 from *Hikaku-bunka, Dai-ni shū* (Comparative Studies of Culture), 2 (Tokyo, 1956).

28. *Pound-Joyce Letters and Essays*, p.58.

29. Ernest Fenollosa, *Certain Noble Plays of Japan*, pp.xii-xiii.

30. In Curtis Bradford, *Yeats at Work*, p.293.

31. Zeami, *Kadensho*, p.72.

32. 'The Book of the Way of the Highest Flower', p.302.

33. Quoted in Suzuki, *Nōgaku*, p.33.

34. Georg Hegel, *Lectures on the Philosophy of Religion*, 2, p.8.

35. *The Renaissance*, p.143.

36. *Four Quartets*, p.7.

Chapter 4. *W. B. YEATS: PLAYS FOR DANCERS*

1. Ronald Gaskell, *Drama and Reality*, p.60.

2. T. S. Eliot, *Notes Toward the Definition of Culture*, p.25.

3. *Inishfallen, Fare Thee Well*, p.290.

4. See 'Choix de pièces du théâtre lyrique japonais', 12-43, reprinted in Renondeau, *Nō*, premier fascicule. Compare *The Noh*, 1, pp.169-201.

5. *The Variorum Edition of the Poems of W. B. Yeats*, p.327.

6. See Tsukimura Reiko, 'A Comparison of Yeats's *At the Hawk's Well* and Its Noh Version *Take no izumi*', p.385-9

7. See *Yeats at Work*, p.190.

8. *Variorum Plays*, p.412.

9. *Ibid.*, p.411.

10. *Ibid.*, p.403.

11. See *Samhain* (December 1906), pp.10-13.

12. In *Frank Pearce Sturm*, ed. Richard Taylor, p.75.

13. *Reflections*, pp.16-17.

14. See Richard Best, *Bibliography of Irish Philology and of Printed Irish Literature*, p.94. A useful plot summary is also given by George Sigerson in *Bards of the Gael and the Gall*, pp.391-5.

15. *Ibid.*, pp.393-4.

16. *Ibid.*, p.394.

17. *The Letters of W. B. Yeats*, p.612.

18. *Variorum Plays*, p.543.

19. *'Noh' or Accomplishment* p.194.

20. *Ibid.*, p.195.

21. *A Vision*, p.213.

22. *'Noh' or Accomplishment*, pp.196-7.

23. See *Cuchulain of Muirthemne*, pp.156-9.

24. *'Noh' or Accomplishment*, p.29.

25. For detailed discussion of this image see David Clark, *'Nishikigi* and Yeats's *Dreaming of the Bones'*, pp.118-19.

26. *Variorum Poems*, p.513.

27. See *The Work of Oscar Wilde*, pp.843-4.

28. *Mythologies*, pp.305-6.

29. *'Noh' or Accomplishment*, pp.220-21.

30. *Variorum Plays*, p.787.

31. *Essays and Introductions*, p.137.

32. *A Vision*, p.275.

33. *Variorum Plays*, p.931. Compare 'I hail the super-human:/ I call it death-in-life and life-in-death', 'Bysantium', *Variorum Poems*, p.497.

34. *Yeats, the Playwright*, pp.113-14.

35. *Variorum Plays*, p.783.

36. *A Vision*, p.275.

Chapter 5. *W. B. YEATS: LATER ASSIMILATION*

1. A Sung poet quoted by Laurence Binyon in *The Flight of the Dragon*, p.84.

2. See *Yeats's Iconography*, pp.241-4.

3. 'Yeats's "Country of the Young"', p.510.

4. See *Yeats at Work*, pp.239-41.

5. *Ibid.*, p.241.

6. See *Variorum Plays*, p.935.

7. *Variorum Poems*, p.563.

8. *Ibid.*, pp.234-5.

9. Terence Gray, *Dance Drama*, p.35.

10. de Valois, *Come Dance with Me*, p.88.

11. *Lady Gregory's Journals*, p.333.

12. *Variorum Plays*, p.950.

13. *Ibid.*, 953.

14. *Ibid.*, p.951.

15. *Ibid.*, p.956.

16. Arthur Symons, *Studies in Seven Arts*, pp.75-6.

17. The Gate Theatre Club continued to produce experimental drama at the Peacock until 1930.

18. Norman Marshall, *The Other Theatre*, p.48.

19. *Variorum Plays*, p.993.

20. *Ah, Sweet Dancer*, p.23.

21. *Autobiographies*, p.321.

22. *Variorum Poems*, p.513.

23. *Variorum Plays*, pp.1009-10.

24. Dennis Donoghue, *The Third Voice*, p.39.

25. Thomas Whitaker, *Swan and Shadow*, p.288.

26. 'Bardic Ireland', p.182. 'The *Tain Bo*, the greatest of all these epics, is full of this devotion. Later, when things were less plastic, men rose against their *ard-reigh* for any and everything: one because at dinner he was given a hen's egg instead of a duck's'.

27. See pp.34-6.

28. *Variorum Plays*, p.1026.

29. *Ibid.*, p.1016.

30. *Ibid.*, p.1016.

31. *The Theosophical Glossary*, pp.262-3.

32. See *The Key to Theosophy*, pp.91-2.

33. *Variorum Plays*, p.1028.

34. *Ibid.*, p.1027.

35. *Ibid.*, p.1027.

36. *Ibid.*, p.1036.

37. *Ibid.*, p.1038.

38. *Ibid.*, p.1040.

39. *Ibid.*, p.1311.

40. *Ibid.*, p.1056.

41. *Ibid.*, p.1059.

42. *Ibid.*, p.1061.

43. *'Noh' or Accomplishment*, pp.247-8.

44. *Variorum Plays*, pp.1051-2.

45. *Ibid.*, p.983.

46. *Ibid.*, p.1049.

47. *'Noh' or Accomplishment*, pp.141-2.

48. *Variorum Plays*, p.1048.

49. *Ibid.*, p.929.

50. *Ibid.*, p.1049.

51. *The Poet in the Theatre*, pp.114-15.

52. Quoted earlier from Curtis Bradford, *Yeats at Work*, p.293.

53. Muriel Bradbrook, *English Dramatic Form*, pp.123-4.

54. *Ibid.*, pp.13-14.

Appendix

1. See Richard McKinnon, 'Zeami on the Art of Training', p.216n.

2. See Noel Peri, *Le Nō*, pp.61-5.   Compare Shimazaki Chifumi, *The Noh*, 1, pp.22-9.

3. Compare Minagawa Tatsuo, '.Japanese *Noh* Music', pp.183-5 and Peri, pp.34-51 and pp.57-61. See also Shimazaki, 1, pp.45-56.

4. See Minagawa, p.193.

5. See p.182 and pp.195-6.

6. See pp.185-93 and Donald Keene, *Nō*, p.76.

7. See Peri, pp.53-4.   Compare Shimazaki, pp.32-8.

8. See Keene, pp.219-22 and Shimazaki, pp.31-2.

Selected Bibliography

A. *NŌ DRAMA*

Arnott, Peter Douglas, *The Theatres of Japan*, London and
    New York, 1969, pp.9-126
Beaujard, André, *Le Théâtre comique des japonais; intro-
    duction à l'étude des Kyōghen*, Paris, 1937
Benazet, Alexandre, *Le Théâtre au Japon: ses rapports avec
    les cultes locaux*, Annales du Musée Guimet, 13, Paris,
    1901
Benl, Oscar, *Seami Motokiyo und der Geist des Nō-Schauspiels*,
    Weisbaden, 1953
Araki, James T., *The Ballad-Drama of Medieval Japan*,
    Berkeley and Los Angeles, 1964
Aston, William George, *A History of Japanese Literature*,
    Short Histories of the Literatures of the World, 6,
    London, 1899, pp.199-214
Bohner, Hermann, *Gestalten und Quellen des Nō*, Tokyo, 1955
----- *Nō: Einführung*, Weisbaden, 1959
----- *Nō: Die Einzelnen Nō*, Weisbaden, 1956
Brinkley, Frank, *Japan: Its History, Arts and Literature*,
    8 vol., London, 1903, 3, pp.28-48
Chamberlain, Basil Hall, *Japanese Poetry*, London, 1911,
    pp.109-44, a revised edition of *The Classical Poetry
    of the Japanese*, London, 1880, pp.135-212
Dickens, Frederick Victor, *Primitive and Mediaeval Japanese
    Texts Translated into English*, Oxford, 1906, pp.391-412
Edwards, Osman, *Japanese Plays and Playfellows*, London, 1901
Furukawa, Hishshi, 'The Noh', in *Japanese Music and Drama
    in the Meiji Era*, compiled by Komiya Toyotaka, trans-
    lated by E. G. Seidensticker and D. Keene, Japanese
    Culture in the Meiji Era, 3, Tokyo, 1965, pp.75-117

-----*O Bei jin no Noh gaku ken kyūu* (European and American
    Studies of Nō), Tokyo Joshi Daigaku Gakkai Sōshi
    (Publication of Tokyo Women's College), 1, Tokyo, 1962
Gundert, Wilhelm, *Der Schintoismus im Japanischen Nō-dramen*,
    Tokyo, 1925
Hinks, Marcelle Azra, *The Japanese Dance*, London, 1910,
    pp.15-23
Japan P.E.N. Club, *Japanese Literature in European Languages:
    a Bibliography*, Tokyo, 1961, pp.23-37
Keene, Donald, *Japanese Literature: an Introduction for
    Western Readers*, London, 1953
-----*Nō: the Classical Theatre of Japan*, Tokyo and Palo
    Alto, 1966
-----editor, *Anthology of Japanese Literature*, New York,
    1955, pp.258-311
-----editor, *Twenty Plays of the Nō Theater*, New York, 1970
Kenney, Don, *A Guide to Kyōgen*, Tokyo, 1968
Kōji, Toita, 'The Kabuki, the Shimpo, the Shingeki', in
    Japanese Music and Drama in the Meiji Era, compiled
    by Komiya Toyotaka, translated by E. G. Seidensticker
    and D. Keene, Japanese Culture in the Meiji Era, 3,
    Tokyo, 1956, pp.177-283
Kokusai Bunka Shinkōkai (The Society for International
    Cultural Relations), *Theatre, Dance and Music*, K.B.S.
    Bibliography of Standard Reference Books for Japanese
    Studies, 7B, Tokyo, 1966
-----*The Noh Drama*, Tokyo, 1937
Konishi, Jin'ichi, 'New Approaches to the Study of the Nō
    Drama', *Kokubungaku Kambungaku Ronso (Bulletin of the
    Tokyo Kyoiku University Literature Department)*, 27
    (1960), pp.1-31
Kōri, Tarahiko, 'Japanese Drama', *Transactions and Procee-
    dings of the Japan Society, London*, 16 (1918), pp.58-74
Lombard, Frank Alanson, *An Outline History of the Japanese
    Drama*, London, 1928, pp.85-180
Magnino, Leo, editor, *Teatro giapponese*, Milan, 1956, pp.
    39-96
Malm, William, P., 'Nohgaku: The Music of Noh Drama', in
    Japanese Music and Musical Instruments, Tokyo and
    Rutland, 1959, pp.105-31
McKinnon, Richard Nichols, 'The Nō and Zeami', *Far Eastern
    Quarterly* 11, No.3 (May 1952), pp.355-61
-----editor, *Selected Plays of Kyōgen*, Tokyo, 1968

-----'Zeami on the Art of Training', *Harvard Journal of Asiatic Studies*, 16, No.1 and 2 (June 1953), pp.200-25

Minagawa, Tatsuo, 'Japanese Noh Music', *Journal of the American Musicological Society*, 10, No.3 (Fall 1957), pp.181-200

Miner, Earl Ray, 'The Technique of Japanese Poetry', *Hudson Review*, 8, No.3 (Autumn 1955), pp.350-66

Nippon Gakujutsu Shinkōkai (Japan Society for the Promotion of Scientific Research), *Japanese Noh Drama*, 3 vol., Tokyo, 1955-60

Nogami, Toyoichiro, *Japanese Noh Plays: How to See Them*, Tokyo, 1934, second edition, 1954

-----*Noh Masks: Classification and Explanation*, Tokyo, 1938

-----*Zeami and His Theories on Noh*, translated by Matsumoto Ryozo, Tokyo, 1955

Noguchi, Yone, *Ten Kiogen in English*, Tokyo, 1907

O'Neill, Patrick G., *Early Nō Drama: Its Background, Character and Development, 1300-1450*, London, 1958

-----*A Guide to Nō*, Tokyo, 1954

-----translator, 'The Nō Plays *Koi no Omoni* and *Yuya*', *Monumenta Nipponica*, 10, No.1 and 2 (April 1954), pp.203-26

Peri, Noël, *Le Nō*, Tokyo, 1944

-----'Sotoba Komachi', *Bulletin de l'Ecole Francaise d'Extrême-Orient*, 13, No.4, (1913), pp.1-43

Perzynski, Friedrich, *Japanishe Masken: Nō und Kyōgen*, 2 vol., Berlin and Leipzig, 1925

Renondeau, Gaston, *Le Bouddhisme dans les Nō*, Tokyo, 1950

-----'Choix de pièces du théâtre lyrique japonais', *Bulletin de l'Ecole Francaise d'Extrême-Orient*, 27 (1927), pp.12-43

-----*Nō*, 2 fasc.,Tokyo, 1953-4

Sadler, Arthur Lindsay, *Japanese Plays: Nō-Kyogen-Kabuki*, Sydney, 1943

Sakanishi, Shio, *Kyōgen: Comic Interludes of Japan*, Boston, 1938, reprinted as *The Ink-Smeared Lady and Other Kyōgen*, Tokyo and Rutland, 1960

Samson, George Bailey, 'Translations from Lyrical Drama: "Nō"', *Transactions of the Asiatic Society of Japan*, 38, No.3 (1911), pp.125-76

-----*The Western World and Japan: a Study in the Interaction of European and Asiatic Cultures*, New York, 1950

Seami, see Zeami

Shimazaki, Chifumi, *The Noh*, 1, Tokyo, 1972
Shimoi, Harukichi, *Kyōgen: xv antiche farce giapponesi*, Naples, 1920
Sieffert, René, translator, *La Tradition secrète du Nō: suivie d'une journée de Nō*, Paris, 1960
Stopes, Marie Carmichael, 'A Japanese Mediaeval Drama', *Transactions of the Royal Society of Literature*, second series, 29, No.3 (1909), pp.153-78
-----and Sakurai Joji, *Plays of Old Japan: the Nō*, London, 1913
Suzuki, Beatrice Lane, *Nōgaku: Japanese Nō Plays*, The Wisdom of the East Series, London, 1932
Taylor, Richard Dean, 'The Notebooks of Ernest Fenollosa', *Literature East and West*, 15, No.4 (December 1971), pp.533-76
Teele, Roy E., 'A Balance Sheet on Pound's Translations of Noh Plays', *Books Abroad*, 39 (Spring 1965), pp.168-70
-----'Formal and Linguistic Problems in Translating a Noh Play', *Studies on Asia*, 4 (1963), pp.43-54
-----'The Structure of the Japanese Noh Play', *Chinese and Japanese Music-Dramas*, edited by J. I. Crump and William P. Malm, Michigan Papers in Chinese Studies, 19, Ann Arbor, 1975
-----'Translations of Noh Plays', *Comparative Literature*, 9, No.4 (Fall 1957), pp.345-68
Toki, Zemmaro, *Japanese Noh Plays*, Tourist Library, 16, Tokyo, 1954
Ueda, Makoto, *Literary and Art Theories in Japan*, Cleveland, 1967
-----'Modern Kyogen and Western Literature', *Literature East and West*, 11, No.4 (1967), pp.373-80
-----*The Old Pine Tree and Other Noh Plays*, Lincoln, 1962
Uyeno, Naoteru, 'The Cultural Background of Meiji Art, with an Outline of Painting', in *Japanese Arts and Crafts in the Meiji Era*, edited by Uyeno Naoteru, adapted into English by Richard Lane, Japanese Culture in the Meiji Era, 8, Tokyo, 1958, pp.1-77
Waley, Arthur, *The Noh Plays of Japan*, London, 1921
Yamasaki, Keiichi, 'Japanese Drama', *Transactions and Proceedings of the Japan Society, London*, 12 (1913-14), pp.112-26
Zeami, Motokiyo, *Blumenspiegel* (Kwa-kyō, Hana-no-kagami), translated by Hermann Bohner, Weisbaden, 1953
-----*The Book of the Way of the Highest Flower*, in

Sources of Japanese Tradition, compiled by Tsunoda
Ryusaku et al, New York, 1958, pp.296-303

-----*Buch von der Höchsten Blume Weg* (Shi-Kwa-dō-sho),
translated by Hermann Bohner, Tokyo, 1943

-----*Fūshi-Kaden* (De la Transmission de la fleur de l'interpretation), in *La Tradition secrète du Nō*, translated by René Sieffert, Paris, 1960, pp.61-112

-----*Kadensho*, translated by Sakurai Chūichi et al, Kyoto,
1968

-----*Kakyō* (Le Miroir de la fleur), in *La Tradition secrète
du Nō*, pp.113-40

-----*Kyūi Shidai* (L'Echelle des neuf degrés), in *La Tradition secrète du Nō*, pp.173-8

-----*Der Neun Stufen Folge* (Kyū-i-shi-dai), translated by
Hermann Bohner, Tokyo, 1943

-----*Nikyoku Santai Ezu* (Etude illustrée des deux elements
et des trois types), in *La Tradition secrète du Nō*,
pp.151-61

-----*The Nine Stages of the Nō in Order*, in *Sources of
Japanese Tradition*, pp.292-6

-----*On Attaining the Stages of Yūgen*, in *Sources of
Japanese Tradition*, pp.288-91

-----*On the One Mind Linking All Powers*, in *Sources of
Japanese Tradition*, pp.291-2

-----'Seami *Jūroku Bushū*: Seami's Sixteen Treatises',
translated by Shidehara Michitarō and Wilfred Whithouse,
Monumenta Nipponica, 4, No.2 (July 1941), pp.530-65
and 5, No.2 (December 1942), pp.466-500

-----'Seami on the Art of the Nō', translated by Tsunoda
Ryusaku and Donald Keene, in *Anthology of Japanese
Literature*, edited by Donald Keene, New York, 1955,
pp.258-62

-----*Yūgaku Shūdō Kempū Sho* (Le Livre de l'étude et de
l'effet visuel des divertissements musicaux), in
La Tradition secrète du Nō, pp.163-71

B. GENERAL

I am not unaware of the many journal articles and unpublished theses on Yeats and the Nō, but only those publications which I have found particularly useful are included.

Adams, Hazard, 'Yeats's "Country of the Young"', *Publications of the Modern Language Association of America*,

72, No.3 (June 1957), pp.510-19

Bentley, Eric Russell, *In Search of Theater*, London, 1954

-----*The Life of the Drama*, New York, 1964

-----editor, *The Theory of the Modern Stage*, Harmondsworth, 1968

Berry, Ralph, 'The Problem of Convention in Drama', *British Journal of Aesthetics*, 9 (July 1969), pp.220-30

Best, Richard Irvine, *Bibliography of Irish Philology and of Printed Irish Literature*, Dublin, 1913

Binyon, (Robert) Laurence, *The Flight of the Dragon*, The Wisdom of the East Series, London, 1911

Blavatsky, Helena Petrovna, *The Key to Theosophy*, London, 1889

-----*The Theosophical Glossary*, London, 1892

Bottomley, Gordon, *A Stage for Poetry: My Purposes with My Plays*, Kendal (privately printed), 1948

Bradbrook, Muriel C., *English Dramatic Form: A History of Its Development*, London, 1965

Bradford, Curtis B., *Yeats at Work*, Carbondale, 1966

Brooks, Van Wyck, *Fenollosa and His Circle: With Other Essays in Biography*, New York, 1962

Bushrui, Suheil Badi, *Yeats's Verse-Plays: The Revisions 1900-1910*, London, 1965

Chambers, Edmund Kerchener, *The Mediaeval Stage*, 2 vol., Oxford, 1903

Chisolm, Lawrence W., *Fenollosa: The Far East and American Culture*, New Haven and London, 1963

Clark, David R., *'Nishikigi* and Yeats's *The Dreaming of the Bones'*, *Modern Drama*, 7 (May 1964), pp.111-25

-----*W. B. Yeats and the Theatre of Desolate Reality*, Dublin, 1965

Capon, Eric, 'Theatre and Reality', *British Journal of Aesthetics*, 5 (July 1965), pp.261-9

Cross, K.G.W. and R. T. Dunlop, *A Bibliography of Yeats Criticism, 1887-1965*, New York, 1971

David-Neel, Alexandra, *With Mystics and Magicians in Tibet*, London, 1931

de Valois, Ninette, *Come Dance with Me*, London, 1957

Donoghue, Dennis, *The Third Voice: Modern British and American Verse Drama*, London and Princeton, 1959

Duncan, Isadora, *The Art of the Dance*, edited by Sheldon Cheney, New York, 1928

-----*My Life*, New York, 1927

Eliot, Thomas Sterns, *Four Quartets*, London, 1943
-----'The Noh and the Image', *Egoist*, 4, No.7 (August 1917),
    pp.102-3
-----*Notes Toward the Definition of Culture*, London, 1948
Ellis-Fermor, Una Mary, *The Irish Dramatic Movement*, second
    edition, London, 1954
Fang, Achilles, 'Fenollosa and Pound', *Harvard Journal of
    Asiatic Studies*, 20 (1957), pp.213-38
Fay, Gerald, *The Abbey Theatre: Cradle of Genius*, London,
    1958
Fay, William George and Catharine Carswell, *The Fays of
    the Abbey Theatre: An Autobiographical Record*, London,
    1953
Fenollosa, Ernest Francisco, 'Awoi No Uye, A Play by Ujinobu',
    edited by Ezra Pound, *Quarterly Notebook*, 1, No.1
    (1916), pp.9-16
-----'The Basis of Art Education, I. The Roots of Art, II.
    The Logic of Art, III. The Individuality of the
    Artist', *Golden Age*, 1 (April 1906), pp.160-2, 1
    (May 1906), pp.230-5 and 1 (June 1906), pp.280-4
-----*Certain Noble Plays of Japan*, edited by Ezra Pound
    with an introductory essay by W. B. Yeats, Dundrum,
    County Dublin, 1916
-----'Chinese and Japanese Traits', *Atlantic Monthly*, 69, No.
    416 (June 1892), pp.769-74
-----'The Classical Drama of Japan', edited by Ezra Pound,
    Quarterly Review, 221, No.441 (October 1914), pp.450-77
-----'The Classical Stage of Japan: Ernest Fenollosa's
    Work on the Japanese Noh', edited by Ezra Pound,
    Drama, 5, No.18 (May 1915), pp.199-247
-----'The Coming Fusion of East and West', *Harpers Maga-
    zine*, 98 (December 1898), pp.115-22
-----'Contemporary Japanese Art', *Century Magazine*, 46, No.4
    (August 1893), pp.577-80
-----*East and West: The Discovery of America and Other
    Poems*, Boston, 1894
-----*Epochs of Chinese and Japanese Art*, edited by Mary
    McNeill Fenollosa, 2 vol, New York and London, 1913
-----*Imagination in Art*, Boston, 1894
-----The Nature of Fine Art', *Lotos*, 9, No.9 (March 1896),
    pp.663-73 and 9, No.10 (April 1896), pp.753-62
-----'Nishikigi', edited by Ezra Pound, *Poetry*, 4, No.2
    (May 1914), pp.35-48

-----*'Noh' or Accomplishment: A Study of the Classical Stage of Japan*, London, 1916 (1917)
-----'Notes on the Japanese Lyric Drama', *Journal of the American Oriental Society*, 22 (1901), pp.129-37
-----'An Outline of Japanese Art', *Century Magazine*, 56, No.1 (May 1898), pp.62-75 and 56 No.2, (June 1898), pp.276-89
Ferguson, Samuel, *Congal*, Dublin and London, 1872
Fergusson, Francis, *The Idea of a Theatre*, Princeton, 1949
Fournier d'Albe, Edmund Edward, *The Life of Sir William Crookes*, London, 1923
Gaskell, Ronald, *Drama and Reality: The European Theatre since Ibsen*, London, 1972
Goldman, Arnold, 'The Oeuvre Takes Shape: Yeats's Early Poetry', in *Victorian Poetry*, edited by Malcolm Bradbury, Stratford-upon-Avon Studies, 15, London, 1973, pp.197-221
Gray, Terence, *Dance Drama: Experiments in the Art of the Theatre*, Cambridge, 1926
Greene, David H. and Edward M. Stephen, *J. M. Synge, 1871-1909*, New York, 1959
Gregory, Lady Augusta, *Cuchulain of Muirthemne*, London, 1902
-----*Lady Gregory's Journals, 1916-1930*, edited by (Esmé Stuart) Lennox Robinson, London, 1946
Hartnoll, Phyllis, editor, *The Oxford Companion to the Theatre*, London, New York and Toronto, 1951
Hegel, Georg Wilhelm Friedrich, *Lectures on the Philosophy of Religion*, 2 vol., translated by E. B. Speirs and J. B. Sanderson, London, 1895
Jeffares, A. Norman and A. S. Knowland, *A Commentary on the Collected Plays of W. B. Yeats*, London, 1975
Kenner, Hugh, *The Pound Era*, Berkeley and Los Angeles, 1971
Marshall, Norman, *The Other Theatre*, London, 1947
-----*The Producer and the Play*, revised edition, London, 1962
Mills, John G. 'W. B. Yeats and Noh', *Japan Quarterly*, 2, No.4 (October-December 1955), pp.496-500
Miner, Earl, *The Japanese Tradition in British and American Literature*, Princeton, 1958
-----'A Poem by Swift and W. B. Yeats's *Words Upon the Window-Pane*', *Modern Language Notes*, 72 (April 1957), pp.273-5
-----'Pound, Haiku, and the Image', *Hudson Review*, 9, No.4 (Winter 1956-57), pp.570-84

Nathan, Leonard, E., *The Tragic Drama of William Butler Yeats: Figures in a Dance*, London and New York, 1965

O'Casey, Sean, *Inishfallen, Fare Thee Well*, London, 1949

Ōshima, Shotarō, 'Yeats and Michio Itō, *Annual Report of the Yeats Society of Japan*, 6 (1971), pp.15-20

-----*W. B. Yeats and Japan*, Tokyo, 1965

Pater, Walter, *Appreciations*, London 1889

-----*The Renaissance: Studies in Art and Poetry*, London, 1888

Peacock, Ronald, *The Poet in the Theatre*, London, 1946

Pound, Ezra Loomis, *Letters of Ezra Pound, 1907-1941*, edited by D. D. Paige, New York, 1950

-----*Pound-Joyce Letters and Essays*, edited by Forrest Read, New York, 1966

-----'Vorticism', *Fortnightly Review*, 96, No.375 (1 September 1914), pp.461-71

-----translator, *Women of Trachis*, London, 1957

Ramsey, Warren, 'Some Twentieth Century Ideas of Verse Theatre', *Comparative Literature Studies*, special advance issue, Proceedings of the First Triennial Meeting of the American Comparative Literature Association (1963), pp.43-50

Robinson, (Esmé Stuart) Lennox, *Ireland's Abbey Theatre: A History, 1899-1951*, London, 1951

Shipley, Joseph T., *Trends in Literature*, New York, 1949

Sigerson, George, *Bards of the Gael and the Gall*, London, 1897

Symons, Arthur, *Studies in Seven Arts*, London, 1906

Taylor, Richard Dean, editor, *Frank Pearce Sturm: His Life, Letters and Collected Work*, London and Chicago, 1968

Tsukimura, Reiko, 'A Comparison of Yeats's *At The Hawk's Well* and Its Noh Version, *Take no izumi, Literature East and West*, 11, No.4 (1967), pp.385-97

Ure, Peter, *Yeats, the Playwright: A Commentary on Character and Design in the Major Plays*, New York, 1963

Vendler, Helen Henessy, *Yeats's Vision and the Later Plays*, Cambridge, Mass., 1963

Waite, Arthur Edward, *The Mysteries of Magic*, London, 1886

Whitaker, Thomas R., *Swan and Shadow: Yeats's Dialogue with History*, Chapel Hill, North Carolina, 1964

Wilde, Oscar, *The Work of Oscar Wilde*, edited by G. F. Maine, London and Glasgow, 1948, pp.843-4

Williams, Raymond, *Drama from Ibsen to Brecht*, second revised edition, London, 1968

Wilson, Francis Alexander Charles, *W. B. Yeats and Tradition*,
    London and New York, 1958
-----*Yeats's Iconography*, London, 1960
Yeats, William Butler, *Ah, Sweet Dancer: A Correspondence*,
    edited by Roger McHugh, London, 1970
-----editor, *The Arrow*, No.1-5, 1906-9
-----*Autobiographies*, London, 1955
-----'Bardic Ireland', *The Scots Observer*, 3 (4 January
    1890), p.182-3
-----editor, *Beltain*, No.1-3, 1899-1900
-----*Essays and Introductions*, London, 1961
-----*Florence Farr, Bernard Shaw, W. B. Yeats Letters*,
    edited by Clifford Bax, London, 1946
-----*L'Oeuf de heron*, translated by R. Giroux, Compagnie
    Madeleine Renaud Cahiers, Paris, 1962
-----*The Letters of W. B. Yeats*, edited by Alan Wade,
    London, 1954
-----*Mythologies*, London, 1959
-----*Reflections*, edited by Curtis Bradford, Dublin, 1970
-----editor, *Samhain*, No.1-8, 1901-8
-----*The Variorum Edition of the Plays of W. B. Yeats*,
    edited by Russell K. Alspach, London, 1966
-----*The Variorum Edition of the Poems of W. B. Yeats*,
    edited by Peter Allt and Russell K. Alspach, New
    York, 1957
-----*A Vision*, revised edition, New York, 1961

Index